D1228552

AL SMITH'S *Treasury of*

Hymn Histories

The authentic, inspiring, and often unknown, stories behind the writing of over 115 favorite hymns and Gospel songs

RESEARCHED AND WRITTEN BY

Alfred B. Smith

COMPLETE SONG included with each story

CREDITS

Typography

Mulligan Printing Corporation

Alberta P. Weingust — typographer

Art and Layout

Paul M. Weingust

Printing and Binding

R. R. Donnelley and Sons

Editorial and Secretarial Assistance

Nancy W. Smith

Ruth Kadioch

Pamela J. Smith

Rev. John James Recene

Technical Assistance

Dwight G. Smith

PRINTED IN THE UNITED STATES OF AMERICA

Distributed by

HERITAGE MUSIC DISTRIBUTORS, INC.

MELODY CENTER

MONTROSE, PENNSYLVANIA 18801

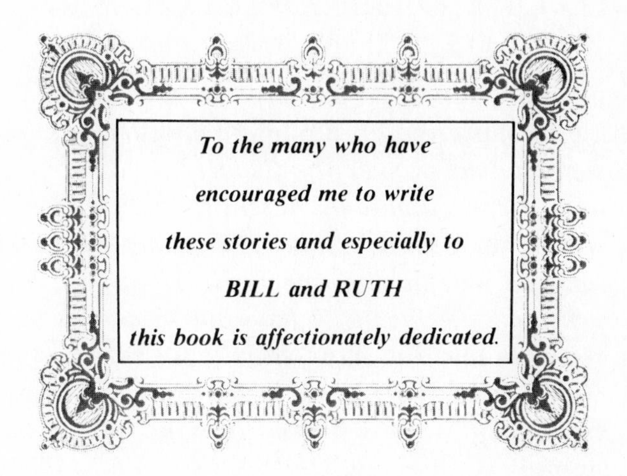

To the many who have
encouraged me to write
these stories and especially to
BILL and RUTH
this book is affectionately dedicated.

Keepsake Edition

A LIMITED PRINTING

A WORD OF COMMENDATION ...

Al Smith has been appropriately called the "Dean" of Gospel music. Dr. Smith has given his life to the ministry of music. There is no man living who can convey the Gospel through music any better than Dr. Smith. He has that unusual sensitivity to the full meaning of every song and he is able to convey that to those who are in the audience.

A very unusual and moving aspect of his ministry is his knowledge of the story behind the hymns. I have sat in awe as he has shared various stories with me. His many years experience and the privilege he has had of being personally acquainted with many of the song writers has given him a depth that is surpassed by no one in Gospel music today. In this book he shares with his readers some of the fond memories and unforgettable stories behind many of the great songs that have been enjoyed by saint and sinner alike down through the years. As you read this book I am sure that Dr. Al's insight into the stories behind these hymns will make you appreciate song and writer as never before.

JERRY FALWELL

Jerry Falwell

An Adventure in Inspiration©

GENERAL INDEX

INDEX OF FIRST LINES AND TITLES

Titles are in CAPITALS; First Lines are in Upper & Lower Case Type

ABS

FOREWORD

THIS IS ONE OF THE HAPPIEST FOREWORDS I HAVE HAD AN OPPORTUNITY TO WRITE IN MY ENTIRE MINISTRY.

DURING THE PAST 40 OR 50 YEARS IT HAS BEEN MY UNIQUE PRIVILEGE TO COUNT AMONG MY FRIENDS MANY OF THE WRITERS OF OUR PRESENT-DAY GOSPEL SONGS. NATURALLY WITH THESE FRIENDSHIPS THERE HAVE ACCUMULATED MANY INCIDENTS AND HAPPENINGS VITALLY RELATED TO THEM AND TO THEIR SONGS. MANY WERE ALSO KIND ENOUGH TO PASS ON TO ME THE STORIES OF OTHER SONGS AND THEIR WRITERS THAT THEY KNEW. THIS PROVED AN ADDED HELP AND INSPIRATION.

AS I BECAME AWARE OF THESE HEART-STIRRING STORIES I BEGAN TO PASS THEM ON AND FOUND THAT OTHER PEOPLE'S HEARTS TOO WERE BLESSED JUST AS MINE HAD BEEN. THIS CREATED A GREATER DESIRE WITHIN ME TO GET TO KNOW MORE ABOUT THE HISTORIES AND THE WRITERS WHO THROUGH THE YEARS HAVE MADE UP THE EVER-WIDENING SPECTRUM OF EVANGELICAL SONG. IT HAS INDEED PROVED TO BE A REWARDING EXPERIENCE.

AUTHORSHIP I'M SURE, HAS ALWAYS BEEN AN ENTRANCING THEME AND WHEN IT CONCERNS A FIELD OF HYMNOLOGY AND THE GOSPEL SONG IT TAKES ON A NEW DIMENSION. CENTURIES AGO SOMEONE SO GRAPHICALLY SAID, "YOU MAY WRITE THE LAWS OF THE LAND BUT LET ME WRITE THE SONGS." GREAT SERMONS HAVE BEEN PREACHED BUT THE REMEMBRANCES OF THEM HAVE FADED OFTEN LONG BEFORE THE PREACHER HIMSELF HAS DIED BUT JOHN NEWTON STILL LIVES ON IN "AMAZING GRACE."

TO PUBLISH ALL THE GLEANINGS OF THIS INTRIGUING SUBJECT THAT I HAVE GAINED THROUGH THE YEARS WOULD TAKE SEVERAL VOLUMES. IN *HYMN HISTORIES* I HAVE CAREFULLY CHOSEN WHAT I CONSIDER OVER 115 OF THE BEST OF THESE.

THE SONGS IN THIS VOLUME HAVE BEEN PARTICULARLY CHOSEN FOR THEIR UNIQUENESS AND HEART APPEAL. IT IS MY PRAYER AND SINCERE HOPE THAT EACH STORY AND SONG MAY BRING ADDED BLESSINGS INTO THE LIFE OF MANY A SINGING PILGRIM AROUND THE WORLD.

"SING"CERELY,

Alfred B Smith

Dr. Alfred B. Smith

How Great Thou Art
Carl Boberg
Tr. by S.K. Hine, 1948
Swedish Melody
Revised by Rev. Jean Staneschi, 1929
Majestically – not rushed
1. O Lord my God! When I in awe-some won-der Con-sid-er all the works Thy hands have made, I see the stars, I hear the might-y thun-der, Thy pow'r thro' out the un-i-verse dis-played,
2. When thro' the woods and for-est glades I wan-der And hear the birds sing sweet-ly in the trees; When I look down from loft-y moun-tain gran-deur, And hear the brook, and feel the gen-tle breeze;
3. And when I think that God, His Son not spar-ing, Sent Him to die— I scarce can take it in;— That on the cross, my bur-den glad-ly bear-ing, He bled and died, to take a-way my sin;
4. When Christ shall come with-shout of ac-cla-ma-tion And take me home-what joy shall fill my heart! Then I shall bow in hum-ble ad-o-ra-tion, And there pro-claim, my God, how great Thou art!
Chorus
Then sings my soul, my Sav-ior God to Thee; How great Thou art, how great Thou art! Then sings my soul, my Sav-ior God to Thee; How great Thou art, how great Thou art!
© Copyright 1953, 1955 by Manna Music, Inc. This arrangement © Copyright 1972 by Alfred B. Smith. Assigned 1978 to Manna Music, Inc., 2111 Kenmere Ave., Burbank, CA 91504. Used by permission.

HOW GREAT THOU ART

I can say without fear of argument that this song has captured the hearts of Christians more than any other song in our generation.

I am indebted to Mr. Stewart K. Hine, who was used of God to literally give this song to the world, for the thrilling story leading to its writing and development.

"How Great Thou Art" in its original form came from Sweden in 1885, almost 100 years ago. It was a poem written by Carl Boberg, a 26-year-old preacher in the summer of 1885 under the title "O Store Gud" which is translated "O Great God." It was a warm summer day. Carl and some of his friends had gone to a meeting some 2 miles from home. On the way back they were caught in a thunder storm. As the storm broke, the lightning flashed, the thunder rolled, and the winds swept across the fields; and then, as quickly as it came, it was all over. The sun again came out and with it appeared a rainbow. Then, as the rainbow disappeared and the sun began to sink in the west in the thrill of the evening, from a distance could be heard the song of the thrush and the church tower sounding the tolling of the bell memorializing a funeral that had been held that afternoon. The very atmosphere, the beauty of the surroundings, and the sound of the bell — all combined to draw from the heart and mind of the young preacher a poem, the subject of which after many translations in many lands and after many years would become known as "How Great Thou Art."

Each translation helped enrich the poem as each country added its own particular "flavor," but it was an English missionary by the name of Stuart K. Hine who worked in the Western Ukraine and later in Sub-Carpathian Russia, who gave us the inspiring original English words as we know them today. As one looks back, one can't help but see the hand of God sending Hine to the particular area in which he worked, for he later said, "God put me amid unforgettable experiences in the Carpathian Mountains." These experiences, plus the grandeur and beauty of his surroundings, did much to flood Hine with the feeling of awe and wonder at so great a God. This would eventually lead him to describe all of this in his own ways and words.

In giving his account of events leading to the writing, Hine recalls the first Carpathian Mountain Village to which he climbed. He stood in the street, sang a Gospel hymn, and read aloud John, chapter three. But a storm was gathering and soon he had taken shelter in the home of a friendly schoolmaster who had been listening. "Awe-inspiring was 'the mighty thunder' echoing through the mountains" was the way he described the experience which would be the seed-thought for his first stanza.

Traveling on, Hine crossed the mountain frontier into Romania. There in the Bukovina (the land of the beech tree) he found believers young and old alike. Together "through woods and forest glades" they wandered and "heard the birds sing sweetly in the trees." To the accompaniment of mandolins and guitars, they too burst into song singing the Russian version of "How Great Thou Art." Thus inspired by the awesome wonder of the surroundings, "the works Thy hands have made," the beautiful melody and the earlier mountain experience with it's "mighty thunder," there burst forth into life from the heart and mind of missionary Hine, the first two stanzas:

O Lord my God! When I in awesome wonder
Consider all the works Thy hands have made,
I see the stars, I hear the mighty thunder,
Thy pow'r throu' out the universe displayed.

When thro' the woods and forest glades I wander
And hear the birds sing sweetly in the trees;
When I look down from lofty mountain grandeur,
And hear the brook and feel the gentle breeze, ...

As Hine continued his work of preaching and distributing Gospels in village after village and had traveled some 125 miles, he had an experience which would give life to verse 3. He met a man and his wife who had owned a Bible for almost 20 years (it had been left by a fleeing Russian soldier) but they could not read it. The very year that Hine met them, the wife had taken the Bible and had made up her mind she would learn to read it. Persevering day by day she began to learn to read it, and in turn began to read it to the villagers who in wonder listened as she slowly and haltingly read the most wonderful story of the crucifixion. Tears began to flow as men and women fell to their knees crying to God. It was at that precise time that Stuart K. Hine came upon the scene and witnessed the amazing happening — people seeing the revelation of God's love at Calvary for the first time. It was then that he conceived stanza three.

And when I think that God, His Son not sparing,
Sent Him to die — I scarce can take it in;
That on the cross, my burden gladly bearing,
He bled and died, to take away my sin.

It was some 10 years later (1948) that he conceived the fourth stanza. God used the years in between to impress upon Hine's heart the importance of the words "home" and "heaven" as he worked among the many World War II refugees in Britain. The first question they would ask was, "When are we going home?" At such a time, what better message could he give to them but of the One who had gone to prepare a better home and who had promised to come someday to take His children home with Him forever to a place called Heaven. And so from his heart and these experiences there came the fourth stanza.

When Christ shall come with shout of acclamation
And take me home — what joy shall fill my heart!
Then I shall bow in humble adoration,
And there proclaim, My God, how great Thou art!

Carl Boberg's poem had traveled long and far but at last it had reached a place in its transformation where it would inspire and bless the English speaking church more than any other song had since the days of the Wesleys. All because of a dedicated missionary servant of God named Stuart K. Hine.

All the facts of this story were taken from a much fuller account by the author Mr. Stuart K. Hine. It is called The Story of How Great Thou Art *and is obtainable by writing Stuart K. Hine, Carpathia, Coast Road, Berrow, Burnham-on-the-Sea, Somerset, England, TA8. A copy will be sent postpaid for $2.00 (for checks, 75¢ bank charges must be added).*

It Took A Miracle
JOHN W. PETERSON
JOHN W. PETERSON
1. My Fa - ther is om - ni - po - tent, And that you can't de - ny;
2. Tho here His glo - ry has been shown, We still can't ful - ly see
3. The Bi - ble tells us of His pow'r And wis - dom all way thru,
A God of might and mir - a - cles— 'Tis writ - ten in the sky.
The won-ders of His might, His throne—'Twill take e - ter - ni - ty.
And ev - 'ry lit - tle bird and flow'r Are tes - ti - mo - nies too.
CHORUS
It took a mir - a - cle to put the stars in place, It took a
mir - a - cle to hang the world in space; But when He saved my soul,
Cleansed and made me whole, It took a mir - a - cle of love and grace.

IT TOOK A MIRACLE

In my opinion, John W. Peterson is one of today's most gifted Gospel songwriters. It was my privilege to collaborate with John for several years as he worked for a publishing company I owned and had founded, named "Singspiration." It was during that time that John told me of the circumstances which led to the writing of this great song.

When World War II came along, John enlisted in the Air Corps and became a pilot and eventually an instructor. As a pilot he served his time in China and flew B47's over the Burma Hump. His payload was 100 octane gas which was used to keep our fighting planes in the air as we fought Japan. Many of John's flights were made at night. During these flights, after he had put the plane on automatic pilot, he would not only spend his time watching out for enemy planes which might attack, but also viewing the mighty works of the heavens which an omnipotent God had made. A God that John knew as his Heavenly Father, for he had accepted Christ as his Saviour while still a young boy. John also told me that often, when the return flight was in the daytime, he would fly his plane in low and wing his way between the rugged mountains passing over many of the native villages. As he did this, his thoughts often dwelt on the fact that the God of miracles and wonders in the heavens was the same God who "So Loved the World," that He had given His all, His only begotten Son, that even these natives, unknown to John but known and loved by God, might experience the greatest miracle of all — eternal life!

The war came to an end, John first went back home to Wichita, Kansas, and then came to Chicago to give himself to the study of music. It was while in Chicago that he reviewed some of his never-to-be-forgotten experiences in the services, and was inspired to write "It Took A Miracle." "My Father is omnipotent and that you can't deny ...; A God of might and miracles, etc.; But when He saved my soul, cleansed and made me whole; It took a miracle of love and grace." ABS

In The Garden
C. AUSTIN MILES
C. AUSTIN MILES
1. I come to the gar - den a - lone, While the dew is
2. He speaks, and the sound of His voice Is so sweet the
3. I'd stay in the gar - den with Him Tho the night a -
still on the ros - es; And the voice I hear, fall - ing on my ear,
birds hush their sing - ing; And the mel - o - dy that He gave to me
round me be fall - ing; But He bids me go— thru the voice of woe,
REFRAIN
The Son of God dis - clos - es.
With - in my heart is ring - ing. And He walks with me, and He
His voice to me is call - ing.
talks with me, And He tells me I am His own; And the joy we
share as we tar - ry there None oth - er has ev - er known.
© Copyright 1912 by Hall-Mack Co. Renewed 1940 The Rodeheaver Co. All rights reserved.
International copyright secured. Used by permission.

IN THE GARDEN

Without a doubt, "In The Garden" is one of the all-time Gospel song favorites. It had its beginning, of all places, in a photographic darkroom. Here's how the story was related to me in Philadelphia by the author, C. Austin Miles. "I had developed a hobby of photography and although my funds were limited, I managed over a period of time to build my own darkroom. I also was able to secure some used equipment which meant that I could now practice my hobby without the worry of spending too much to have the pictures developed.

"I had been writing songs before this and had formed a habit of reading my Bible with the express purpose of getting ideas for them. To my amazement, I found that I could read my Bible in the special light of the darkroom. This was a great help, for it meant I could 'kill two birds with one stone' — that is, carry on my hobby and at the same time get ideas for new Gospel songs.

"One day as I waited for some film to develop, I picked up my Bible which fell open to the Gospel of John, chapter 20. I began to read the story of Jesus and Mary on Resurrection morning.

"As I read it I seemed to be transported to the actual garden and I became a silent witness to that dramatic moment. I saw the very movements; I heard the very words of Mary as she thought she was talking to the gardener; and I heard Jesus say, 'Mary,' after which I saw her kneel before her Lord and say, 'Rabboni!'

"When I awakened, I was gripping my Bible. My muscles were tense and vibrating. I thought of myself, 'This is not an experience limited to a happening almost 2000 years ago but it is the daily companionship with the Saviour that makes up the Christian's daily walk.' It was under the inspiration of that holy moment that I wrote, as quickly as the words came, the poem exactly as it appears today; and that evening I wrote the music.

And He walks with me, And He talks with me,
And he tells me I am His Own,
And the joy we share as we tarry there,
None other has ever known.

ABS

The Lily Of The Valley

Charles W. Fry
William S. Hays
1. I have found a friend in Je-sus, He's ev - 'ry-thing to me, He's the
2. He all my grief has tak - en, and all my sor-rows borne; In temp-
3. He will nev -er, nev - er leave me, nor yet for-sake me here, While I
fair-est of ten thou-sand to my soul; The Lil - ly of the Val - ley, in
ta-tion He's my strong and migh-ty Tow'r; I have all for Him for-sak-en, and
live by faith and do His bless-ed will; A wall of fire a - bout me, I've
D.S. Lil - y of the Val - ley, the
Fine
Him a - lone I see All I need to cleanse and make me ful-ly whole.
all my i-dols torn From my heart, and now He keeps me by His pow'r.
noth-ing now to fear, With His man-na He my hun-gry soul shall fill.
bright and Morn-ing Star, He's the fair - est of ten thou - sand to my soul.
In sor-row He's my Com-fort in troub - le He's my Stay,
Though all the world for - sake me, and Sa - tan tempts me sore,
Then sweep-ing up to glo - ry, I'll see His bless - ed face,
D.S
He tells me ev - 'ry care on Him to roll. He's the
Through Je - sus I shall safe - ly reach the goal; He's the
Where riv - ers of de - light shall ev - er roll! He's the
Hal-le-lu-jah!

THE LILY OF THE VALLEY

This happy and enjoyable song has a very interesting history and here it is in a "nut shell."

An early minstrel song written in America finds its way to England where it becomes a favorite. Its catchy melody attracts the attention of a Salvation Army musician who writes a set of Gospel verses for it and this combination immediately becomes a favorite among the Salvation Army folk. When Ira Sankey comes to England with D. L. Moody, he hears the song, likes it, and takes a copy back to America where he publishes it and soon it becomes an all-time Sunday school favorite. This is the story, in short, of "The Lily Of The Valley."

Now, may I give you the intriguing details as they were told to me.

"Charles Fry was the eldest son of an unusual Salvation Army group called 'The Musical Frys.' They traveled about England and were known particularly for the fact that they never used printed music. All of them had a talent for shorthand; so, when they would hear a new song, all of them except elder brother Charles, would take down the words. Brother Charles' job was to write down the music using the sol-fa system where the initials of each syllable are used to designate the notes. Thus they were able to retain many songs which would have been lost if they had had to rely upon memory alone.

"Brother Charles died in 1882 and among the things he left was a paper upon which several verses had been written. At the bottom he had attached a sol-fa copy of a melody to be used. He, however, had not included the information as to who had written it or where it had come from. These papers were given to the Salvation Army who published the song in the early part of 1885. It immediately found favor among the Army but it was Moody's and Sankey's second visit to England in the fall of 1885 that really made the song popular, for a newly published copy had been given to Mr. Sankey, who then taught it to the great crowds. In a few short weeks it had become the most requested song of the campaign and had winged itself over the entire British Isles.

"When Mr. Sankey returned to America, the song came back with him and soon it had become a great favorite in the Moody and Sankey meetings in America also. In 1887 he published it in *Gospel Hymns Number Five.* In this edition he gave credit to Fry for the words but, as yet, the author of the music was unknown. It was only after the song had become well-known in our country, that the true source of its origin was discovered. It was not an old English folk tune as many had thought but had been written in 1871 in Louisville, Kentucky, by William S. Hays. He had composed it under the title, 'The Little Ole Log Cabin Down the Lane' — a typical minstrel song of the era which majored in memory songs. Somehow it had found its way to England.

"Charles Fry had several changes in his rendition of the melody. Perhaps it was to smooth it out and make it more adaptable for his sacred words. But whatever his reason may have been, he did succeed in giving the music something which would outlast, by far, the minstrel days for which it had been written originally." ABS

MORE LOVE TO THEE

The year was 1856, and into the already troubled life of Elizabeth Prentiss had come more waves of anxiety and distress. She had been an invalid most of her 38 years, but now the bodily suffering was beyond human endurance and in her heart were raging the storm clouds of doubt and despair. "Does God really care?" "Does He know that I even exist?" "I just can't take any more!" Over and over again like the pounding of the merciless waves of the sea her soul was pounded to and fro. Then through the storm there shone God's precious promises — "I will never leave you nor forsake you"; "Casting all your care upon Him for He careth for you." On and on they came, as God began to paint a rainbow of hope, and soon her life was flooded with the "peace that passeth understanding." It was then that she wrote with a heart full of gratitude, "More Love to Thee, Oh Christ."

It was simply a prayer put into verse. It was said by her husband, that she wrote it so hastily she forgot to write down the last line of the last stanza and this she wrote in with pencil many years after, when she was asked to submit some of her poems for publication. Its success was always a wonder to her.

From that day on until the Lord took her home at the age of 60, Elizabeth Prentiss' life was marked with radiancy and devotion to Christ and the family of God. She once said, "To love Christ more is our deepest need. The constant cry of my soul, be it out in the woods, on my bed, out driving, or when I am happy and busy, sad and not able to do anything, the whisper of more love — more love — more love keeps filling my soul."

Is it any wonder that a hundred years after Miss Prentiss' homegoing, her testimony in song, "More Love To Thee, Oh Christ," is still a favorite?

I Have Never Lost The Wonder Of It All

* This was the reply of beloved evangelist "Gypsy" Smith to the question – "What is your secret – you are now over 80 years of age yet you still preach with the same sincerity and enthusiasm you had 50 years ago?"

Gone my days of sin and wan-d'ring, Since the Sav-iour made me whole.
'Tis the peace of sins for-giv-en— Joy that makes my glad heart glow.
Chorus
I have nev-er lost the won-der of it all. I have
nev-er lost the won-der of it all! Since the day that Je-sus saved me and a
whole new life He gave me, I have nev-er lost the won-der of it all!

I HAVE NEVER LOST THE WONDER OF IT ALL

The writing of this song really had its beginning with this story. Moody and Sankey were in their first crusade in the British Isles and after having meetings in such places as New Castle, Glasgow, they were now in London. There were great crowds attending. One day Mr. Moody remarked to Mr. Sankey, "Ira, I've heard some news today that bothers me. They're not allowing the Gypsies to attend our meetings here in London. It seems that a few of the several hundred Gypsies are expert pick-pockets and the police have decided that by keeping the Gypsies out of the meetings they will eliminate this hazard from our meetings. But you know, Ira, the Gypsies need to be saved too." Mr. Sankey readily concurred with Mr. Moody and they worked out a plan. They would put on a meeting just for the Gypsies. Mr. Moody had found out where their camp was located in Epping Forest, and had also found a place where they could hire a horse and buggy to take them out there.

They agreed that one day when someone else took the afternoon meeting, Mr. Moody and Mr. Sankey would go out to the camp.

It wasn't very many days later, that they had the opportunity they had been waiting for and so they hired the horse and buggy and headed for the Gypsy camp. They were first given a warm welcome of appreciation by the Gypsies and then Mr. Sankey and Mr. Moody sang and preached for them. How the Gypsies were blessed and how they appreciated that these two men of God had taken time out of their busy schedule to come to them alone. This feeling was not only shared by the older members of the Gypsy family but also by the young people. When the meeting was over and Moody and Sankey had gotten back into the buggy to head back to London and the evening meeting, a group of young Gypsies gathered around the buggy and began to thank them for coming and telling them about Jesus. These youngsters knew how busy and important these two men were, for in the last few weeks they had often seen their pictures on the front page of the London papers. And to think they had taken time to come to be with them!

As the two men gazed down into their faces, one especially attracted the attention of Mr. Sankey. It was a Gypsy boy with dark curley hair and great big soft brown eyes. Mr. Sankey quickly leaned out of the buggy, put his hand upon the head of the boy and then prayed out loud, "Oh Lord, if this dear boy has never accepted Thee as Saviour, may he do so and, Lord, make a preacher out of him. Amen." With that Mr. Moody gave the reins to the horse and headed back to London.

The London campaign had become history. Years had gone by and Moody and Sankey were back in America, when one day a New York paper carried the headline "Famous British Evangelist Coming To America." In his article the editor told in glowing terms about a great preacher who had taken Britain by storm. Why he never had less than 10,000 persons attend his Sunday evening meetings and at many of them the royal family was in attendance! He concluded his article saying that this great preacher of renown had started as a barefoot boy in a Gypsy camp in Epping Forest just outside London.

When the Evangelist arrived in America he asked the welcoming party that met him if they would be kind enough to take him to see Mr. Ira Sankey in Brooklyn. This they readily did.

They tell me that by this time Mr. Sankey was already becoming blind. He would eventually become totally blind some years before his death, and it was during this time that he wrote "Under His Wings" and "There'll Be No Dark Valley When Jesus Comes."

The young Evangelist was taken to the home of Mr. Sankey and after they had been introduced, he said, "Mr. Sankey, do you remember a visit you and Mr. Moody made to a Gypsy camp while you were in England?" Mr. Sankey thought a moment and then replied, "You know, I do remember. Mr. Moody and I rented a horse and buggy and that day we went out to Epping Forest where the Gypsies had their camp." The young Evangelist then continued, "And do you remember that just before you and Mr. Moody went back to London and after you had gotten back into the buggy, a group of teenage youngsters gathered around your buggy to thank you and to bid you farewell? You leaned out of your buggy, put your hand on a curley haired boy's head and prayed out loud, 'Dear

Lord, if this boy has not accepted Jesus as Saviour, may he do so and Lord make a preacher out of him.' Mr. Sankey, do you remember?" Sankey replied, "So many things have happened through the years that I have forgotten but I've never forgotten that moment." The young Evangelist, whose name was Gypsy Smith, then replied, "Mr. Sankey, I was that curley haired barefoot boy and you know, Mr. Sankey, I never get into the pulpit to preach the unsearchable riches of Christ but that I still feel the pressure of your hand on my head."

Moody and Sankey's "cup of cold water" given to the Gypsy camp so many years ago had paid a rich dividend.

I am indebted to Dr. Vance Havner for the sequel to this story. I'll tell it as he told me. "Al, it was my privilege to hear the Gypsy preach at meetings which proved to be the last time he came to America. He was in his 80's. My, how he preached that night! I had never heard him any better. At the end of the meeting, I decided that this might be the last time I would see him this side of Heaven and I just had to go up and shake his hand and thank him. As I came near the Gypsy, an older man came up to him and I heard him say, 'Gypsy, I heard you preach when you first came to America over 50 years ago — my how you blessed my heart then. I have never forgotten it — but again tonight, how my heart was warmed and thrilled! Gypsy, tell me — what's the secret?' I'll never forget his reply," said Dr. Havner as Gypsy answered, 'Sir, I have never lost the wonder of it all.' "

These stories are the seed thought from which grew "I Have Never Lost The Wonder Of It All." ABS

The Ninety And Nine

THE NINETY AND NINE

Perhaps no Gospel song has ever captured the hearts of the people as did "The Ninety and Nine." And, as one becomes better acquainted with the unusual circumstances leading to the writing of both the words and the music, one can see that the hand of the Lord was very evident in its creation.

The story really begins in Fifeshire, Scotland, where lived Elizabeth Clephane — daughter of the sheriff and a devoted Christian. Estranged from the family and wandering through the world was a prodigal brother for whom she prayed and about whom she wrote the poem. The unusual facts of how the music for the song came to be written, are as follows.

D. L. Moody and Ira Sankey were holding one of their great missions in the British Isles. The year was 1874. One day in Glasgow, as they boarded a train for Edinburgh, the mail was handed to Mr. Moody who immediately became engrossed in reading his letters. Mr. Sankey bought a paper and began to read it for the latest American news. He had about exhausted all of the paper, when in a corner he found a poem entitled, "The Ninety and Nine." As he read it he exclaimed to Mr. Moody, "This is just what I have been looking for — a shepherd hymn."

Mr. Moody was so engrossed with his letters that he did not hear Mr. Sankey's remark and so the incident passed but not before Mr. Sankey had carefully torn the poem from the paper and put it in his pocket.

Some nights later, Dr. Horatius Bonar was asked to participate in the service with Mr. Moody. He chose as his subject "The Good Shepherd." Mr. Sankey knew that at the conclusion he would be called upon to sing an appropriate hymn. Mr. Sankey always played his own accompaniments on the little organ he had taken with him from America and so did not have to worry about an accompanist.

For a time Mr. Sankey was puzzled as to what song to sing and began to review in his mind which one he might use when the time came. He decided that he should jot down some titles and as he reached into his pocket for a piece of paper upon which to write, lo — he pulled out the piece of newspaper on which was printed the words of "The Ninety and

Nine." As Mr. Sankey began to reread the words, he was to later say, "A voice seemed to say to me, 'Sing that hymn.' 'But I have no music,' I replied. But again the voice insisted, 'Sing that hymn!' It was then that I heard Mr. Moody say, 'And now Mr. Sankey will sing.' I arose, went over and sat down at the organ. As I touched the keys, there came to me, note by note, the tune as it is sung today. I must admit that as I finished the first stanza I wondered if the melody would stay with me for the remaining stanzas, but God was good. Nothing changed, not a single note. When I had finished, Mr. Moody came and leaned over the little organ. I could see tears in his eyes and I heard him say, 'Where in the world did you get that?' At the moment I could not reply for to me, also, it had been an unusual experience."

At the time it was not known who had written the words of "The Ninety and Nine." It was some years later that it was found that they had been written by 21-year-old Elizabeth Clephane and that she had died two years before they had been published. This was, also, the case of another hymn she had written entitled, "Beneath The Cross Of Jesus." AES

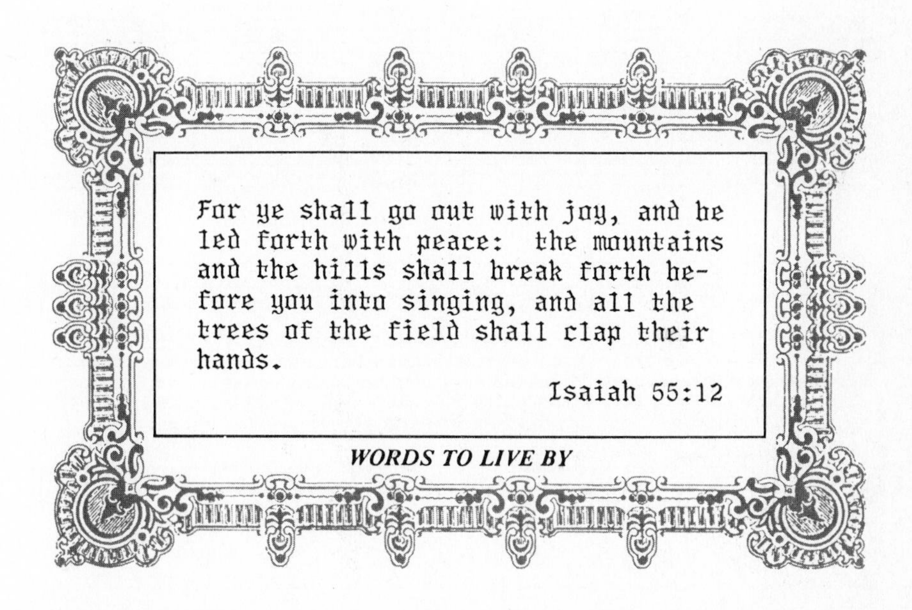

Pass It On
Henry Burton
George C. Stebbins
Moderato.
1. Have you had a kindness shown? Pass it on; 'Twas not giv'n for
2. Did you hear the lov - ing word— Pass it on; Like the sing - ing
3. 'Twas the sun-shine of a smile— Pass it on; Stay - ing but a
4. Have you found the heav'nly light? Pass it on; Souls are grop - ing
5. Be not self - ish in thy greed, Pass it on; Look up - on thy
thee a - lone, Pass it on; Let it trav - el down the years, Let it
of a bird? Pass it on; Let its mu - sic live and grow, Let it
lit - tle while! Pass it on; A - pril beam, the lit - tle thing, Still it
in the night, Day-light gone; Hold thy light-ed lamp on high, Be a
brother's need, Pass it on; Live for self, you live in vain; Live for
wipe an - oth - er's tears, Till in heav'n the deed appears—Pass it on.
cheer an - oth - er's woe, You have reap'd what others sow, Pass it on.
wakes the flow'rs of spring, Makes the si - lent birds to sing—Pass it on.
star in some one's sky, He may live who else would die, Pass it on.
Christ, you live a - gain; Live for Him, with Him you reign—Pass it on.

PASS IT ON

The incident which gave rise to the writing of this song was an experience told by a young Englishman named Mark Pearse. Here it is as he told it.

"Once when I was a schoolboy going home from the far-away little town of Zeist, Holland, where I went to school, I first had to go to Bristol, England, and there catch a boat for home. When I got onboard the steamer, I had just enough money to pay my fare. After paying what I thought also took care of all my expenses — even the meals — I prepared for an enjoyable time. The trip went nicely and I enjoyed my meals as long as there was smooth water, but then came the rough Atlantic where I lost my appetite and became wretchedly seasick. I had been lying in my bunk a long time, not caring about anything, when the steward came into my stateroom. Holding out a piece of paper he said, 'Here's your bill for your meals, Sir.' Somewhat taken back, I replied, 'But Sir, I have no money and I'm ill.' 'I am sorry about that but I shall have to keep your luggage as security. What is your name and address?' When I told him that my name was Mark Pearse and that I lived in London, he took off his cap with the gilt band and thrust out his hand. 'I want to shake your hand,' he said. He then explained.

"'Many years ago when I was a little lad, my father died leaving my mother to care for us children. She had it very hard but insisted that she would not give us up. In the sorrow and burdens of widowhood, your father did many kindnesses for my mother. I never thought the chance would ever come for me to repay even a little,' he said pleasantly, 'but I'm glad that I now have the opportunity.' As soon as I got ashore, I told my father what had happened. His reply was, 'See how a bit of kindness lives? Now he has passed it on to you and remember, if you meet anybody who needs a friendly hand, you must pass it on to him!'"

It was Mark Guy Pearse's son-in-law Henry Burton who, catching the inspiration of the story, wrote the song "Pass It On."

It Is Well With My Soul

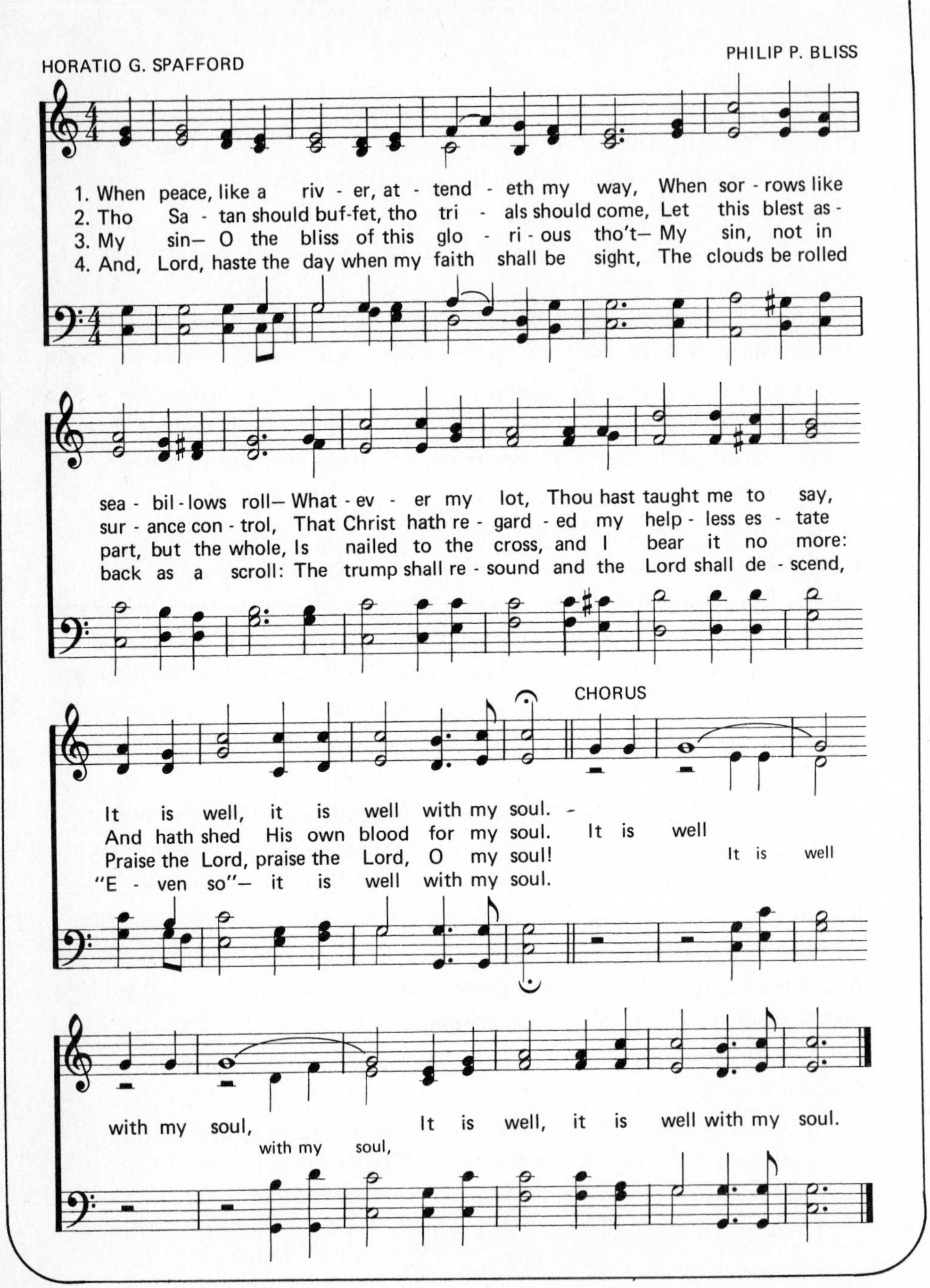
HORATIO G. SPAFFORD
PHILIP P. BLISS
1. When peace, like a riv - er, at - tend - eth my way, When sor - rows like
2. Tho Sa - tan should buf-fet, tho tri - als should come, Let this blest as -
3. My sin— O the bliss of this glo - ri - ous tho't— My sin, not in
4. And, Lord, haste the day when my faith shall be sight, The clouds be rolled
sea - bil - lows roll— What - ev - er my lot, Thou hast taught me to say,
sur - ance con - trol, That Christ hath re - gard - ed my help - less es - tate
part, but the whole, Is nailed to the cross, and I bear it no more:
back as a scroll: The trump shall re - sound and the Lord shall de - scend,
CHORUS
It is well, it is well with my soul.
And hath shed His own blood for my soul. It is well
Praise the Lord, praise the Lord, O my soul! It is well
"E - ven so"— it is well with my soul.
with my soul, It is well, it is well with my soul.
with my soul,

IT IS WELL WITH MY SOUL

Perhaps no other Gospel song has proven what the longevity of a scripturally based song can be, as has "It Is Well With My Soul." Hardly a week goes by but that I hear it on some radio or television program or hear it sung in a church. Yet it was written over 100 years ago in 1873.

I'll relay the story of its writing as it was told to me back in the early 1940's by George C. Stebbins, an associate of D. L. Moody and a man who knew both Horatio Spafford and P. P. Bliss, the writers of this song.

"Mr. Spafford was a well-known Christian lawyer, in Chicago, who also had great holdings in real estate in the fast-growing frontier town. He had been led into a deeper dedication of his life and wealth to the Lord through his association with D. L. Moody and Henry Moorehouse, the English Bible teacher who had come to Chicago and had preached seven sermons on John 3:16. In 1871 the great tragedy of fire struck Chicago and in a matter of a few hours much of Mr. Spafford's real estate holdings were nothing but ashes. This proved a real test for him, but little did he know there would be a far greater testing for him in the not-too-distant future.

"After the fire, most of young Chicago lay in ruins. The first building erected on the ashes was a building built by Mr. Moody called the North Side Tabernacle. It was at this place that Mr. Spafford kept himself occupied in helping those whose loss in actual money was not as great as his; but, like the widow who gave all, they had lost all. He was fortunate for he still had his law practice, his family, and also had some equity left.

"In November of 1873, some two years after the fire, many of the schools in Chicago had not yet been rebuilt and so Mr. Spafford decided that he would take his family to England where his children could enroll in an English Academy and not be held back in their education.

"Just before they were to leave, a last-minute business development made it necessary for Mr. Spafford to remain in Chicago and to send his wife and children on ahead. He would come later, on another ship.

"The Spafford family arrived safely in New York and boarded the ship Villa de Havre. Soon they were on their way to England, but in mid-ocean there was a collision between their ship and an English sailing ship. The Villa de Havre floundered and sank, taking with her to the bottom of the ocean most of those onboard, including the Spaffords' four daughters. Mrs. Spafford was found barely conscious but clinging to a piece of the wreckage. While aboard the rescue ship which was taking her and the other survivors to England, she was able to draft a short message which was sent to her husband in Chicago. It read, "Saved, alone."

"When Mr. Spafford received this message, the tragedy of the fire seemed but nothing in comparison to what this cablegram implied. Money and burned buildings could be replaced but his children were gone! It was through these clouds of darkness and despair that there shone, into the heart of H. G. Spafford, the bright light of God's promise. God would not forsake him in the trying hour no matter what the circumstances. Peace like a river or sorrows like sea billows — with God all is well!

"Captured by this thought, Mr. Spafford quickly penned the words of the song that soon would herald its way through the Christian church and encourage multitudes. It would continue doing so for over a hundred years. When he finished writing the words, Mr. Spafford took the poem over to a friend and neighbor who also lived on May Street. His name was P. P. Bliss, the composer who gave the words a most fitting melody — one that has kept the message of the song alive and vibrant all of these years." ABS

His Banner Over Me Is Love

1. Point up with index finger. 2. Hit left palm with right fist. 3. Point to self. 4. Arms extended above head fingertip touching. 5. Arms thrown around chest implying hug.

This little song lends itself easily to other verses such as:

2. Ask and receive that your joy may be full, His banner over me is love.
3. He feeds me at His banqueting table, His banner over me is love.
4. His sheep love Him and know His voice, His banner over me is love.
5. Jesus is the Way, the Truth, the Life, His banner over me is love.

HIS BANNER OVER ME IS LOVE

Perhaps no song, that I have ever been permitted to have part in writing, has traveled the world so quickly and gained as many friends both young and old as has this little Gospel chorus.

It was written in public in the early part of the 1960's. I was giving a concert at a little Baptist church in a place called Laurelton. The first half of the program had been completed and, before the concluding half, there was a time given for announcements and the offering. It was often my custom, in those days, to use this time to write an original song with a title supplied by someone in the audience. That night the title was suggested by a teenager who called out, "His Banner Over Me Is Love." We had just finished singing "Faith Is The Victory" in which the second stanza begins with "His banner over us is love." I am sure that this line had appealed to her and so she had thought it worthy to be used as a title for the song I would endeavor to write.

Though the church was filled, it was not a very large one, which meant the offering would not take long and I would not have long to write down my ideas. So in a matter of a few minutes, a very simple melody had been composed and two phrases of words written which were to be repeated three times. I then ended with the words of what is now the title, "His Banner Over Me Is Love."

There was great enthusiasm as the song was introduced that night. Little did I dream that this was the beginning of a song in which people, young and old from all over the world, would take part in writing literally dozens of new stanzas.

As is so often the case, it is not up to the composer to say if a song will succeed or not. The final vote always is in the hands of the people. I must confess that when "His Banner Over Me" was written, I felt that it would have a one-night stand and would be forgotten within a few days. How wrong I was; for soon I was receiving requests for copies from people who had heard it sung by some of the young people who had attended the concert that night. These requests I hurriedly filled with copies I made on my duplicator. To keep track of where the song had been written I put B. C. Laurelton (Baptist Church Laurelton 1965) on them. At the time I did not bother to put my name on it as the composer. Soon the requests increased and people also began asking for the song by B. C. Laurelton and so in 1969 when I finally had a music plate made for printing, I decided why not use the name B. C. Laurelton as a pen name? (Fanny Crosby had used some 100 fictitious names on her songs.) This would also be of help. I had made some changes in the arrangement and had included some of the new verses that had been sent to me and so I could add revised and arranged by Alfred B. Smith.

This has proven both an enjoyment and an embarrassment to me — an enjoyment in that I can listen to the song being sung and know that it is being sung because Christians (particularly the boys and girls) enjoy singing it and it is not being sung because the composer is present. The embarrassment has been when folks ask the address of Mr. Laurelton so that they may write and thank him for the song.

Someday it will be interesting to find out just how many different sets of words have been written for this little action song. But, in the meantime, I feel sure that it would easily win the prize for having more co-authors than any other song ever written. ABS

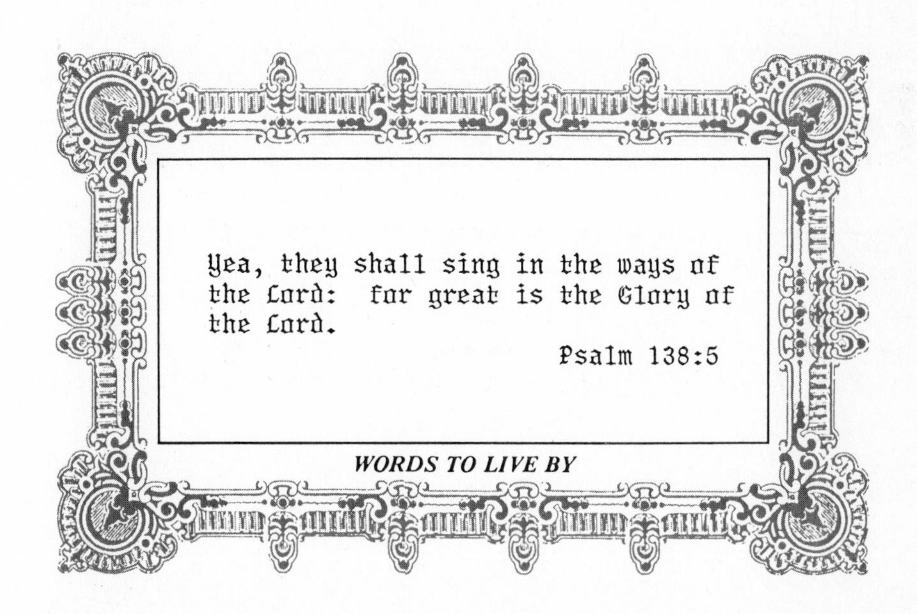

My Faith Looks Up To Thee
RAY PALMER
LOWELL MASON
1. My faith looks up to thee, Thou Lamb of Cal - va - ry,
2. May thy rich grace im - part Strength to my faint - ing heart,
3. While life's dark maze I tread, And griefs a - round me spread,
4. When ends life's tran - sient dream, When death's cold, sul - len stream
Sav - ior di - vine! Now hear me while I pray, Take all my
My zeal in - spire; As thou hast died for me, O may my
Be thou my guide; Bid dark - ness turn to day, Wipe sor - row's
Shall o'er me roll; Blest Sav - ior, then, in love, Fear and dis -
guilt a - way, O let me from this day Be whol - ly thine!
love to thee Pure, warm, and change-less be, A liv - ing fire!
tears a - way, Nor let me ev - er stray From thee a - side.
trust re - move; O bear me safe a - bove, A ran-somed soul! A - men.

MY FAITH LOOKS UP TO THEE

After the Revolution, the theological climate of America changed considerably. It became popular to adapt views of disbelief in the Bible. the deity of Christ, and to scoff at religion as superstition. Intemperance, profanity, gambling, and licentiousness were common. But God, in His perfect planning and undying love, caused "The Second Great Awakening" which, as it swept across our country, overflowed its bounds; and many unconcerned, unbelieving college students became new creatures in Christ.

One such student was Ray Palmer who, after he graduated from Yale in the fall of 1830, became a teacher in New York City. One evening while alone in his room, he began to review the wonder of God's love and its effect upon his young life. In the hush and solemnity of that moment, he penned these beautiful words of testimony and assurance. He carefully copied the six-stanza text in a small leather book he carried. This for his own use, for he had not the slightest idea that it would be of use to anyone else.

Sometime later, while visiting in Boston, he was met on the street by Dr. Lowell Mason, who asked him if he might have any hymns he could submit for a hymn and tune book he was compiling with Dr. Hastings of New York. Ray Palmer showed "My Faith" to Dr. Mason who copied it and took it with him.

Two or three days later they met again on the street. Dr. Mason exclaimed in greeting, "Mr. Palmer, you may live to do many great things but I feel that you will be known best as the author of 'My Faith Looks Up To Thee.'" ABS

The Peace That Jesus Gives

THE PEACE THAT JESUS GIVES

"Life is full of contrasts — bitter and sweet — the drab and the brilliant — the harsh and the gentle — the chord and the discord — the shadow and the sunshine. Today we may suffer the icy blasts of winter; tomorrow we may come to the gentle zephyrs of spring. Today the gold and green of harvest days; tomorrow the brown and crimson of autumn. All these things have to do with the molding of our characters, with the shaping of our destinies, with our preparation for the life that is to come, of which we know so little.

"The peace that Jesus gives, is the most satisfying of all experiences. We enjoy human fellowship, the precious ties of the home, the communion of the saints, professional or literary attainments — any success in life brings a deep sense of satisfaction but all of them are transitory. This peace that Jesus gives is more satisfying than any human emotion and is as enduring as the Eternal hills."

Speaking was Dr. Haldor Lillenas, the well-known composer and author of this song. I was his guest in Kansas City, Missouri. The year was 1942. He continued, "I'll never forget that day in the little Illinois town of Auburn when 'The Peace That Jesus Gives' was written. It had been very hot and sultry and then came a downpour of cloud-burst proportions accompanied by thunder and lightning. After the heavy shadows and strong wind had subsided, the sun appeared and the air was fragrant with the breath of flowers.

"On the parsonage lot, behind our garage, we had our little flower garden. This garden had been planted and attended with painstaking care. Naturally I was anxious to see how the flowers had fared during the storm. The flowers were somewhat drooped, but they were radiant in the late afternoon sun and with the rain drops still clinging to them they seemed to be ablaze with a thousand diamonds. In the sky hung a brilliant rainbow. The God who spoke 'Peace be still' to the boistrous waves of the Sea of Galilee had brought peace and calm to the little town of Auburn and its inhabitants. From this experience was born this song that seems to have won its way into many hearts." ABS

I'm Going Through
HERBERT BUFFUM
HERBERT BUFFUM
1. Lord, I have start-ed to walk in the light, Shin-ing up-on me from
2. I'd rath-er walk with Je-sus a-lone, Have for my pil-low, like
3. And when the gates of pearl shall un-fold, I shall my Sav-ior in
heav-en so bright; I've bade the world and its fol-lies a-dieu, I've
Ja-cob, a stone, Liv-ing each mo-ment with His face in view, Than to
Glo-ry be-hold; He'll bid me wel-come be-cause He is true; I'll
REFRAIN.
start-ed for Glo-ry, and I'm go-ing through.
turn from the path-way and fail to go through. I'm go-ing through, yes,
shout, "Blessed Je-sus, I'm sure com-ing through."
I'm go-ing through, I'll pay the price what-ev-er oth-ers do; I'll take the

I'M GOING THROUGH

The name, Herbert Buffum, is found as the writer of many enjoyable and unusual Gospel songs such as "I'm Going Higher Someday," "The Old-Fashioned Meeting," "When I Take My Vacation In Heaven." It was one of his first songs which has affected the lives of more people than all of the rest combined. The song is "I'm Going Through."

It all started when young Pastor Buffum left his small church in Salt Lake City. There had been a misunderstanding and in the heat of it all, he had resigned. Disheartened, disillusioned, and discouraged, he boarded the train for Los Angeles. He had tried to preach the Word without compromise, but what had it gotten him? He was out of a job and no one cared — so reasoned the Devil with him, but young Buffum remembered the story of Job. God hadn't forsaken him and He wouldn't forsake Herbert Buffum either! He determined not to quit the ministry but would keep right on going whatever the price might be. On the back of an old envelope he began to write, 'I'm going through, Jesus, I'm going through; I'll pay the price whatever others do."

When he reached Los Angeles, he introduced the song in the first meeting he was able to hold and in a short time it had become widely used.

At the time, Herbert Buffum knew nothing about the procedure of copyrighting a song and so in a matter of months, several publishers were publishing their own arrangements of "I'm Going Through." Young Buffum never realized any immediate compensation for this song but in eternity I know his reward will be great. ABS

The Star-Spangled Banner

THE STAR-SPANGLED BANNER

Because of a persistent British interference against American commerce, which existed after the War for Independence, the United States declared war on England on June 18, 1812. The War of 1812 lasted two-and-one-half years. Later in August, 1814, the British, under General Ross, landed at Chesapeake Bay and set fire to the Capital, the White House, and other public buildings in Washington. During this attack, a Doctor Binet of Upper Marlboro, Maryland, was taken prisoner.

Because of his political influence, Francis Scott Key, a Christian attorney, was persuaded to negotiate Binet's release. Key and his party reached the British fleet in Chesapeake Bay off the mouth of the Potomac River on September 7, and were successful in securing the agreement for the release of Binet. However, fearing that Key's party might alert the American forces of the proposed attack on Baltimore, the British detained them. After the British fleet had arrived in Baltimore, Key's party was returned to their sloop under guard. There they fearfully witnessed the British bombardment of Fort McHenry on September 13, which lasted all day and into the night.

Although the firing ceased shortly after midnight, it was not until they saw the United States flag flying over Fort McHenry in the early morning mist, that they knew the British had been unsuccessful in their attack.

Still on the sloop, Key, inspired by this experience, began sketching these lines beginning, "Oh, say can you see by the dawn's early light."

In his hotel room at Baltimore that evening, he wrote out a clean copy which is now preserved at the Walters Art Gallery in Baltimore. The following day it was printed in handbill form and within a week it had been reprinted in two Baltimore papers.

About a month later, Joseph Carr published the song in sheet music form. Many patriotic songs have been written and publicized, but this song has outlived them all and was acclaimed our National Anthem by public acceptance long before the Act of Congress which was on March 13, 1931 — one hundred and seventeen years after it was first written. ABS

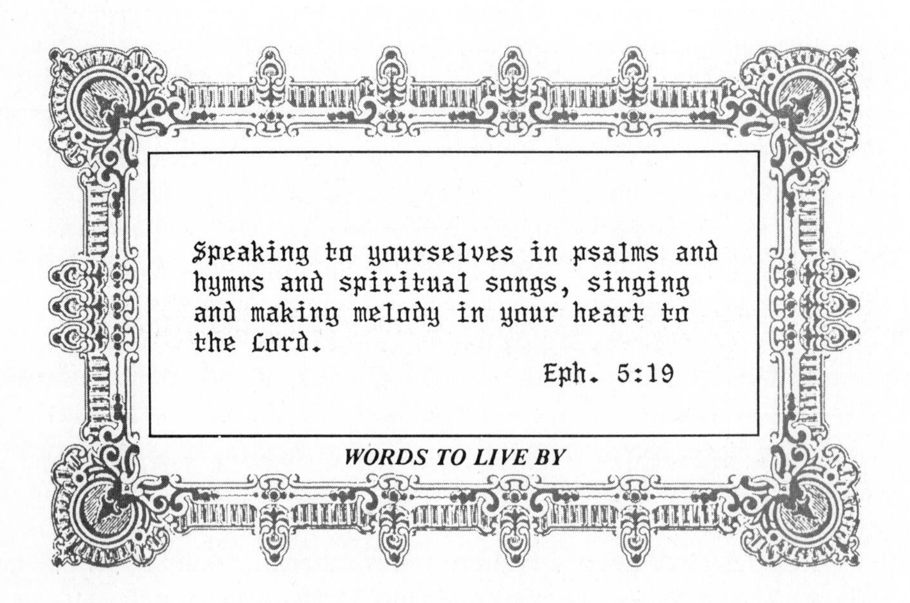

Ye Must Be Born Again
Based on John 3:3
WILLIAM T. SLEEPER
GEORGE C. STEBBINS
1. A rul - er once came to Je - sus by night To ask Him the way of sal - va - tion and light; The Mas - ter made an - swer in words true and plain, "Ye must be born a - gain."
2. Ye chil-dren of men, at - tend to the word So sol-emn - ly ut - tered by Je - sus the Lord; And let not this mes - sage to you be in vain, "Ye must be born a - gain."
3. O ye who would en - ter that glo - ri - ous rest And sing with the ran-somed the song of the blest, The life ev - er - last - ing if ye would ob - tain, "Ye must be born a - gain."
CHORUS
"Ye must be born a - gain, Ye must be born a - gain; I ver - i - ly, ver - i - ly say un - to thee, Ye must be born a - gain."

YE MUST BE BORN AGAIN

D. L. Moody saw early that it would be impossible for him and Sankey to fill all of the requests for meetings that were coming in during and after their great meetings in Britain. Realizing that it was important to get out the Gospel at once, he encouraged other men to form teams as he and Sankey had, and he promised to see to it that they were kept busy. The first team formed was Major Whittle and P. P. Bliss in 1874, and in 1876 there was Dr. Pentecost and George Stebbins.

It was while in Worchester, Massachusetts, that "Ye Must Be Born Again" was written. Dr. Pentecost and Mr. Stebbins were conducting a summer campaign there and one evening the subject preached on was "The New Birth." I'll let George Stebbins tell the story.

"While presenting the truth, enforcing it by referring to various passages of Scripture, Dr. Pentecost quoted our Lord's words to Nicodemus, 'Verily, verily I say unto you, ye must be born again,' [John 3:3-7]. It occurred to me that by taking the line 'Verily, verily I say unto thee,' from the third verse, and putting it with the line, 'Ye must be born again,' and by transferring the word 'I' from the middle of the first line to the beginning so it would read, 'I verily, verily say until thee, ye must be born again,' those passages would then fall into rhythmical form and, by the use of some repetition, could be made available for a musical setting and also for a chorus to a hymn, if some suitable verses could be found.

"I had long been impressed by the fact that that truth lay at the foundation of God's plan for the salvation of men, and that it was of the greatest importance that it should be made known everywhere. It also came to me with special force that a good hymn using those lines as the refrain, would be a means of emphasizing that truth and thereby doing great good. I spoke to Rev. William T. Sleeper, one of the pastors of the city of Worchester who sometimes wrote hymns at my suggestion, and asked him if he would write some verses on the subject. He acted at once upon my suggestion and soon after, came to me with the hymn that bears his name. Before the meeting closed, a musical setting was made and, when *Gospel Hymns #3* came out, the song was sent on its mission carrying the solemn message to the hearts and consciences of men and women with the importance of being born again."

Mr. Stebbins also related the following story which I know will be of interest.

"The following incident is of interest as showing not only the magnetic attraction of song, but its power in carrying a message to the heart, and its tendency to awaken the careless to a sense of need.

"'One evening in November 1886,' said the superintendent of a boy's school, 'I was walking along a street in St. Joseph, Missouri, when I saw before me a great crowd gathered around a door. On approaching, I discovered it to be the entrance to the Young Men's Christian Association Hall. In the doorway stood some young men singing. Just as I came near enough to hear, they began:

A ruler once came to Jesus by night
To ask Him the way of salvation and light;
The Master made answer in words, true and plain,
"Ye Must be born again."

CHORUS:

Ye must be born again,
Ye must be born again,
I verily say unto you,
Ye must be born again!

When they came to the chorus, the sword of the Spirit entered my soul. It seemed to me that I was brought face to face with the Lord Jesus. There on the street, while the song was being sung, I asked Him to teach me how to be born again, and He did. I accepted an invitation to the service of the evening and after that service, for the first time in my life, I publicly acknowledged Christ as my Saviour. I have always considered that it was through the influence of that hymn that I was awakened. Many times have I thanked God for the song, as well as for the courage He gave to those young men to sing it that public way.'" ABS

Must I Go, And Empty-Handed?

MUST I GO, AND EMPTY-HANDED?

In 1877 Evangelist A. G. Upham was leading a series of meetings in a church in New England where Rev. C. C. Luther was the pastor. At the start of the campaign, Rev. Upham had given out the topics for the first few days. It was the custom, in those days, to address the first sermons to the Christians. The reason was to get the Christians right with the Lord and involved in witnessing and bringing others to the meetings. This proved to be a very workable approach.

On one of the evenings, Evangelist Upham chose as his topic, "Stars for Your Crown" or "The Importance of Witnessing." In his discourse he gave as an illustration — the true story of a young man who, a month after being saved, was fatally injured in an accident. As the seriousness of his condition became evident, one of his Christian friends who was at his bedside, asked him if he was afraid to die. He replied, "Friend, no I am not afraid to die for Jesus has saved me. But, I have not been able to lead even one such as I was, to Christ in the time I have known Him. No, I am not afraid to die; but oh! If I go — must I go and empty-handed?"

Mr. George C. Stebbins told me this story and then added, "I was in Providence, Rhode Island, in meetings with Dr. Pentecost when I received the words and a letter of explanation from Rev. Luther. He informed me of the story told by Evangelist Upham, and how it had so gripped him that right in the meetings he took a piece of paper he had in his Bible and jotted down the lines as quickly as he could write them. Mr. Stebbins then added, "This proved to be one of the easiest melodies for me to write. ABS

I'm Going Higher Someday
ALFRED B. SMITH
and H. B.
HERBERT BUFFUM
Arranged by Alfred B. Smith
1. Of-ten I've watched the clouds up in the sky. Al-ways I've heard they were man-y miles high; Then as they sailed out of sight far a-way I said I'm go-ing far high-er some day.
2. Men fly the o-ceans and probe out-er space Their earthly fame time will dull and e-race. Christ gave this promise when He went a-way "I'm go-ing high-er, yes, high-er some day."
3. Of-ten my soul has been lift-ed a-bove Lost in the o-cean of God's mighty love; Though this is won-der-ful yet I can say "I'm go-ing high-er, yes, high-er some day."
4. Soon will the Sav-iour from Heav-en ap-pear Com-ing in clouds for His chil-dren so dear, Friend are you read-y—with me can you say "I'm go-ing high-er, yes, high-er some day?"
CHORUS 4 parts
I'm go-ing high-er, yes, high-er some day, I'm go-ing high-er to stay; Ov-er the clouds and be-yond the blue sky, *To be with Je-sus for-ev-er on high— Loved ones I'll
*Optional phrase (Going where none ever sicken or die)
© Copyright 1981 by Alfred B. Smith. All rights reserved.

I'M GOING HIGHER SOMEDAY

It was a beautiful clear day in Kansas City, Missouri. The year was 1924 and Herbert Buffum, an itinerant preacher and singer, was walking along Main Street enjoying himself when he was attracted by the faint whir of an engine. As he stopped and listened he reasoned that it had to be coming from the sky above and as his eyes searched they eventually focused upon a small plane flying among the fleecy clouds in the great expanse of the blue heavens. It was flying so high that he could hardly see it. It was for this reason that Buffum hardly heard the whir of its engine. As he stood enthralled at the sight, for flying was then in its infancy, his eyes began suddenly to search deeper and deeper into the depths of the wide blue expanse. He mused "It must be wonderful to fly that high." He became so engrossed with the scene and with his thoughts that he became unaware of the people and noise about him.

With a start he awoke from his daydreaming for it seemed that the faint whir of the engine had become a loud audible voice saying, "Herbert Buffum, you're going higher someday!"

It was with this experience still warm upon his memory that he wrote "I'm Going Higher Someday."

Herbert Buffum was born in Lafayette, Illinois in 1879. He preached his first sermon when he was seventeen years of age and also wrote his first song the same year. At the time he was serving with a Christian service organization called "The Volunteers of America." It was while he was sweeping the floor of the gospel mission that he received the inspiration to write his first song. ABS

God Understands

GOD UNDERSTANDS

This song was born out of deep bereavement and sorrow. I'll let Dr. Oswald J. Smith tell it as he told it to me years ago.

"My youngest sister, Ruth, and her husband, Clifford Bicker, were finishing their first term as missionaries to Peru, South America. During their stay, God had blessed their home with two happy boys. We had received word that their first furlough tickets had been purchased for the boat passage and all that remained were a few last minute details. Soon we would have the joy of being united with them and seeing the boys for the first time — this after several years of separation. We could hardly wait. Then came the tragic news — Ruth's husband, Cliff, had been killed instantly in an auto accident! Our jubilation was turned to sorrow. Along with this was the deep concern for my little sister of twenty-six and her two fatherless boys, alone now in a foreign land. Far from loved ones — yet not alone; for I reasoned it is for times such as this that God has said, 'I will never leave you.'

"It was at that moment, and I am sure directed by the Lord, that I wrote a poem especially for my sister, Ruth. It began:

God understands your sorrow
He sees the falling tear,
And whispers 'I am with thee,'
Then falter not, nor fear.

"I sent it off to her immediately and God in a wonderful way used it to lift the burdens and sorrows and prepare her heart for the trip home.

"I later sent the poem to Mr. B. D. Ackley who wrote the beautiful and strong musical setting which God has used to send it around the world." ABS

I've Found The Way
Paul Rader
Arr. By C. & D. Kreiger
P. R.
1. Oft - en my heart longed to pray; Sin - ner, so what could I say?
2. Right-eous-ness now I have found; Cal - va-ry's cleans-ings a - bound;
3. Wan - der-ing days now are done; Guess-ing days now are all gone;
4. Ask - ing, I now may re - ceive; Seek - ing, I know He'll re - lieve;
Then I was told of the blood-cleans-ing way O - pened by Je - sus, my Lord.
Tak - ing this blood-way I'm on sol - id ground, Ground of Christ's me-rits a - lone.
Now a new path-way of prayer is be - gun, O - pened by Je - sus a - lone.
Knock-ing, I get, for I take and be-lieve Je - sus is pray-ing for me.
REFRAIN
1. 2.
I've found the way thro' the blood past the veil To the Ho-ly of Ho-lies with God.
There, by His pow'r, o-ver sin I pre-vail, I can walk in the path that He trod.
There in the pres-ence of Je-sus I stand, Glo-ri-fied Son at the Fa-ther's right hand;
There I can plead, I can claim, I can have All that He pur-chased for me.
©Copyright 1956 Renewal. The Rodeheaver Co., Owner.
Arr. ©Copyright 1967 by The Rodeheaver Co., in "Golden Series, Low Voice Collection No. 2." All Rights Reserved.

I'VE FOUND THE WAY

The great preacher and evangelist, Paul Rader, was holding a special city-wide evangelistic campaign in Toronto, Canada. The year was 1928 and playing at the hotel in which the Rader party was staying, was a newly formed orchestra which advertised itself as playing "the sweetest music this side of heaven." Mr. Rader had seen the picture of the orchestra leader and his band and the slogan each time he entered the hotel but because of the great demands of the meetings, he had not had a chance to hear them. He was, however, curious to know what their interpretation of "the sweetest music this side of heaven" would be. His opportunity came a few days later when after a meeting he invited Merrill Dunlop, the party's pianist, to join him for an evening snack, for Mr. Rader had not had time for dinner before the meeting. The only place available for food, was the hotel's main dining room in which this orchestra was playing. Now Paul Rader would have his curiosity satisfied. They were seated at the edge of the dining area but close enough to see and hear the "band" without any difficulty. The music began to rise and flood the area with beautiful sounds — every musician was an expert following the baton of his leader who was a master. Merrill Dunlop remarked to me, "Al, it was a great orchestra and the music they played was carefully chosen. I enjoyed the blending of chords and the interpretation — it was all done in such good taste. After finishing our meal and as we prepared to leave, Mr. Rader said to me, 'Merrill, that's a good orchestra and I'm sure it will go places. But you know, they may say they are playing the "sweetest music this side of heaven" but I disagree with them; for I feel that there is nothing sweeter this side of heaven than a song that tells people about Jesus and His love. Merrill, I feel a song coming on — one that will beat anything we've heard tonight. Good-night, Merrill, see you in the morning!" Merrill Dunlop continued, "Al, I said good-night to Mr. Rader and went to my room and in a matter of minutes I was sound asleep. It was bright and early the next morning that I received a call from Mr. Rader. He said, 'Merrill, I've got to see you before breakfast. Meet me in a half hour at the piano in the big dining room where we were last night and bring some manuscript paper with you.'

"When I met Mr. Rader, he had a paper in hand. He sat me down at the piano and began to sing the melody and words he had written. I followed along the best I could and soon the song that Mr. Rader had promised the night before had become a reality. Its strong and lilting melody carried a truth that would outlast time and eternity as it proclaimed, 'I've Found the Way,' a message of hope and assurance — truly the sweetest music this side of heaven." ABS

I GAVE MY LIFE FOR THEE

"Yes, 'I Gave My Life For Thee' is mine and perhaps it will interest you to know how nearly it went into the fire instead of all over the world." It was Frances Ridley Havergal writing to a friend who had asked the authorship of the song. I'll let Miss Havergal continue with her story. "I was twenty-three at the time and was visiting friends in Germany. I had been sightseeing and was very tired. I was staying as a guest in the home of a well-known pastor. On the wall of this home, was a picture of the curcifixion with the words, 'I Gave My Life For Thee' written underneath it. Earlier in my visit, I had noticed this painting but its significance had not gotten hold of me. This day I sat down and looked at it intently. I re-read the words 'I Gave My Life For Thee' and then it seemed as if I heard a voice asking 'What hast thou given for me?' Immediately in a flash the words came to me. I scribbled them in a few minutes of the back of a circular I had in my purse. I read them over and thought, well, this is not worthwhile poetry anyhow, so I won't bother to write it out on paper. I then thought, why keep it at all? So I threw it into the burning fire in the fireplace. Somehow it did not ignite but fell out onto the hearth. As I saw it there a sudden impulse made me pick it up. It was crumpled and singed but I put it in my purse.

"Some days later when I was back in England, I went to see an old woman in the poor house. She began talking to me about her Saviour as she always did. I thought I would see if she, a simple woman, would care for these verses which I felt sure were of no value to anyone.

"I read them to her and to my delight and surprise she was so pleased that she requested a copy for herself. This I gave her and soon I was sending copies of it in all directions."

This hymn proved to be the first of many written by Miss Havergal. Some of her others are: "I Am Trusting Thee Lord Jesus," "Who Is On The Lord's Side?", "O Saviour, Precious Saviour," and "Take My Life And Let It Be."

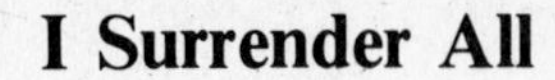
I Surrender All

JUDSON W. VAN de VENTER
WINFIELD S. WEEDEN
1. All to Je - sus I sur-ren - der, All to Him I free - ly give;
2. All to Je - sus I sur-ren - der, Hum-bly at His feet I bow;
3. All to Je - sus I sur-ren - der, Make me, Sav - ior, whol-ly Thine;
4. All to Je - sus I sur-ren - der, Lord, I give my - self to Thee;
I will ev - er love and trust Him, In His pres - ence dai - ly live.
World - y pleas - ures all for - sak - en, Take me, Je - sus, take me now.
Let me feel the Ho - ly Spir - it— Tru - ly know that Thou art mine.
Fill me with Thy love and pow - er, Let Thy bless-ings fall on me.
CHORUS
I sur-ren - der all, I sur-ren - der all,
I sur - ren - der, I sur - ren-der all, I sur - ren - der, I sur - ren-der all,
All to Thee, my bless - ed Sav - ior, I sur - ren - der all.

I SURRENDER ALL

"For many years I had been studying art. My whole life was wrapped up in its pursuit and the thing farthest from my mind was active Christian service," so spoke Judson W. Van DeVenter. "My dream was to become an outstanding and famous artist. After graduating from college I studied drawing and painting under a well-known German teacher. To help me financially, I taught school and eventually I became supervisor of art in the public schools of Sharon, Pennsylvania.

"It was during this period in my life that a revival was held in the First Methodist Church of which I was a member. I became very interested in these meetings as a personal worker. It was not very long after that, I was licensed as a lay preacher. God blessed my efforts and many souls were saved in the meetings I conducted. The Spirit of God was strongly urging me to give up teaching and to enter the evangelistic field but I would not yield. I still had the burning desire to be an artist. This battle raged for five years. At last the time came when I could hold out no longer and I surrendered my all — my time and my talents. It was then that a new day was ushered into my life. I became an Evangelist and discovered that deep down in my soul was hidden a talent hitherto unknown to me. God had hidden a song in my heart and touching a tender chord He caused me to sing songs I had never sung before.

"I wrote 'I Surrender All' in memory of the time when, after the long struggle, I had surrendered and dedicated my life to active Christian service for the Lord. It was written in the home of Mr. George Sebring in East Palestine, Ohio. It was Mr. Sebring who later founded the city of Sebring, Florida." ABS

Is It The Crowning Day?
HENRY OSTROM
CHARLES H. MARSH
1. Je - sus may come to - day— Glad day! glad day! And I would see my Friend; Dan - gers and trou - bles would end If Je - sus should come to - day.
2. I may go home to - day— Glad day! glad day! Seems like I hear their song: Hail to the ra - di - ant throng If I should go home to - day.
3. Faith-ful I'll be to - day— Glad day! glad day! And I will free - ly tell Why I should love Him so well, For He is my all to - day.
CHORUS
Glad day! glad day! Is it the crown-ing day? I'll live for to - day, nor anx - ious be, Je - sus, my Lord, I soon shall see; Glad day! glad day! Is it the crown-ing day?
© Copyright 1910 by The Praise Publishing Co. Renewed 1938 The Rodeheaver Co. Used by permission.

IS IT THE CROWNING DAY?

While a student at the Moody Bible Institute in Chicago, Illinois, in the 1930's, I would often see and hear speak, an older man who visited the campus. He was an outstanding Bible teacher and evangelist. He also had been a friend and associate of D. L. Moody and R. A. Torrey. His messages were always forceful and challenging. He would remind the students that the Lord was coming soon and it was our privilege and duty to get out the Gospel to the ends of the earth as quickly as possible. There was always the challenge: "This may be the crowning day!"

At the time, I did not dream that one of my favorite Gospel songs had been written by this wonderful man. Here's the story.

One of the first Gospel songs I learned after I had been saved was written by two men. The music was by a Mr. Charles H. Marsh, who had been the pianist for Charles M. Alexander. The words were written by a man with the illustriouis name of George Walker Whitcomb. This man I did not know (or at least was not aware of it). The song was "Is It The Crowning Day?"

It was not until the 1940's that I found out who George Walker Whitcomb was. Mr. George Sanville, manager of the Rodeheaver Company, who had been the first to publish "Is It The Crowning Day" when it was written in 1910, told me, "It was none other than Dr. Henry Ostrom, our Moody Institute visitor and Bible teacher."

The truth of the imminent return of Our Lord had become a very important part in the preaching and teaching of such men as Moody, Torrey, Lowry, Pierson, Pentecost, Riley, Billy Sunday, W. R. Newell, and others. Songs on this theme, in those days, were rather scarce and so one day Dr. Ostrom had put into words the challenge he had often given to us students — "Is It The Crowning Day?"

It was while at the Bible Conference at Winona Lake, Indiana, that he gave these words to the pianist, Charles H. Marsh, who immediately put them to melody — a very, very good one at that, for "Glad day! Glad day! Is it the crowning day?" ABS

I Must Tell Jesus

I MUST TELL JESUS

It was while he was a pastor in Lebanon, Pennsylvania, that the Rev. Elisha A Hoffman wrote "I Must Tell Jesus."

On the membership roll of the church was a lady who just seemed to be troubled with sorrows and trials all of the time. Because of this, Rev. Hoffman made a determined effort to visit with her more often than the others in the church for he sensed her need of the prayer and the reading of the Bible which accompanied each of his visits. This did much to lift her spirits and lighten her load.

Coming into her home one day, he found that a new calamity had befallen her and she was chestfallen and oh, so discouraged! As she unburdened her heart to her pastor, and as she told him what had happened, she would wring her hands and exclaim, "Oh, Brother Hoffman, what shall I do? What shall I do?" When she had finished her tale of woe, Pastor Hoffman opened the Bible and began to quote verses of assurance, trust, and the faithfulness of God. After he had read a few of them, he remarked, "You see, my dear sister, God wants to bear all of these sorrows whether great or small. The best thing we can do is to take them to Jesus. We must tell Jesus!" For a moment there was silence and then with face aglow and her eyes shining she exclaimed, "Yes, Pastor, you are so right. I must tell Jesus! I must tell Jesus!"

Pastor Hoffman said that he made no further pastoral calls that day, for in his heart was burning the phrase, "I must tell Jesus." He knew it was a message the whole world should know and what better way to send it forth than with a song. He went back to his church study and wrote "I Must Tell Jesus" that very afternoon. ABS

Battle Hymn Of The Republic

BATTLE HYMN OF THE REPUBLIC

It was in the early part of the Civil War, while on a visit to Washington, D.C., that Julia Ward Howe, her husband, and her pastor, Dr. James Clark, were the guests of Governor Andrews of Massachusetts. During their stay, they were invited to visit some of the wounded servicemen in the hospital some distance from the city. The agony and sorrow witnessed that day would long be remembered. On the return to the Capital, they found the road they were using was crowded along the way with troops who were singing, "John Brown's Body Lies Amolderin' in the Grave." They were struck with the stirring character of the melody and Dr. Clark suggested to Mrs. Howe that it deserved a better text. They finished their journey back into Washington and, for the present, the troops and the suggestion were forgotten. That evening, Mr. and Mrs. Howe retired to their room at the Willard Hotel with plans for a full night of rest and another day of visiting and travel on the morrow. But toward early morning, Mrs. Howe awoke and began to review all that she had witnessed the day before: the agony, the suffering, the terrible price of war. When would it stop? Only when the Lord returns with great power and glory, answered her heart. Her mind then focused on the troops and the catchy tune with the unsuitable words and Dr. Clark's suggestion. She could remain in bed no longer. Even though it was still dark, she carefully found her way, without disturbing her husband, to the little desk in her hotel room. She found the steel pen, put it in the ink well, and began to write, "Mine eyes have seen the glory of the coming of the Lord," on and on until she had completed five stanzas. On her return to Boston, she showed the poem to her neighbor, Mr. James T. Field, who was also the editor of the Atlantic Monthly. He was so stirred as he read it that he exclaimed, "This should be called, 'The Battle Hymn of the Republic.'"

It was published in the Monthly in February of 1862. ABS

Amazing Grace
Early American Melody
Virginia Harmony, 1831
JOHN NEWTON, 1725-1807
1. A - maz - ing grace! how sweet the sound That saved a
2. 'Twas grace that taught my heart to fear, And grace my
3. Through man - y dan - gers, toils, and snares, I have al
4. The Lord has prom - ised good to me, His word my
5. Yea, when this flesh and heart shall fail, And mor - tal
wretch like me! I once was lost, but now am
fears re - lieved; How pre - cious did that grace ap -
read - y come; 'Tis grace hath brought me safe thus
hope se - cures; He will my shield and por - tion
life shall cease, I shall pos - sess, with - in the
found, Was blind, but now I see.
pear The hour I first be - lieved!
far, And grace will lead me home.
be As long as life en - dures.
veil, A life of joy and peace. A - men.

AMAZING GRACE

The Psalmist tells us, "God works in mysterious ways, His wonders to perform." We can see His "mysterious workings" in connection with this great hymn since its writing over 200 years ago (1779). For years "Amazing Grace" has been a favorite, particularly in our Southern churches and no convention, especially a Baptist convention, is ever complete unless it has been sung at least once.

But a few years ago, through an "accident," it became the number-one song of the recording world and it stayed at the top for weeks. This so-called accident, in which I can see the hand of God, occurred when a young woman made a pop recording and needed a "back-up" for the "flip-side"; preferably something on which no copyright fee would have to be paid. She suggested a song she learned in Sunday School. "It was a religious song but no one would play that side anyway." And so, "Amazing Grace" became the flip-side, or so they thought; for when the record was released, for some unknown reason the "disc-jockeys" began to use the flip-side. Soon every radio station in the country was playing "Amazing Grace." In a matter of a few short weeks, it had become number one on the hit parade and millions were hearing the testimony of John Newton written 200 years before.

It was my privilege to know and work with the late Dr. Donald Grey Barnhouse, the great preacher and Bible teacher. Dr. Barnhouse considered the life of John Newton to be second only to the life of the apostle Paul and it was he who first acquainted me with the life of this unusual man.

John Newton was born in London in the year 1725. His father was a sea captain. His mother, a devout Christian woman who, realizing that an illness she had would take her life within a short time, taught her son to know the Bible at an early age.

When John was seven, his mother died and he became a cabin boy aboard a sailing ship. His experiences through the years on the sea were dangerous and exciting, even to being shanghaied. That is, he was forced to join the crew of a Man of War. Here he was cruelly treated, being flogged and abused. After this experience, he joined the crew of a slave ship and eventually became a captain. During all of this, John drifted far from his mother's God and the Bible. He later wrote, "I often saw the necessity of being a Christian as a means of escaping hell, but I loved sin and was unwilling to forsake it."

Each year saw him sinking lower into the pits of sin and soon he had gotten so low that even the ship's crew despised him as being no more than an animal. On one occasion, the drunk captain fell overboard but the men did not so much as make an effort to drop a boat over the side to rescue him. They simply took a whaling harpoon and threw it at him. It caught him in his hip and the crew hauled him aboard, much the same as they would a large fish. Because of this occurrence, John Newton limped the rest of his life, but as he would say, "Each limp is a constant reminder of God's grace to this wretched sinner."

Amazing Grace is really the life story and testimony of John Newton. It was in 1779 while working on the hymnal "Olney Hymns" with William Cowper, author of "There Is a Fountain Filled with Blood" that he wrote this gem of hymnology using as its title "Faiths Review and Expectation."

ABS

God Leads Us Along
G. A. Young
G. A. Young
1. In shad-y, green pas-tures, so rich and so sweet, God leads His dear
2. Some-times on the mount where the sun shines so bright, God leads His dear
3. Tho sor-rows be-fall us and Sa-tan op-pose, God leads His dear
4. A - way from the mire and a - way from the clay, God leads His dear
chil-dren a - long; Where the wa-ter's cool flow bathes the wea-ry one's feet,
chil-dren a - long; Some - times in the val-ley, in dark-est of night,
chil-dren a - long; Thru grace we can con-quer, de-feat all our foes,
chil-dren a - long; A - way up in glo-ry, e - ter-ni-ty's day,
God leads His dear chil-dren a - long.
CHORUS
Some thru the wa-ters, some thru the flood,
Some thru the fire, but all thru the blood; Some thru great sor-row, but
God gives a song, In the night sea-son and all the day long.

GOD LEADS US ALONG

Story Number One ...

It was while visiting Dr. Haldor Lillenas in his private office at the Lillenas Publishing House in Kansas City, Missouri, that he gave me a story in connection with "God Leads Us Along" that I have never been able to forget and one that I have often used and God has blessed in a special way to the hearts of many. I am including it with a prayer that it will bless many more.

It seems but yesterday but the year was 1942. I was still a student at Wheaton College and I was working on my first "Favorites" songbook which in the years to come would make music history. My just starting in the publishing business I am sure had something to do in opening the windows of memory in the heart and mind of Dr. Lillenas and he began to tell me how he had come to America as a young boy from Norway. It had not been too easy for him for it meant that he not only had to earn his living but had to learn a new way and a new language. But God in His providence had sent a dear Christian woman across his path who had led him to Christ. Her name was Manie Payne Ferguson, in later years (1902) she would write the hymn "Blessed Quietness" but during this early acquaintance she had taught him the song "God Leads Us Along." She had not written it but it was her favorite.

With Christ in his heart and a new purpose in his life young Haldor went forth, determined to serve the Lord and singing his "new" song. In due time God called him into a unique ministry. He not only preached but wrote and sang many songs which he himself composed. Eventually he was led to devote all of his time to music, not only in writing but in publishing and that is why I was sitting in his music office and not in a preacher's study.

He continued, "Al, some time ago I was recounting how wonderfully God had led me and through the years had given me the very desires of my heart. I, a former immigrant boy, now a child of the King, having his own music company to send the good news around the world. I thought of Mrs. Ferguson and of the song that had become my theme song since that wonderful day when she introduced me to Jesus. I mused, "Could the writer of the song be alive? How I'd love to have the story of how he wrote it for I'm sure it would be a good one."

I began to make inquiry and soon the word came back. Rev. Young had passed away but some thought his widow was still alive. I reasoned — well, I'll have to wait 'til I get to "glory" to get it from Brother Young but maybe his wife would know. In a short time I was able to obtain her address and one morning bright and early I started off from Kansas City. It was quite a drive and when I came to the small town in which the woman lived, I pulled into a service station. The attendant came out bright and cheerful but as I showed him the address I had in the letter his face clouded. "Why sir — that's the County Poor House up that road about three miles and mister when I say poor house I really mean poor house!" His description was not too inviting and for a moment I almost said to him, "Fill up my gas tank. I've got to get back to Kansas City." For I reasoned "How can I go into a place such as this fellow describes and comfort a woman who perhaps is spending the rest of her life there?" But something seemed to say, "Haldor, you've come all this way so you had better go." "Well, Al, I went and am I ever glad I did for that day I met one of the most unusual women I ever met in my life. After we had been introduced she said, "Why you're Dr. Lillenas and you've come all the way from Kansas City to see Little Me?' Then she smiled and straightened her whole 4′10″ form and said — 'Of course, that's just the way Our Blessed Lord leads — doesn't He?'

"She continued, 'You know, Doctor, I came to know Jesus Christ when I was a young girl. One day I met a young man. He, too, was a Christian. Soon we had fallen in love. As we began to make plans for our marriage we did not forget to include our best friend. Together we pledged that we would go anywhere and do anything that the Lord

Jesus would want us to. God would do the leading and we would do the following.'

"'Oh, Dr. Lillenas, it was so wonderful as we saw Him do miracles in our lives! And you know through the many years we never went hungry! Oh, sometimes we didn't have too much of this world's goods but, Dr. Lillenas, we always had so much of Jesus.'

"As she continued to talk her face turned serious as she said, 'One day God took my sweet husband home. Oh, how I missed him for we had always served the Lord together. In my heart I wondered — 'Where will God now lead me?'

"The seriousness vanished from her face as it became radiant and she exclaimed, 'Dr. Lillenas, God led me here! I'm so glad he did, for you know, about every month someone comes into this place to spend the rest of their days and Dr. Lillenas, so many of them don't know my Jesus. I'm having the time of my life introducing them to Jesus! Dr. Lillenas, isn't it wonderful how God leads?'"

Tears had filled the eyes of Dr. Lillenas as he told me the story. After some of the tears had run down his rough cheeks and he had wriped his eyes he said, "You know, Al Smith — I forgot to ask the dear lady for the story I had come for, for I was so blessed and overwhelmed with what I had just heard — two young people starting out in life to serve the Lord and though to some it would seem to be a life of privation yet to this dedicated saint the thing that mattered was to serve the Saviour and though even her husband had been taken and she had to spend the remaining days in a not-too-luxurious poor farm, even for that — she was thankful for here she could lead men and women to know her Christ."

Away from the mire and away from the clay,
God leads His dear children along,
Away up in Glory — Eternity's day,
God leads His dear children along.

How I thank the Lord that Dr. Lillenas took time out of his busy life to give a then "beginner" publisher the story. In later years I was able to get the story leading to the actual writing of "God Leads Us Along" — the story which follows.

Story Number Two ...

George A. Young was a preacher who much of his life made his living doing carpentry work — a skill he was proud to have; for was not our Lord known as the carpenter from Nazareth? Young and his wife had started out early in their married life to serve the Lord. Theirs was a dedication which eventually led to full-time Christian service — going from small church to small church in the country areas.

Their experiences were many — some good and some heartbreaking — as they faithfully ministered in season and out of season. Often those with whom they worked were too poor to help in supplying the needs of the preacher and his wife and family. Sometimes there were those who just didn't care. Through it all, George Young and his wife did not waver but as they often said, "God is doing the leading and all we have to do is follow. He will not forsake us in time of need and is also very much aware of our situation wherever we are." It was in times such as these, that Young's saw and hammer came in very handy.

It also came in handy when, after years of living in "borrowed tents and from hand to mouth" (George Young would always remind you that it was God's hand) the Youngs were able to commence building a small home of their own. By working extra hours at his trade whenever he could, and by the family often doing without the "extras," enough money had been put aside to eventually purchase a piece of land made available at a low price by a friend. Now after waiting all these years, a dream that often seemed impossible would become a reality. The house would take several more years of sacrifice and dreaming before it would be completed, but in the end it would be well worth the waiting. Had not Our Blessed Lord promised a mansion in Heaven and could He not provide a home for his pilgrims while here on earth?

At last the day came, and the Young family moved into their own home. How wonderful it was! It was almost too good to be true — but it was true! Together they sang the Doxology to the God who also gave them songs to sing, even in the darkest of nights, and who had faithfully led them all the way. Because they were now living in their own home did not mean that George Young would curtail his service and stay home more to enjoy it. No, he kept on preaching and witnessing; for after all, this world was not his lasting home — he was just passing through.

Then disaster struck while George Young and his family were away holding meetings. It is thought that someone, not in sympathy with Young and his preaching and not in favor that the likes of him should have a home of his own, set fire to it. When George returned he found but a heap of ashes. All that he and his family had sacrificed for and dreamed of was now but a memory. The home, clothing, cherished keepsakes that never could be replaced, were all lost in the conflagration. As Mr. Young stood there, his heart was sad but he found a deep consolation as he remembered the priceless things he possessed which could not be destroyed by fire. Perhaps, like Job, this could be an attack of Satan but he was not alone, for God was aware of it all.

In his mind, words began to form —

Tho' sorrows befall us and Satan oppose,
God leads His dear children along.
Some thro' the waters, some thro' the flood,
Some thro' the fire, but all thro' the blood;
Some thro' great sorrow, but God gives a song.
In the night season and all the day long.

George A. Young had been given the beginning of a song in his deep night of despair — a song that would lift many a burden and give light and encouragement to untold thousands in the years ahead. Within a few days he had written three other stanzas and in 1903 it was first published.

ABS

At Calvary

WILLIAM R. NEWELL
DANIEL B. TOWNER
1. Years I spent in van - i - ty and pride, Car - ing not my Lord was
2. By God's Word at last my sin I learned— Then I trem-bled at the
3. Now I've giv'n to Je - sus ev - 'ry - thing, Now I glad - ly own Him
4. O the love that drew sal - va - tion's plan! O the grace that bro't it
cru - ci - fied, Know-ing not it was for me He died On Cal - va - ry.
law I'd spurned, Till my guilt - y soul im - plor-ing turned To Cal - va - ry.
as my King, Now my rap-tured soul can on - ly sing Of Cal - va - ry
down to man! O the might - y gulf that God did span At Cal - va - ry.
CHORUS
Mer - cy there was great and grace was free, Par - don there was mul - ti -
plied to me, There my bur-dened soul found lib-er - ty—At Cal - va - ry.

AT CALVARY

This gospel song of testimony, which is enjoyed by so many and is one of my favorites, would not have been written had it not been for a concerned father and a Bible School official who made an exception to the rules because he felt God wanted him to do so.

I'll let Dr. R. A. Torrey tell the story as he told it in a Torrey-Alexander meeting in Birmingham, England, in 1905.

"When I was President of the Moody Bible Institute, I received a letter from a very concerned pastor father who told me of a son who was causing himself and his family a great deal of trouble. His life was really mixed up, and the father felt that the only thing that could help would be if his son could be under the daily teaching of the Bible as well as Christian fellowship with other young people. I, at first, advised the father that even though I sympathized with him, for I too was a father, yet, because I was running a Bible school and not a reform school, I had to deny his request. The broken-hearted father contacted me immediately upon receipt of my reply and again pleaded his son's cause. This time I capitulated with the stipulation that the son was to see me each day and that he would make every effort to abide by the rules and requirements of the Institute. If he failed in any of these terms, I would have to ask him to leave.

"The son came and at first it almost seemed hopeless. Never have I met someone with so many problems, and particularly in the spiritual realm. He did however, abide by the rules as he had promised. As I look back, I feel that this was his first step to recovery. But each day as he came, he would reveal by his questions the turmoil and raging turbulence which was almost tearing him apart. Each day I would answer his questions with God's Word. I felt that this would do more than all of the human reasoning I might be able to give. The days became weeks, the weeks became months, and though some improvement seemed to have been made yet there was not the total deliverance for which we prayed. One day he came in with his face aglow, like the rain on parched ground — God had answered our prayers for his needs. From that time on he became an exemplary student and today in our country, he is one of our fine Bible teachers — his name is William R. Newell."

It was my privilege to know Dr. Newell personally and he confirmed all that Dr. Torrey had said but then he added, "You know, Al, if I hadn't gone through that experience, and may I assure you it wasn't pleasant at the time, I perhaps never would have come to know the importance of God's Word and the wonderful truth of salvation by grace — that my place had been taken at Calvary by God's only begotten Son. It was one day, as I was rejoicing in the reality of this, that I decided I would write it out as a poem — more or less giving an account of God's leading in my life. I thought how I gave little thought to the Gospel, but how through Dr. Torrey and his faithfulness in presenting God's Word as the answer to my problems, I realized I was a sinner and had to come God's way. There followed the wonderful day when I surrendered my all — that wonderful day when I came rushing into Dr. Torrey's office to tell him. It was then I decided that the poem needed one more stanza and so, led by the Holy Spirit I am sure, I wrote:

'O the Love that drew salvation's plan,
O the grace that brought it down to man;
O the mighty gulf that God did span,
At Calvary!'

"As I read what I had written, I realized that this not only was a word picture of what had happened in my life but could also apply to many more in the family of God.

"I was, at that time, teaching at the Moody Bible Institute and so with a copy of the poem in my hand, I made my way to the office of Dr. D. B. Towner, who was the head of the music department and also a well-known composer of Gospel music. I hoped that perhaps he might find the poem good enough to write some music for it. I met him in the hallway and handed it to him and then went on to a class I was teaching. After teaching the class, I was on my way back to my office when Dr. Towner met me and said, 'Bill, I was so taken with the poem you gave me that I went immediately to my studio and composed a tune. I feel that it could be the best song that either of us will ever write in our lifetime.

"And you know, Al," continued Newell, "I don't know how much merit my song has as far as literary value is concerned but I'll tell you one thing — that song has affected more people around the world than the many books the Lord has permitted me to write. God is good, isn't He?"

ABS

Face To Face
Based on I Corinthians 13:12
CARRIE E. BRECK
GRANT COLFAX TULLAR
1. Face to face with Christ, my Sav - ior, Face to face—what will it be?
2. On - ly faint - ly now I see Him, With the dark-ling veil be - tween;
3. What re-joic - ing in His pres - ence, When are ban-ished grief and pain,
4. Face to face—O bliss - ful mo - ment! Face to face—to see and know;
When with rap-ture I be - hold Him, Je - sus Christ who died for me!
But a bless-ed day is com - ing, When His glo - ry shall be seen.
When the crook-ed ways are straightened And the dark things shall be plain.
Face to face with my Re - deem - er, Je - sus Christ who loves me so!
CHORUS
Face to face I shall be - hold Him, Far be-yond the star - ry sky;
Face to face, in all His glo - ry, I shall see Him by and by!

FACE TO FACE

The melody of this wonderful song went through an experience similar to the melody by William Bradbury which is now used with Charlotte Elliott's words "Just As I Am." Both melodies were first written for a different set of words. Here is the story of "Face To Face."

Grant Colfax Tullar was holding meetings in Rutherford, New Jersey, in 1898. He decided that he would introduce something new for the Sunday evening service and so he quickly jotted down a melody and a set of words that had been forming in his mind for several days. It was entitled "All for Me the Saviour Suffered." He played it on the piano for the Pastor, Charles L. Mead, and asked him to sing it that evening. The people were blessed by the new song and were very pleased that a new song had been introduced in their church. At that time I'm sure neither they, nor the composer, felt it would "set the world on fire," but a letter Brother Tuller received the next day changed all of this. It was a letter from a Mrs. Frank Breck, and in it she had enclosed some poems for him to put to music. As he looked over the poems, one of them caught his eye. It was entitled "Face To Face." As Mr. Tuller reviewed the words, he found that they fitted exactly to the melody he had written the day before. Without a moment's hesitation he said to himself, "These words convey a stronger message with my tune than my own. I'll use these, for I feel God will bless these words to many hearts." And bless them God did!

From the day when it first appeared in print in 1898, until now, "Face To Face" has been a favorite of pilgrim hearts around the world.

ABS

Anywhere With Jesus
1,2 -JESSIE B. POUNDS
3 - HELEN G. ALEXANDER
DANIEL B. TOWNER
1. An-y-where with Je-sus I can safe-ly go, An-y-where He leads me in this world be-low; An-y-where with-out Him dear-est joys would fade, An-y-where with Je-sus I am not a-fraid.
2. An-y-where with Je-sus I am not a-lone, Oth-er friends may fail me—He is still my own; Tho His hand may lead me o-ver drear-y ways, An-y-where with Je-sus is a house of praise.
3. An-y-where with Je-sus o-ver land and sea, Tell-ing souls in dark-ness of sal-va-tion free; Read-y as He sum-mons me to go or stay, An-y-where with Je-sus when He points the way.
REFRAIN
An-y-where! an-y-where! Fear I can-not know; An-y-where with Je-sus I can safe-ly go.

ANYWHERE WITH JESUS

The theme for this song came to Dr. D. B. Towner as he was listening to a message given by D. L. Moody. It was in Binghamton, New York, in 1866 and it was one of the first meetings in which Dr. Towner was associated with Mr. Moody. It is also one of the first songs that he wrote.

Mr. Moody's sermon was filled with the challenge that with Christ as the captain of one's life you could go anywhere without fear for God would see you through. He drew his illustrations from the Bible and introduced Daniel in the Lion's Den, the Hebrew children in the fiery furnace, the Apostle Paul, and others — Moody made them come to life!

Mused Towner, "There ought to be a song written with that theme." Usually, a writer of that time would first secure the words before attempting a melody; but he decided that he would write the melody first and try to put into it the special feeling he felt was needed for such a song. After he had complete the music, he sent it on to Cleveland, Ohio. There lived a young lady named Jessie Brown who had a God-given gift for writing sacred poems. With the song, Mr. Towner included a note telling Miss Brown that he wanted the song to say "Anywhere With Jesus." As Miss Brown played the music, she was able to catch the spirit in which Mr. Towner had written it and in a very short time had written a set of words making "Anywhere With Jesus" a complete song. Soon the Sunday Schools and Christian Endeavor societies had made it their most popular Gospel song.

In 1896, Jessie Brown became the wife of Rev. John E. Pounds. It is because of this, that the name Jessie Brown Pounds is now usually used on her songs. ABS

A Charge to Keep

A CHARGE TO KEEP

There are many stories of hymns being written after reading the Bible but this is the only one I know of, which was inspired through the reading of a Bible commentary.

One day Charles Wesley was reading Matthew Henry's comments on Leviticus 8, verse 35. Henry had written, "We shall every one of us have a charge to keep, an Eternal God to glorify, an immortal soul to provide for, to serve our generation." The verse he was commenting on reads, "Therefore, shall ye abide at the door of the tabernacle of the congregation day and night seven days, and keep the charge of the Lord that ye did not." The last part of this verse is reflected in the final stanzas of the hymn as Wesley writes, "Assured, if I my trust betray, I shall forever die." This complete dedication is that which so vividly reflects the quality which made up the early Methodist Church.

It wasn't a case of being afraid of physical death but the fear of the possibility of being estranged from God because of unfaithfulness. Of physical death the early Methodists held no fear. "Our people die well," said John Wesley. Often at their funeral services there were shouts of joy at the "homegoing" of a fellow Christian. A doctor at the time of the Wesley's said, "Most people die for fear of dying but I never met such people as the Methodists; none of them are afraid of death but calm and patient and resigned to the end."

As is so often the case with older hymns, they are sometimes used with more than one melody and "A Charge to Keep" is no exception. In 1832 Dr. Lowell Mason wrote a short but beautiful setting of 8 measures fitting these words. In *Hymn Histories* I have chosen one written by George J. Elvy which is 16 measures long and which I feel helps illuminate the repetitious feeling so often associated with the shorter versions.

Beyond The Sunset

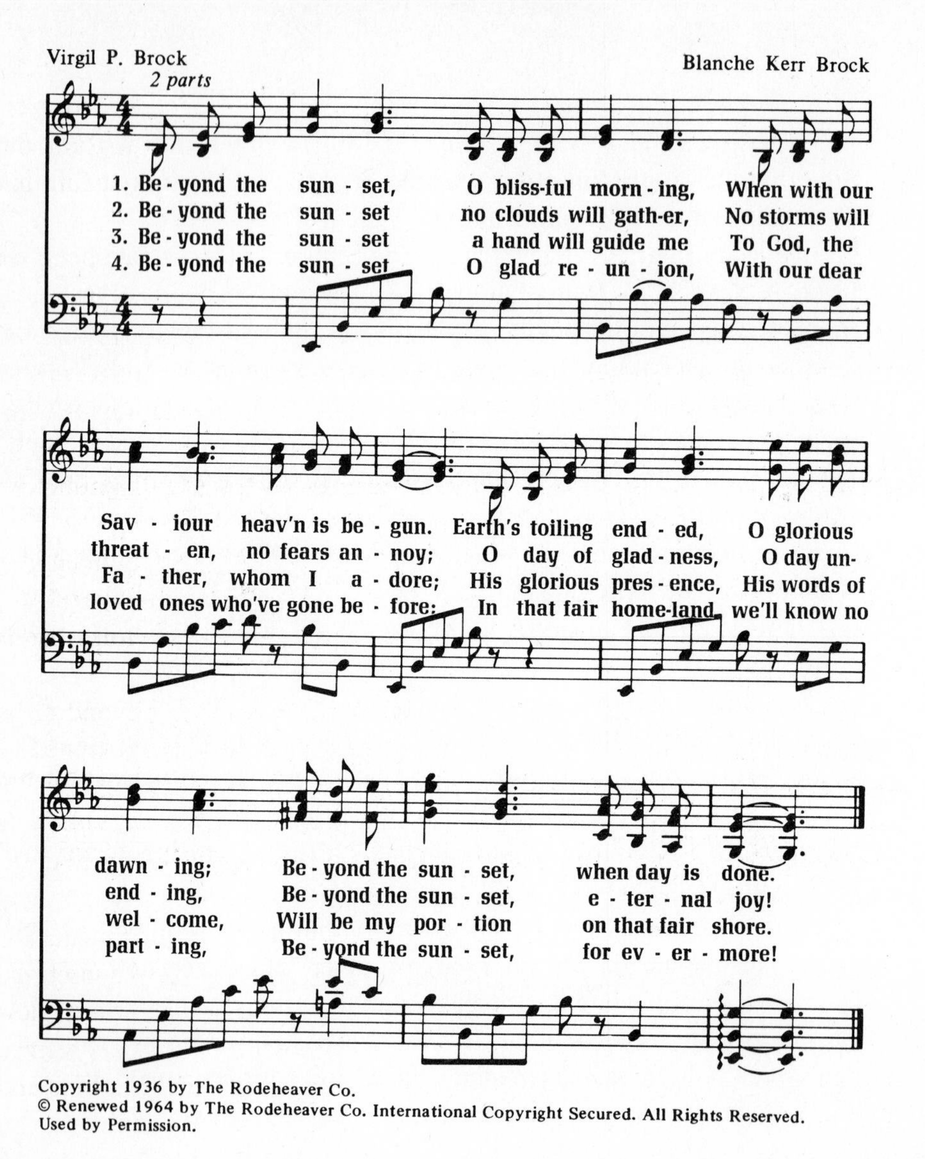
Virgil P. Brock
Blanche Kerr Brock
2 parts
1. Be - yond the sun - set, O bliss-ful morn - ing, When with our
2. Be - yond the sun - set no clouds will gath-er, No storms will
3. Be - yond the sun - set a hand will guide me To God, the
4. Be - yond the sun - set O glad re - un - ion, With our dear
Sav - iour heav'n is be - gun. Earth's toiling end - ed, O glorious
threat - en, no fears an - noy; O day of glad - ness, O day un-
Fa - ther, whom I a - dore; His glorious pres - ence, His words of
loved ones who've gone be - fore: In that fair home-land, we'll know no
dawn - ing; Be - yond the sun - set, when day is done.
end - ing, Be - yond the sun - set, e - ter - nal joy!
wel - come, Will be my por - tion on that fair shore.
part - ing, Be - yond the sun - set, for ev - er - more!

BEYOND THE SUNSET

"It was at the invitation of its genial host, Dr. Homer Rodeheaver, that we were to have a time of food and Christian fellowship at 'Rainbow Point' on Winona Lake." Mr. Virgil Brock, himself, was telling me the story.

"It was during the time of the Rodeheaver School of Music at the Winona Lake Bible Conference and Dr. Rodeheaver had asked the faculty to be his guests. Many times I had witnessed breathtaking sunsets from Rainbow Point but this particular evening words were inadequate to describe this one. The more we grasped for words, the more paltry they seemed — we stood entranced! We were watching our Heavenly Father slowly draw the curtains of heaven amid a symphony of breathtaking color as only He could do it.

"In our group was a blind man named Horace Burr. Suddenly he exclaimed, 'My, that sure is a wonderful sunset. Thanks so much for picturing it for me. I sure would have missed a lot if you folks hadn't been here to describe it.'

"Someone then raised the question, 'I wonder what's beyond all of this?' Immediately the answer began to form in my mind. I reasoned — Horace Burr has never seen the glory of an earthly sunset, yet was blessed as we tried to describe it to him — so we too, as Christians, have never seen what is beyond but God in His love and promise has told us in the Bible of the glory that is awaiting us beyond.

"In an hour my wife and I were back at our hillside apartment. The night had fallen but the thrill and inspiration of the glorious sunset had not faded. Together we sat down at the old piano, and amid the afterglow of the sunset the poem took form and was set to music. To us it seemed as if a bright light of truth had streamed into our hearts and lives and had become a song to answer our questions about the beyond.

"Our final touch, as we finished the manuscript, was to inscribe the words 'Dedicated to Horace and Grace Burr.'" ABS

Good Night And Good Morning

GOOD NIGHT AND GOOD MORNING

"God, why should you take my lovely daughter, you know how much I needed her — why, God, why?" A sudden illness had taken the life of Mrs. DeArmond's daughter. The experience had left her despondent and bitter. Later on in recounting the experience, she said, "This discordant symphony of words and thoughts raced back and forth through my mind night and day. Month after month passed until one night, after I had tried to sleep and could not, I went out into the yard and began to walk back and forth on my lawn. The bright stars in the heavens and the stillness of the night were in stark contrast to the bitter darkness and turmoil that was raging within. Then words came to me — not words of thunder but words as if spoken directly from heaven assuring me, 'Lizzie, Christians do sorrow but they also have this blessed hope — we do not say good-bye to our loved ones when they leave us, we only say good-night here, but it will be good-morning up there!' The raging seas were stilled, God's peace flooded my heart and soul and, through this experience, God gave me a song."

The musical setting of this song has played no small part in its popularity. Dr. Homer Rodeheaver, its composer, was born in the mountains of East Tennessee, and through the influence of another Gospel song, "I'll Go Where You Want Me To Go, Dear Lord," was led into Christian service. He became associated with Evangelist Billy Sunday as his song-leader and soloist. He also founded the Rodeheaver Company which first published the great Gospel song favorites of the Sunday era and eventually developed this company into one of the leading church music publishers. Dr. Rodeheaver, himself, did not have time to do very much in the way of composing, but as one realizes the effect that "Good Night And Good Morning" and the song "Then Jesus Came" (another Rodeheaver setting) have had, how one wishes that he could have spent more time in the composing field. ABS

Heartaches

A. H. A.
Rev. A. H. Ackley
1. When your heart is ach-ing, turn to Je - sus, He's the dear-est Friend that you can know; You will find Him standing close beside you, Wait-ing peace and com-fort to be - stow. . .
2. There is joy for ev - 'ry blight-ing sor - row, Sweet re - lief for ev - 'ry bit - ter pain, Je - sus Christ is still the great Phy-si-cian, No one ev - er sought His help in vain. . .
3. Je - sus un-der-stands, what-e'er the trou-ble, And He waits to heal your wound-ed soul; Will you trust His love so strong and tender, He a - lone can make your spir-it whole. . .
CHORUS
Heart-aches, take them all to Je - sus, Go to Him to - day, do it now with-out de - lay; Heart-aches, take them all to Je - sus, He will take your heartaches all a-way.
He will take them all a-way.

HEARTACHES

"Kick him into the street," said a neighbor, "I cannot," said the father. "He is my son and I love him!"

The drama that was unfolding was caused by a stubborn, rebellious, defiant, and impenitent son — a son who was so sin-hardened that the appeals and tears of a loving father were of no avail. He had brought disgrace upon the family name. His wild life of crime had caused his mother's early death and now his rebellious, unrepentent, ungodly attitudes and actions were breaking the heart and health of his father. How long could this go on?

The brokenhearted father went to Rev. A. H. Ackley and told his story. The story of a son who had defied everyone as he lead his life of recklessness and now was sentenced to serve many years in prison at hard labor. "The numbing heartache and agony of the father could not be described as his son remained unrepentent and blatantly defiant," said Rev. Ackley as he told me the story. He continued, "Together we prayed for the prodigal son, that somehow God would stop him in his mad rush and save him. We also thanked the Lord that He was a very present help in time of trouble and that we could come to Him at just such a time when our hearts were aching. In Him we had someone who understood and it was He who had told us to cast all of our care upon Him, for He cared for us.

"As I said good-bye to the father, I found that our talk with the Lord had made a difference. He remarked to me, 'I'll never forget this time and, come what may, I'll always remember to take my heartaches to Jesus,' and I responded, 'He will take your heartaches all away.'

"Al Smith, I knew I could never forget the picture of that father who's heart was aching almost beyond human endurance. Neither could I forget that we have a Saviour who cares and wants us to take all of our heartaches to Him. It was that evening I wrote 'Heartaches.'" ABS

Jesus Led Me All The Way
JOHN W. PETERSON
JOHN W. PETERSON
1. Some day life's jour - ney will be o'er, And I shall reach that dis - tant shore; I'll sing while en - t'ring heav - en's door, "Je - sus led me all the way."
2. If God should let me there re - view The wind - ing paths of earth I knew, It would be prov - en clear and true— Je - sus led me all the way.
3. And hith - er - to my Lord hath led, To - day He guides each step I tread; And soon in heav'n it will be said, "Je - sus led me all the way."
CHORUS
Je - sus led me all the way, Led me step by step each day; I will tell the saints and an - gels as I lay my bur - dens down, "Je - sus led me all the way."
© Copyright 1954 by Singspiration, Inc. All rights reserved. Used by permission.

JESUS LED ME ALL THE WAY

For a good number of years it was my privilege to direct the singing at the Founder's Week Conference of the Moody Bible Institute in Chicago, Illinois. Never will I forget the thrill of the great congregational singing in the Moody Memorial Church, as some 5000 Christians raised their voices in praise and thanksgiving.

Because so many in attendance were preachers, missionaries, and Christian workers, it made the songleading easy; in fact, because of this, the large congregation could be treated just like one great choir. This I often did, with the result that one could attain effects and inspiration not equaled at any other place.

One afternoon I chose as the concluding song for the session, and following the message, Fanny Crosby's song, "All The Way My Saviour Leads Me." Each stanza seemed to take on a greater dimension until, when we reached the great concluding phrase, "This my song thru endless ages, Jesus led me all the way," it seemed as if all that was needed was the sound of the trumpet heralding us to come up higher. I could have dismissed the congregation but never before in all of the times I had sung the song, had the truth of the fact "Jesus led me all the way" been brought so close to my heart. I was overwhelmed! Turning to the audience, I asked if they, without the help of the great organ and the two concert grand pianos, would softly repeat that last line of the song as the benediction for the meeting. As the great host of believers began to softly voice the proclamation that Fanny Crosby had written over 80 years before, "This my song through endless ages, Jesus led me all the way," a holy hush seemed to envelop each singer. When the last faint strains had melted away, each left reassured that a nail-scarred hand was leading them.

Listening to the meeting on a speaker, because they were unable to attend, was the staff of Radio Station WMBI. Included among them was the young musician and composer, John W. Peterson. When I met him a short time after, he remarked how he had been blessed by the meeting and particularly the last song. To this I replied, "Thanks, John. By the way, why don't you write a complete song using Fanny's last line as the title for yours?"

Some days later, I received a manuscript from John. It was entitled, "Jesus Led Me All The Way." ABS

Jesus Paid It All

Jesus Paid It All
ELVINA M. HALL
JOHN T. GRAPE
1. I hear the Sav - ior say, "Thy strength in - deed is small!
2. Lord, now in - deed I find Thy pow'r, and Thine a - lone,
3. For noth - ing good have I Where - by Thy grace to claim—
4. And when be - fore the throne I stand in Him com - plete,
Child of weak - ness, watch and pray, Find in Me thine all in all."
Can change the lep - er's spots And melt the heart of stone.
I'll wash my gar - ments white In the blood of Cal - v'ry's Lamb.
"Je - sus died my soul to save," My lips shall still re - peat.
CHORUS
Je - sus paid it all, All to Him I owe;
Sin had left a crim - son stain— He washed it white as snow.

JESUS PAID IT ALL

In all of sacred music, I doubt if there is a better wedding of music and words.

The words burst upon the heart of the writer, Elvina Hall, in the Monument Street Methodist Church in Baltimore as the pastor of her church was leading in the morning prayer. He was thanking God for so perfect and complete a salvation as found in Jesus Christ. Later she would tell how the thought so overwhelmed her that she took a copy of the church hymnal, "The New Lute of Zion," and wrote the words as quickly as they came, upon the flyleaf of the hymnal. Later that day, she recopied them and gave them to her pastor and then forgot all about them.

Sometime later, the pastor was visiting the church organist, Mr. John T. Grape. For some months the church had been undergoing some repairs which soon would be finished. They then could move back into the main auditorium and they were making plans for this. The church cabinet-organ had been kept at Brother Grape's home during the remodeling and the pastor asked him, if perchance, he had had time to write any new music since having the organ at his home. Brother Grape replied that he had and began to play a melody he had just recently written. Upon hearing it, the pastor exclaimed, "Why you know, Elvina Hall gave me a beautiful set of words some time ago and, if I'm not mistaken, the melody sounded as if it had been written just for her words." With that he opened his Bible and produced the poem. As together they sang and played the new melody and the new words, an experience enveloped them that they had never witnessed before — a uniting of words and music in such a way that God had to be doing it. They were witnessing a miracle!

Soon the song was being sung in the churches of Baltimore. It was first published in 1868 in the book "Sabbath Chords." However, it gained worldwide fame after it was published in 1875 by P. P. Bliss and Ira D. Sankey in "Gospel Hymns." ABS

Beyond God's Sunset

A. B. S.
Alfred B. Smith
F C7 F Bb C7 C7
1. I've oft - en watched the clouds go by up in the sky so blue.
2. "Let not your heart be troub-led," How these words bring hope and cheer;
3. And if you'd know with-out a doubt that all of this is true,
Gm7 C7 Gm7 C7 F Bb Bbm F
I've stood a-mazed to see the sun-set in the west-ern view.
"And if I go, I'll come a-gain," His prom-ise bright and clear.
And in your life you'd know the joy the Lord has saved for you,
© Copyright 1968 by The Rodeheaver Co.
All rights reserved.

F7 F7 D7 Gm D7 Gm
But all these scenes that thrill me so soon fade and can't com - pare
"That where I am, there ye may be;" Good-bye to toil and tears!
Give Him your heart, be - lieve His Word, and He will see you through;
C7 Gm7 C7 Gm7 C7 F
With all the glo - ries that a - wait me in that land so fair.
What joy 'twill be His face to see and sing ten mil - lion years.
Then you will live e - ter - nal - ly, be - yond God's sun - set, too.
CHORUS
F C C7 B♭ F
Be - yond God's sun - set I'll nev - er roam;
rit.
F7 B♭ B♭m C C7 F
Be - yond God's sun - set, my "Home, Sweet Home."
rit.

BEYOND GOD'S SUNSET

It was Haldor Lillenas and Virgil Brock who both wrote songs entitled "Beyond The Sunset," W. C. Poole wrote "Sunrise Tomorrow," and John W. Peterson wrote "Over The Sunset Mountains." All wonderful and graphic ways of describing Heaven, that beautiful place Our Blessed Lord has prepared for them that love and serve Him. Somewhere in the life of a composer he will eventually write a song on this theme which never seems to grow old and so it was not at all unusual that one day as I viewed a Western sky tinted in colors that only God could paint I exclaimed — "How wonderful and yet the Lord has told me that He is preparing a place and a life so beautiful for me that no human eye has seen anything to compare with it, no description man ever gave with words could truthfully picture it and no man, no matter how vivid his imagination could ever envision the wonderful things that God has prepared for His children. (I Corinthians 2:9)

I felt inspired to translate into a song that which I had experienced in those few but exciting moments. The result was "Beyond God's Sunset."

Often when I sing this song I will use the following letter instead of the story. It was written by Dr. Harry Rimmer who was a cherished friend and one of the most inspiring and challenging Bible teachers and conference speakers of the last generation. He was always a favorite of young people because he had a wonderful way of making the Bible live. Dr. Rimmer was also a scientist and archaeologist in his own right and his informative lectures on science and the Bible have long been remembered.

Dr. Rimmer spent his last year in California where he had gone to live after a diagnosis that he had terminal cancer. Each Sunday he listened on the radio to his good friend in the bonds of the Gospel — Dr. Charles E. Fuller of the Old Fashioned Revival Hour. One broadcast Dr. Fuller advised his audience that on the next Sunday he would speak on his favorite subject — Heaven.

After the broadcast Dr. Rimmer wrote Dr. Fuller the following letter:

My dear Charlie:

Next Sunday you are to talk about Heaven. I am interested in that land, because I have a clear title to a bit of property there for over 50 years. I did not buy it, for it was given to me without money and without price. But the donor purchased it for me at tremendous cost. I am not holding it for speculation, for the deed is not transferrable. It is not a vacant lot, for I have been sending materials there for over fifty years out of which the greatest Architect and Builder of the Universe has been building a home for me which will suit me perfectly and will never need to be repaired. Termites cannot undermine its foundations, for it rests upon the "Rock of Ages." Fire cannot destroy it. Floods cannot wash it away. No locks or bolts will ever be placed upon its doors, for no devious person can ever enter that land where my dwelling stands, almost completed. It is ready for me to enter in and rest in peace eternally, without fear of being ejected. There is a valley of deep shadow between the place where I live in California and that to which I shall journey in a short time. I cannot reach my home in that city of gold without passing through this dark valley of shadows. But, I am not afraid, because the best Friend I ever had went through the same valley long ago, and drove away its gloom. He has stuck with me through thick and thin since we first became acquainted fifty-five years ago, and I hold His promise in printed form never to forsake me nor to leave me alone. He will be with me as I walk through the valley of the shadows, and I shall not lose my way when He is with me.

I hope to hear your sermon on Sunday next from my home here, but I have no assurance that I shall. My ticket to Heaven has no date stamped upon it, no return coupon, and no permit for baggage. I am all ready to go, and I may not be here when you are talking next Sunday, but if not, I shall meet you there someday.

Signed,
Harry Rimmer, Sc.D.

This letter was placed upon the desk of Dr. Fuller the next Wednesday. By that time Dr. Rimmer was already in that land which is fairer than day. The land that he had seen by faith for over 50 years.

Shall We Gather At The River

SHALL WE GATHER AT THE RIVER

Dr. Robert Lowry, who wrote both the words and the music for this song, was the pastor in a Baptist church in Brooklyn, New York, when he wrote "Shall We Gather At The River?" He gives the following account of his writing it.

"One afternoon in July, 1864, when I was pastor at Hanson Place Baptist Church, Brooklyn, the weather was oppressively hot, and I was lying on a lounge in a state of physical exhaustion. I was almost incapable of bodily exertion and my imagination began to take wings. Visions of the future passed before me with startling vividness. The imagery of the apocalypse took the form of a tableau. Brightest of all were the throne, the heavenly river, and the gathering of the saints. My soul seemed to take new life from that celestial outlook. I began to wonder why the hymn-writers had said so much about the 'River of Death' and so little about 'The pure water of life, clear as crystal, proceeding out of the throne of God and the Lamb.' As I mused, the words began to construct themselves. They came first as a question of Christian inquiry, 'Shall we gather?' Then they broke out in a chorus, as an answer of Christian faith, 'Yes, we'll gather!' On this question and answer form the hymn developed itself. The music came with the hymn."

This is a song that keeps living on. To some it's so much a part of America that its source is often mistaken. It was in a nationwide telecast by the Philadelphia Orchestra in 1962 in which the commentary read: "It was an early Southern Camp Meeting song and came from American folk song tradition." My friend, Dr. Bill Reynolds, in his book *Hymns Of Our Faith*, says, "Aside from the fact that it was written in Brooklyn, published in New York, not in the South, and was originally a Sunday school song not a camp meeting song — the commentator was correct!"

Draw Me Nearer

DRAW ME NEARER

This blessed song was the result of a visit made by Fanny Crosby to the home of the man who composed so many of the musical settings for her hymns. She was the guest of Dr. William Howard Doane and family in Cincinnati, Ohio.

She looked forward to these visits not only because they afforded a change of location and relief from an even-then busy New York City, but also for the wonderful Christian fellowship which she found in the Doane household.

Late one afternoon, as they were all seated on the front porch of the lovely Doane home, they witnessed the glory of a mid-west sunset with all of the riot of color which only the Creator, Himself, could paint. Though Fanny was blind yet she had witnessed many a sunset through the eyes of her Grandmother Crosby. This day members of the Doane family were her eyes. Then, as the sun began to lose itself beyond the horizon and the evening shadows began to fall, Dr. Doane spoke to Fanny of the nearness of God at a time like this — the marvel of the reality that the great Creator had become the Saviour, and day by day our desire should be to live more pleasing in His sight. Suddenly, in a moment of inspiration, Fanny asked Dr. Doane if he would write down a poem which had started in her mind during their discussion. She dictated it line by line, verse by verse, and then a chorus — and so another heart-warming Gospel song had been composed by Fanny Crosby. The next day Dr. Doane wrote the musical setting which has played such an important part in making it one of Fanny Crosby's best-loved songs.

Standing Somewhere In The Shadows

STANDING SOMEWHERE IN THE SHADOWS

Often it has been an unusual circumstance, a trying experience, or perhaps a stirring sermon, that has triggered the inspiration for the writing of a Gospel song. It was when he had lost his children in a disaster at sea that Horatio Spafford wrote "It Is Well With My Soul." "He Keeps Me Singing" came through the carnage of a fire in which Luther Bridgers lost his entire family including his wife. P. P. Bliss wrote "Almost Persuaded" after hearing a soul-searching message by a Rev. Brundage on the apostle Paul standing before King Agrippa.

"Standing Somewhere in the Shadows" was born amidst a time of heartbreak and discouragement. Rev. E. J. Rollings had often preached on God's sustaining power in times of trial, he had often reminded his congregations that God's grace was sufficient for any circumstance in life and that through all of these happenings we had the assurance that He would not forsake us, in fact, the promise was "I will *never* leave you." But now it was striking nearer home. Now he was not on the giving end but the receiver. Now he was the one being buffeted and tossed to and fro on the waves of despair. Now he began to ask the questions and it seemed as if no one was there to answer them. Why was this happening to him? Didn't the Lord know about it or worse still — did He really care? The master buffer and the author of discouragement, Satan, was having a field day and it looked as if he were winning.

It was in the midst of this experience when things looked the darkest, when Rollings was feeling as if he were forsaken by both God and man that he received a letter. It may have had a U.S.A. stamp and postmark but to Rollings it was sent directly from Heaven. It was from a preacher friend, Rev. A. P. Gouthrey. Gouthrey's letter informed him that he had heard of his circumstances and had been praying for him but that he had also felt led to write him this letter to remind him that though things may look hopeless and though he might feel that he was alone and forsaken, and surrounded by shadows of doubt and despair, just to remember that "standing somewhere in the shadows you'll find Jesus."

A ray of hope flooded Rollings heart, and soon the rainbow of God's promises began to form as the sunshine of God's love dispelled the clouds of despair — to Rollings, Pastor Gouthrey's letter had been a message from the Lord. Soon after he wrote this song of comfort and encouragement.

ABS

Someday He'll Make It Plain To Me

SOMEDAY HE'LL MAKE IT PLAIN TO ME

Like Fanny Crosby, Adam Geibel too, was a blind hymnwriter and it was a tragedy in his life that gave to us the song "Someday He'll Make It Plain To Me."

It was Easter week and for months the Geibel family, including a married daughter and her husband, had planned to spend the weekend at the great Methodist Community of Ocean Grove located on the Atlantic Seashore in New Jersey. In the providence of God this was not to be, for tragedy struck through the unexpected.

Here's the story as related to me by the famous composer, C. Austin Miles, who was a co-worker of Dr. Geibel's.

"Adam Geibel's son-in-law, after he had graduated from college, took a position with a steel manufacturing company. He had shown great promise and was assigned to the various departments in the plant so that eventually he would be acquainted with all of the workings of the process of making steel. At this particular time, he was working in the open hearth department from which originated the molten metal used to make the steel. On Thursday evening the man who was to relieve him for two days called to say that he had an emergency which had to be taken care of and would it be possible for Dr. Geibel's son-in-law to continue to work on Friday and then he could take his place for Saturday. This Dr. Geibel's son-in-law agreed to do and thanked him for taking his place on Saturday so that he then could join the family at the seashore.

On Friday the Geibels left for the shore with the expectation that the son-in-law would join them Friday evening after work. But this was not to be. For on that Good Friday a great conveyor loaded with molten liquid steel jumped the track spewing its contents in all directions. Dr. Geibel's son-in-law, seeing what was happening, literally threw himself in front of some of his co-workers in an effort to protect them and in so doing, he was burned to death.

"The Geibels were crushed and, for a long period of time, the usually happy and jovial Dr. Geibel became disconsolate and heartbroken. It was impossible to cheer him up and so we continued to pray.

"Then one day the 'old' Geibel came back to the office. Something had happened — he told us the reason. 'Without a doubt the hardest thing I have ever had to face was not my blindness but the tragedy of losing my son-in-law. I had expected so much fromhim and loved him as if he were my own son and now he was gone. I kept asking God why. Then last night as I was praying about it, for I felt I could go on no longer in this attitude, the Lord, Himself, seemed to say to me, "Adam, someday you'll understand all about it for someday I'll make it plain to you." With that he sat down at the piano in our office and began to sing, 'I do not know why oft round me — my hopes all shattered seem to be — God's perfect plan I cannot see — but someday I'll understand.' He had written the music and words for one stanza and the chorus. We then sent the song to Lida Shivers Leech who carefully and prayerfully wrote the beautiful expressive second and third stanzas." ABS

JESUS LOVES ME

It seems very appropriate that the music for the two Gospel songs that have influenced, more than any others, the hearts of young and old alike for Christ, are still on the preferred list today — even though they were written over 100 years ago by William B. Bradbury. Bradbury is often called the Father of the Gospel hymn. The two songs referred to are the invitation song "Just As I Am" and the children's worldwide favorite "Jesus Loves Me."

The burden for this type of song had first been laid upon the heart of Mr. Bradbury when he saw children of his day faced with hymns that were, as he said, "Almost impossible to sing." To him, many of the songs had the same effect as if one were to force young, happy, alert, and healthy youngsters to walk slowly and haltingly with canes. Why not free them and write happy, bright, and simple songs that would fit in with their tempo of life and teach the precious truths of the Bible. With this mission in his heart and mind, Bradbury began to write and eventually publish the songs which would revolutionize the music of the American Sunday Schools.

Bradbury was not gifted in writing the words for his songs but had to rely upon the talents of others. He was the first to use Fanny Crosby. With "Jesus Loves Me" he used words written by Annie B. Warner.

The words of "Jesus Loves Me" came from a best-selling book of the day entitled "Say and Seal." In its time, this novel was to rank second only to "Uncle Tom's Cabin." In the book, little Johnny Fox is dying and a Mr. Linden, a real friend to children, comforts little Johnny by reading this simple poem to him. Mr. Bradbury read the book and when he came to this part of the story he realized that here was a set of words that he could use for a children's song. He wrote a melody for them and added his own chorus. The chorus was to be the trademark for Bradbury's Gospel song form, and thus, "Jesus Loves Me" was on its way. Soon every Sunday School in America was singing it and before many months had passed, it had found its way around the world and had so taken hold that it was then already destined to remain the number-one song in the hearts of boys and girls — should I say — forever? ABS

Jesus Loves Even Me
PHILIP P. BLISS
PHILIP P. BLISS
1. I am so glad that our Fa - ther in heav'n Tells of His
2. Tho I for - get Him and wan - der a - way, Still He doth
3. O if there's on - ly one song I can sing When in His
love in the Book He has giv'n; Won - der - ful things in the
love me wher - ev - er I stray; Back to His dear lov - ing
beau - ty I see the great King, This shall my song in e -
Bi - ble I see— This is the dear - est, that Je - sus loves me.
arms would I flee When I re - mem - ber that Je - sus loves me.
ter - ni - ty be: "O what a won - der that Je - sus loves me!"
CHORUS
I am so glad that Je-sus loves me, Je - sus loves me, Je-sus loves me;
I am so glad that Je - sus loves me, Je-sus loves e - ven me.

JESUS LOVES EVEN ME

I am indebted to George C. Stebbins, who gave us many favorite Gospel songs, for the story of "Jesus Loves Even Me." Here it is as he told it to me.

"Around the year 1870 the song 'O How I Love Jesus' was new and very popular. It seemed that wherever folks sang, you would be sure to hear it at least once in a service — sometimes several times. At the time, Mr. Bliss was compiling his first Sunday School songbook which he entitled 'The Charm.' Because of its popularity, Mr. Bliss wanted very much to use 'O How I Love Jesus.' But when he wrote the owner of the copyright, he was refused permission to use it, for the owner felt it would hurt the sale of his own books. It is needless to say that Mr. Bliss was very disappointed — not so much that he could not use the song, but the mercinary attitude of the owner of the copyright.

"In the days that followed, Mr. Bliss often thought of the incident and then one day the thought suddenly dawned upon him. 'It is important that I love Jesus, but it is a greater and a more wonderful truth that He loves me!' That night Bliss went to bed with the thought in his heart and on his mind. He and Mrs. Bliss were staying in the home of Mr. and Mrs. D. W. Whittle in Chicago at the time. When he came to the breakfast table he said, 'Lucy, the Lord gave me a new song early this morning and here's how it goes, 'I am so glad that the Father in Heaven tells of His love in the book He has given . . .'"

God had given Bliss a song that he could put in his book on the very page he had planned for "O, How I Love Jesus" and his song, too, was destined to become a Sunday School favorite and is still being sung a hundred or more years later. ABS

He Leadeth Me
JOSEPH H. GILMORE
WILLIAM B. BRADBURY
1. He lead - eth me! O bless-ed thought! O words with heav'n - ly
2. Some-times 'mid scenes of deep-est gloom, Some-times where E - den's
3. Lord, I would clasp Thy hand in mine, Nor ev - er mur - mur
4. And when my task on earth is done, When by Thy grace the
com - fort fraught! What - e'er I do, wher - e'er I be, Still
bow - ers bloom, By wa - ters still, o'er trou - bled sea, Still
nor re - pine; Con - tent, what-ev - er lot I see, Since
vic - t'ry's won, E'en death's cold wave I will not flee, Since
'tis God's hand that lead - eth me.
'tis His hand that lead - eth me!
'tis my God that lead - eth me!
God thru Jor - dan lead - eth me.
CHORUS
He lead - eth me, He
lead - eth me, By His own hand He lead-eth me; His faith-ful
fol - l'wer I would be, For by His hand He lead - eth me.

HE LEADETH ME

Through the years, Philadelphia has been the birthplace of many church hymns and Gospel songs. But perhaps the one for which it is best known, is the great assurance hymn, "He Leadeth Me."

John Henry Gilmore was born in Boston in 1834. In 1861 he was supply pastor at the First Baptist Church in Philadelphia. After a mid-week praise and prayer service in which he had been speaking on the twenty-third Psalm, he visited the home of Deacon Watson, where there was further discussion on this beautiful portion of scripture. It was during the discussion that he jotted down this hymn, as he said, and handed it to his wife. She in turn, without his knowledge, sent it off to a Baptist publication. Some years after its publication in that paper, and when visiting a church in Rochester, New York, he happened to pick up a new little hymnal they were using. As he turned its pages, his eyes fell upon his hymn. You see, William Bradbury, often called the "Father Of the Gospel Song," had found the words in the Baptist magazine and had composed a tune which exactly caught the tone and spirit of the text. Such is the story of Joseph H. Gilmore's great hymn. On a bronze tablet, on the side of the UGI Building in Philadelphia are found these words; "'He Leadeth Me,' sung throughout the world, was written by the Reverend Doctor Joseph H. Gilmore, a son of a governor of New Hampshire, in the home of Deacon Watson, immediately after preaching in the First Baptist Church, northwest corner Broad and Arch Streets, on the twenty-sixth day of March, 1862. The church and Deacon Watson's home stood on the ground upon which this building was erected." ABS

Lead Me To Calvary
JENNIE EVELYN HUSSEY
WILLIAM J. KIRKPATRICK
1. King of my life I crown Thee now— Thine shall the glo - ry be;
2. Show me the tomb where Thou wast laid, Ten - der - ly mourned and wept;
3. Let me like Ma - ry, thru the gloom, Come with a gift to Thee;
4. May I be will - ing, Lord, to bear Dai - ly my cross for Thee;
Lest I for - get Thy thorn-crowned brow, Lead me to Cal - va - ry.
An - gels in robes of light ar - rayed Guard - ed Thee whilst Thou slept.
Show to me now the emp - ty tomb— Lead me to Cal - va - ry.
E - ven Thy cup of grief to share— Thou hast borne all for me.
CHORUS
Lest I for - get Geth - sem - a - ne, Lest I for - get Thine ag - o - ny,
Lest I for - get Thy love for me, Lead me to Cal - va - ry.*
© Copyright 1921. Copyright Renewed. Hope Publishing Co., Carol Stream, IL 60187.
All rights reserved. Used by permission.

LEAD ME TO CALVARY

"I've spent much of my life hidden away in the country, and I'd like to have the opportunity before God takes me home to tell everybody, 'I love Jesus.'" With these words addressed to the pastor of the First Baptist Church of Concord, New Hampshire, Jennie Evelyn Hussey applied for Baptism.

Miss Hussey had come from a long line of Friends, often called Quakers. Her forebearers had settled in New England many generations before. Jennie's life had not been one of D.A.R. and History Club meetings but of taking care of a helpless invalid sister. She never complained and, instead of growing bitter, had accepted it as "from the Lord." As she daily labored, doing the menial and thankless tasks, she "practiced the presence of Jesus," as Gypsy Smith used to say.

It was after a time, in which she had been tried almost beyond endurance with deformative arthritis, that she was led to write the words that would eventually place her name among the immortals of Gospel hymnwriters. Jennie had come through the experience saying, "Please, Lord, make me willing to bear my cross daily without complaining because you bore yours for me." It was then that she wrote,

May I be willing Lord
To bear daily my cross for Thee;
Even the cup of grief to share —
Thou hast borne all for me.

This was to eventually become stanza four of "Lead Me To Calvary."

From this experience had been planted in the heart and mind of Evelyn Hussey the seed-thought for a complete song. Before many days had gone by the song had been written, but it had developed in reverse. It was only after the petitions which became verses two, thee, and four had been written, that the proclamation verse beginning, "King of my life, I crown Thee now" burst forth from her heart. Jennie Evelyn Hussey had learned the lessons of submission and, in so doing, had blessed the world with a song. ABS

I Need Thee Every Hour
ANNIE S. HAWKS
ROBERT LOWRY
1. I need thee ev - ery hour, Most gra - cious Lord;
2. I need thee ev - ery hour; Stay thou near by;
3. I need thee ev - ery hour, In joy or pain;
4. I need thee ev - ery hour; Teach me thy will;
5. I need thee ev - ery hour, Most Ho - ly One;
No ten - der voice like thine Can peace af - ford.
Temp - ta - tions lose their power When thou art nigh.
Come quick - ly and a - bide, Or life is vain.
And thy rich prom - is - es In me ful - fill.
O make me thine in - deed, Thou bless - ed Son.
Refrain
I need thee, O I need thee, Ev - ery hour I need thee;
O bless me now, my Sav - ior, I come to thee! A - men.

I NEED THEE EVERY HOUR

"I remember well the morning many years ago, when in the midst of the daily cares of my home, I was so filled with the sense of nearness to the Master. While wondering how one could live without Him either in joy or pain for any period of time, these words "I Need Thee Every Hour" were ushered into my mind — the thought at once taking full possession of me.

"Seating myself by the open window in the balmy air of that bright June day, I took up my pencil and the words were soon committed to paper, almost as they are sung today. It was only by accident, it seemed at the time, that a few months later my pastor, Robert Lowry, set them to music and for the first time, they were sung at a Sunday School Convention held in Cincinnati, Ohio. Now of course, I can see God's hand in it all. From there they were taken farther West and sung by many thousands of voices before the echo came back to me — thrilling my heart with surprise and gladness.

"For me the hymn was prophetic rather than expressive of my own experiences at the time it was written, and I did not fully understand why it so touched the great throbbing heart of humanity. It was not until long years after, when the shadow of a great loss fell over my way, that I understood something of the comforting in the words I had been permitted to write and give out to others.

"Now when I hear them sung, as I have sometimes by hundreds of voices in chorus, I find it difficult to think they were ever, consciously, my own thoughts or penned by my own hand."

Thus wrote Mrs. Annie Sherwood Hawks, regarding the writing of this great Gospel hymn.

Mrs. Hawks was born at Hoosack, New York, in May 1835 and died in 1918. Her maiden name was Annie Sherwood.

How Can I Be Lonely?

HOW CAN I BE LONELY?

"This is my 'basement song' but it has climbed out of the basement to become a source of consolation to many lonely hearts." It was Haldor Lillenas speaking and he was telling me the story of "How Can I Be Lonely?" As he continued, he said, "It was cold and dreary on that November day in 1928. I had, for some weeks, been traveling through several states in convention work. Driving along in a 1923 Buick, I finally topped a range of hills from which could be seen, in the distance, the smoky outlines of the great city of Pittsburgh, Pennsylvania. As I reached the outskirts of the city, the fog and smoke (smog) for which Pittsburgh was noted in those days, became more noticeable. It finally became necessary to turn on the lights in order to drive with safety.

"Finally locating the First Church of the Nazarene, atop Mount Washington, I arrived at four o'clock. The building, a large and rambling wooden structure was well-painted but showed the effects of the smoke-laden atmosphere of the great steel manufacturing center. Deciding to survey the situation, I entered the building to see what could be seen. Having been away from home a considerable time and being alone in that dimly lighted building, I felt a deep sense of loneliness. In the half light of a classroom in the basement, I discovered a folding Bilhorn organ. Procuring a chair, I sat at the organ and began playing, for my own entertainment, whatever I could discover in the little noisy instrument. From somewhere came both the words and music:

How can I be lonely, When I've Jesus only
To be my companion and unfailing guide?
Why should I be weary, Or my path seem dreary,
When He's walking by my side?

"A great peace and a deep sense of His nearness came to me in that hour. Truly He is 'a friend that sticketh closer than a brother.'" ABS

Rescue The Perishing
FANNY J. CROSBY
WILLIAM H. DOANE
1. Res - cue the per - ish - ing, care for the dy - ing, Snatch them in
2. Tho they are slight-ing Him, still He is wait - ing, Wait - ing the
3. Down in the hu - man heart, crushed by the tempt - er, Feel - ings lie
4. Res - cue the per - ish - ing, du - ty de - mands it— Strength for your
pit - y from sin and the grave; Weep o'er the err - ing one, lift up the
pen - i - tent child to re - ceive; Plead with them ear-nest-ly, plead with them
bur - ied that grace can re - store; Touched by a lov - ing heart, wak-ened by
la - bor the Lord will pro-vide; Back to the nar-row way pa - tient-ly
REFRAIN
fall - en, Tell them of Je - sus, the might - y to save.
gen - tly, He will for - give if they on - ly be - lieve.
kind - ness, Cords that are bro - ken will vi - brate once more.
win them, Tell the poor wan - d'rer a Sav - ior has died.
Res - cue the
per-ish-ing, Care for the dy - ing; Je - sus is mer - ci - ful, Je - sus will save.

RESCUE THE PERISHING

For years on a pew in the old Bowery Mission in New York City (now torn down) was a brass plaque which read "Fanny Crosby occupied this seat on her many visits to this mission for over a period of 50 years. It was while sitting here that she received the inspiration for the great Gospel song "Rescue The Perishing." This is how Fanny told the story of its writing.

"It was written in the year 1869, when I was forty-nine years old. Many of my hymns were written after experiences in New York mission work. This one was thus written. I was addressing a large company of working men one hot summer evening, when the thought kept forcing itself on my mind that some mother's boy must be rescued that night or not at all. So I made a pressing plea that if there was a boy present who had wandered from his mother's home and teaching, would he come to me at the close of the service. A young man of eighteen came forward and said, "Did you mean me? I promised my mother to meet her in Heaven, but as I am now living that will be impossible.' We prayed for him and finally he arose with a new light in his eyes and exclaimed in triumph, 'Now I can meet my mother in Heaven, for I have found God.'

"A few days before, Mr. Doane had sent me the subject 'Rescue the Perishing, Care for the Dying.' I could think of nothing else that night. When I arrived home I went to work on the hymn at once and before I retired it was ready for the melody. The next day my song was written out and forwarded to Mr. Doane who wrote the beautiful and touching music as it now stands to my hymn.

"This blessed song so wonderfully shows how God blends experience and even suggestions from others and in His timing makes 'All things work together for good!'" ABS

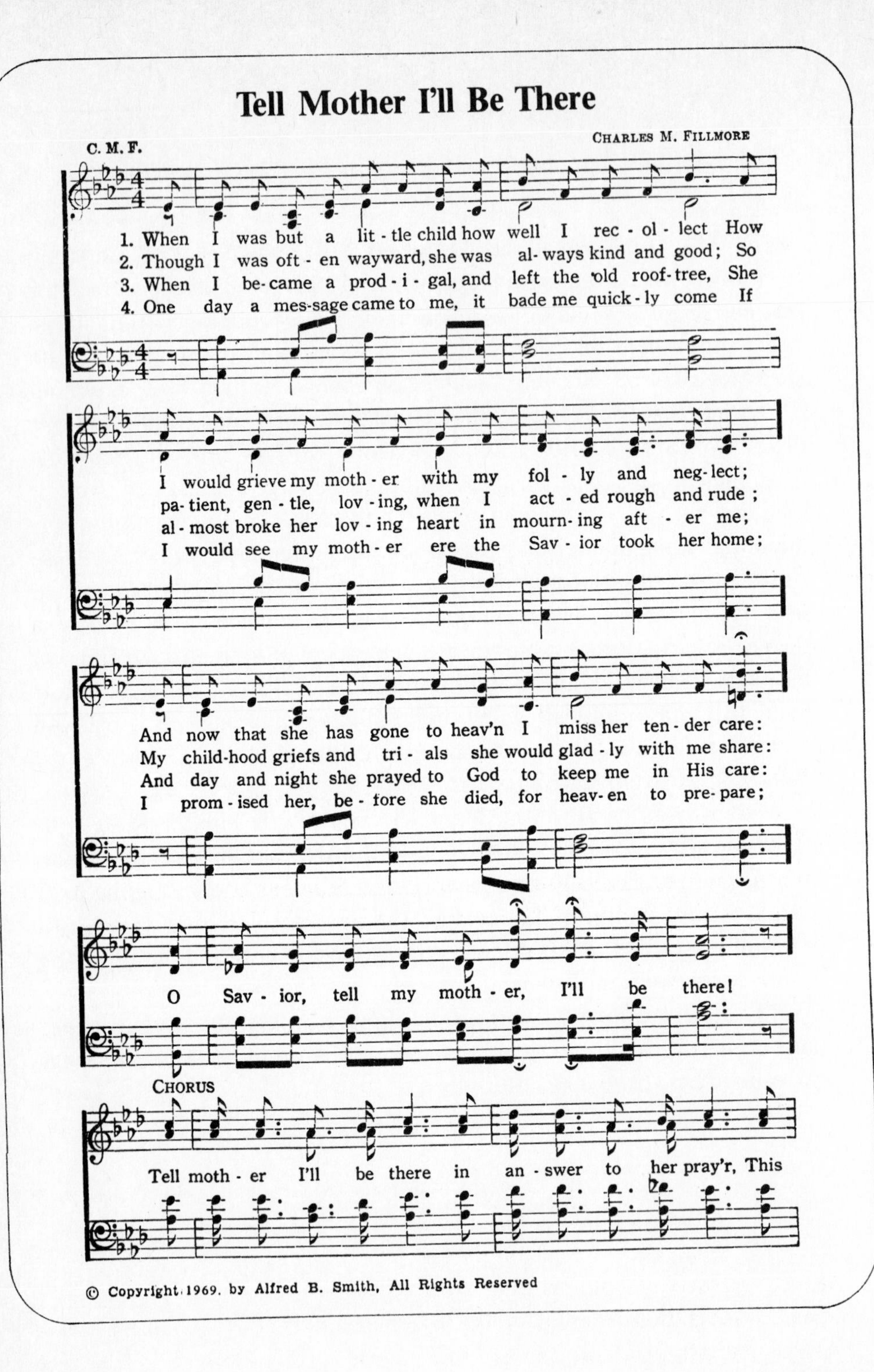
Tell Mother I'll Be There
C. M. F.
CHARLES M. FILLMORE
1. When I was but a lit - tle child how well I rec - ol - lect How
2. Though I was oft - en wayward, she was al - ways kind and good; So
3. When I be - came a prod - i - gal, and left the old roof - tree, She
4. One day a mes - sage came to me, it bade me quick - ly come If
I would grieve my moth - er with my fol - ly and neg - lect;
pa - tient, gen - tle, lov - ing, when I act - ed rough and rude;
al - most broke her lov - ing heart in mourn - ing aft - er me;
I would see my moth - er ere the Sav - ior took her home;
And now that she has gone to heav'n I miss her ten - der care:
My child - hood griefs and tri - als she would glad - ly with me share:
And day and night she prayed to God to keep me in His care:
I prom - ised her, be - fore she died, for heav - en to pre - pare;
O Sav - ior, tell my moth - er, I'll be there!
CHORUS
Tell moth - er I'll be there in an - swer to her pray'r, This
© Copyright 1969, by Alfred B. Smith, All Rights Reserved

TELL MOTHER I'LL BE THERE

No less than five prominent musicians and publishers turned this song down. Finally the Fillmore Music House, of which Charles Fillmore was a part, decided that they would publish it themselves even though they too had some misgiving. A published copy was sent to Charles M. Alexander who was the songleader for Dr. R. A. Torrey. He, too, looked at the song and wondered if he could ever use it but decided he would put it in his briefcase for reference. He carried it with him for over two years and had really never thought about the song again until one Sunday afternoon the meeting was just for railroad men, and Charlie needed a solo that would speak to men's hearts. "Where is My Wandering Boy" was getting almost threadbare. What else could he use? His mind went to the song that Fillmore had sent. He soon found it and that afternoon sang it as an invitation. Hundreds of men responded and, in the years that followed, he sang it around the world and declared that "Tell Mother I'll Be There" had brought more men to decide for Christ than any other song he ever used.

The inspiration for its writing came from a telegram sent by President McKinley to his family when his mother was dying and calling for him. He had wired, "Tell Mother I'll Be There." Charles Fillmore had read the newspaper account of this and had caught the idea for a song — one which experts thought not good but one that God would use to change the lives and destinies of thousands of men. ABS

Living For Jesus

THOMAS O. CHISHOLM

C. HAROLD LOWDEN

LIVING FOR JESUS

It was a melody written to a set of words to be used in a Children's Day service and after the program was finished it would no doubt be filed away and forgotten for it would have served its purpose. This would have been the logical conclusion but this song proved to be the "exception to the rule." After the program numerous people came up to Mr. C. Harold Lowden commending him for a fine program and especially thanking him for the new and beautiful song. Among the many complementers was one who suggested that the melody was so beautiful it should have a new setting of words so it could be used more often. Mr. Lowden thanked his many well-wishers for their appreciation and told the one who made the suggestion he would keep it in mind.

Two years went by and one day as Mr. Lowden was working on a new book his mind went back to the children's program and the song he had written for the occasion. He went to his files, found it, and began to play it over on the piano. He realized that the present words would not be acceptable for general use but perhaps if he played it over, forgetting the present words, the music would suggest something new to him. As he rehearsed the song it seemed to say, "I'll live for Jesus."

With this thought in mind Mr. Lowden hurriedly dropped a note to a hymnwriter, Mr. T. O. Chisholm, with a copy of the music and telling him what the song seemed to say to him and suggesting the title, "Living for Jesus." In a matter of a few days the completed song came back and "Living for Jesus" was a reality.

As he anxiously read Mr. Chisholm's words Mr. Lowden breathed a prayer of thanksgiving to God for directing him to send the music to Mr. Chisholm for it said exactly what he had felt it should and the chorus was a prayer of dedication. Truly God was in it and would bless the song.

Through the years God has blessed "Living for Jesus" in a special way, particularly among young people. It has been translated into 15 foreign languages, no hymnal is really complete without it, and it still rates high in the hearts of young and old alike, though it was written over sixty years ago. ABS

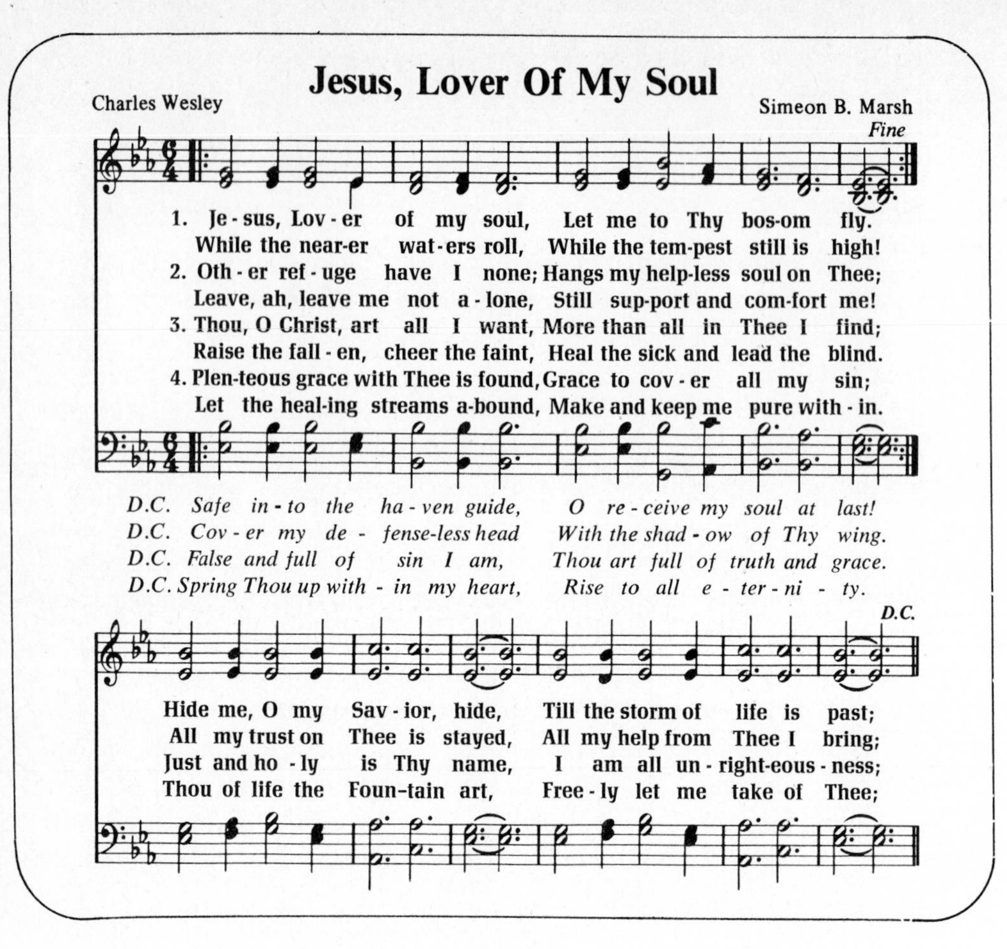

JESUS, LOVER OF MY SOUL

"I would rather have written that hymn of Wesley's, than to have the fame of all the kings that ever ruled on earth. It is more glorious, it has more power to it. I would rather be the author of that hymn than to hold the wealth of the richest man in New York. It will go on singing until the trump brings forth the angel band and I think it will mount up on some lips to the very presence of God." Thus spoke the famous preacher, Henry Ward Beecher, of Charles Wesley's immortal hymn, "Jesus, Lover Of My Soul."

As in the case of the writing of "Rock Of Ages," this hymn also has more than one story attributed to its origin and, as with "Rock Of Ages," not all of them could be true. I do feel, however, that God allowed two happenings — either of which would have been enough. But God used both of them to inspire the writing of this immortal hymn.

One incident, to which Charles Wesley referred often through his life, happened while on his first missionary journey to Savannah, Georgia. He was aboard ship along with his brother, John, and a group of Moravian missionaries. Both he and John were impressed with their love for the Word of God, their love for one another, and the beautiful hymns they sang. But a lasting impression was made as the ship was in the midst of a turbulent storm. From all outward signs, all onboard would, for a certainty, perish. Charles Wesley said, "My heart was seized with terror but as I looked around about me, I saw in the midst of all the pending destruction and danger, that group of Moravians showing no sign of outward fear. In fact, they were singing of One who loved them and cared for them amidst the storms of life — One who loved them so much He had died on the cross to save them from the guilt of sin and the storm of a Holy God's wrath. It was something both brothers would never forget, especially Charles. Through the years that followed, he thought of this experience often and each time it would engrave itself deeper upon his heart.

The other incident which has come down through family tradition, and yet I feel has credence, I found in Sankey's "Story of The Gospel Hymns." I quote: "Mrs. Mary Hoover, of Bellefonte, Pennsylvania, whose grandmother was the heroine of the story, had related to her pastor this family tradition. 'Charles Wesley was preaching in the field of the parish of Killyleagh, County Down, Ireland, when he was attacked by men who did not approve of his doctrines. He sought refuge in a house located on what was known as the Island Band Farm. The farmer's wife, Jane Lowrie Moore, told him to hide in the milkhouse, down in the garden. Soon the mob came and demanded the fugitive. She tried to quiet them by offering them refreshments. Going down to the milkhouse, she directed Mr. Wesley to get through the rear window and hide under the hedge, by which ran a little brook. In his hiding place, with the cries of his pursuers all about him, he was inspired to write a hymn of the Saviour's protecting and loving care. This he did a day later. The result was this immortal hymn."

It was first published in 1740 in a book entitled "Hymns and Sacred Songs of Prayer and Temptation." ABS

Moment By Moment
DANIEL W. WHITTLE
MAY WHITTLE MOODY
1. Dy - ing with Je - sus by death reck-oned mine, Liv - ing with Je - sus a
2. Nev - er a tri - al that He is not there, Nev - er a bur-den that
3. Nev - er a weak-ness that He doth not feel, Nev - er a sick-ness that
new life di - vine, Look-ing to Je - sus till glo - ry doth shine—
He doth not bear; Nev - er a sor - row that He doth not share—
He can - not heal; Mo - ment by mo-ment, in woe or in weal,
CHORUS
Mo-ment by mo-ment, O Lord, I am Thine.
Mo-ment by mo-ment, I'm un - der His care. Mo-ment by mo-ment I'm
Je - sus, my Sav-ior, a - bides with me still.
kept in His love, Mo-ment by mo-ment I've life from a - bove; Look-ing to
Je - sus till glo - ry doth shine, Mo-ment by mo-ment, O Lord, I am Thine.

MOMENT BY MOMENT

It was a chance remark that really became the spark which eventually led to the writing of this beautiful and meaningful song.

The English businessman and preacher, Henry Varley, was walking to catch a streetcar after the Sunday afternoon service held at the 1893 World's Fair Exposition in Chicago. He was in company with Daniel W. Whittle, an associate evangelist of D. L. Moody, and with Mr. Whittle's daughter, May, and her husband, Will R. Moody, the son of D. L. Moody. As they walked along, they were reviewing the inspirational service that they had just attended. There was quite some discussion about the wonderful message and its application for everyday living. The Englishman Varley had been more or less the listener to the conversation — adding from time to time his agreement with what was said. There came a little lull in the conversation at which time Mr. Varley said, "You know we sang a song this morning that I know is a favorite of many, but you know, I feel that instead of singing "I Need Thee Every Hour" we should have a song that really shows our dependence on God every moment of the day."

I can still see Mrs. May Whittle Moody as she told me this story and then went on to say, "You know, dad loved to write Gospel songs and as I looked at him I knew exactly what was going through his mind; for what Mr. Varley said was, to my father, like saying sic-um to a dog. It wasn't many hours later that my father handed me the words of 'Moment By Moment' and asked if I would try my hand at composing a tune. This I did, and the rest is history. It was first printed as a leaflet in 1893, and then in 1896 Mr. Sankey included it in 'Sacred Songs Number 1.'" ABS

No One Ever Cared For Me Like Jesus

NO ONE EVER CARED FOR ME LIKE JESUS

Charles F. Weigle spent much of his time as an itinerant evangelist. It was not an easy life but a rewarding one. I first met him on the campus of Tennessee Temple University at Chattanooga, Tennessee. I had often sung his songs and now I had the chance to ask him how he had been led to write "No One Ever Cared For Me Like Jesus." I felt that there had to be something special connected with its writing. Here is the story as it was told to me by "Uncle Charlie."

"I had been actively engaged in evangelistic work for quite a few years. To some it may have seemed a life of sacrifice, but to me the reward of seeing souls saved was worth more than money. God had given me a definite call. I was obeying Him and He had promised to keep me and supply all my needs. In all of this I thought I had the support of my wife, but, somewhere along the way, she began to be influenced by relatives who cared not about the things of the Lord nor understood the calling of God. One day I found a note waiting for me. It said, 'Charlie, I've been a fool. I've done without a lot of things long enough. From here on out, I'm getting all I can of what the world owes me. I know you'll continue to be a fool for Jesus but for me it's good-bye!' "

Uncle Charlie's eyes filled with tears as he told the story. He continued, "The bottom of my world seemed to fall out at that moment, for I loved my wife very much. I found her and tried to reason with her and pleaded with her not to go through with her plans, but it was to no avail. One day as I sat on the porch of a cottage in Florida overlooking a lake, I felt so depressed and forsaken I thought why not end it all. Your work is finished — no one cares whether you're dead or alive anyway, why not walk off the pier. But through the appalling gloom of that moment, there seemed to flash a voice in my soul that said, 'Charlie, I haven't forgotten you. Charlie, I care for you — let not your heart be troubled.' I threw myself down beside my chair and asked the Lord to forgive me for not fully trusting Him and promised that come what may, from here on out I'd never again let such a thought cross my mind.

"I began serving the Lord again. At first, it wasn't easy, for some folks did not understand the situation and were reluctant to use me. But slowly the Lord began to heal this hurt also and soon I was again busy for the Lord.

"One day I received the sad news that my wife had died and under very heartbreaking and tragic circumstances. She had had less than five years in which to "try the world" and eternity had begun for her. What did the future hold for me? It was while reviewing the heart-rending experiences of the past three years and reflecting upon the goodness and love of the Saviour who never forsook me thru it all, that there was rekindled in my soul the desire to write a song. This song would be the summation of my whole life experience with this wonderful friend. It was a story the whole world needed to know and it came to me as fast as I could put it down. It was the first song I had written since the day my world seemed to fall apart. Now, I wanted the whole wide world to know that 'No One Ever Cared For Me Like Jesus.'"

I said, "Uncle Charlie, was it worth it all — to go through the heartache and heartbreak? Don't you often wish that it had never happened?" His reply I'll never forget, "Al Smith, it is not for me to question the testings of the Lord no matter how hard they may seem to be. God, in His love, knows what is best and someday He'll tell me why it all happened. Until then I'll go on singing and telling the world that 'No One Ever Cared For Me Like Jesus.'" ABS

Calvary Covers It All
ETHEL ROBINSON TAYLOR
ETHEL ROBINSON TAYLOR
1. Far dear - er than all that the world can im - part Was the
2. The stripes that He bore and the thorns that He wore Told His
3. How match - less the grace, when I looked in the face Of this
4. How bless - ed the thought that my soul, by Him bought, Shall be
mes - sage that came to my heart, How that Je - sus a - lone
mer - cy and love ev - er - more; And my heart bowed in shame
Je - sus, my cru - ci - fied Lord; My re - demp-tion com - plete
His in the glo - ry on high, Where with glad-ness and song
for my sin did a - tone— And Cal - va - ry cov - ers it all.
as I called on His name— And Cal - va - ry cov - ers it all.
I then found at His feet— And Cal - va - ry cov - ers it all.
I'll be one of the throng— And Cal - va - ry cov - ers it all.
CHORUS
Cal - va - ry cov - ers it all, My past with its sin and stain; My
guilt and de-spair Je-sus took on Him there, And Cal - va - ry cov-ers it all.
© Copyright 1934 by Walter G. Taylor. Renewed 1962 The Rodeheaver Co. All rights reserved.
International copyright secured. Used by permission.

CALVARY COVERS IT ALL

While a student at Moody Bible Institute in Chicago, Illinois, I was assigned every Saturday night to take part in the service at the Pacific Garden Mission. For me, it was an experience I shall never forget. "The Old Lighthouse" as it is called, has been shelter for many a homeless and helpless victim of sin and circumstance. There, many have not only found a shelter from the heat or the cold, and some food to keep them from starving, but many have also found "The Shelter In The Time Of Storm" and "The Bread Of Life." Among the many, there were three who went on to be used mightily of the Lord. Mel Trotter went on to start, all over America, 57 other "Lighthouses" and win thousands of men and women to Christ. Billy Sunday, the professional baseball player extraordinare, had gone out to preach the Gospel. At his invitation, it is said that over 1,000,000 walked the "sawdust trail" to accept Christ. The third man? — well, you will meet him in this story.

One night there came into the mission a man, rather slight of build and like so many who came in, under the influence of liquor. He had not been seen there before. That night he did not respond to the invitation but left the mission. He did, however, come back the next night and the next; but always with the same ending — he did not respond. By this time, some of the workers at the mission had gotten to know who he was. He was not the general run of the mission circuit but was a professional entertainer. A man whom Eddie Cantor had advertised as having the fastest feet in the world, that is, when he was sober. "Mac," as he was called, had hit town in between bookings. He was also hitting the bottle; for he was, as he later said, "a slave of Satan, sin and suds."

Mr. and Mrs. Walter Taylor, better known as Ma and Pa Taylor, were running the mission at the time. Ma, too, had been in the entertainment field before she was saved and knew of its many pitfalls and temptations. She also knew of the terrible loneliness which can envelope one when he or she is alone and when there aren't the crowds and the bright lights to keep one's mind off oneself and the emptiness of the life one is living.

Her heart went out to Mac as she prayed, "Dear Lord, please help us say and do the right things so that we may win Mac to Thee. Please touch his heart."

It was about Mac's fourth or fifth visit to the Old Lighthouse. The meeting was in progress and Ma Taylor was playing one of the big, nine-foot Steinway Grands that Billy Sunday had given the mission. At the other piano was a student from the Moody Bible Institute. As Ma Taylor looked toward Mac, she saw that he was trying the best he could to sing and seemed to be enjoying it. When the singing was over, she noticed that he was staying awake and listening to every word the speaker was saying. When the speaker finished, Pa Taylor gave the invitation. The first one to respond was Mac, who came and knelt at the front. As the invitation continued, Ma Taylor could see that Mac was having some sort of trouble and, after beckoning the girl at the piano to take over, she went and knelt by Mac. As she did so, she heard him say, "But you don't understand, you don't know how bad I am, Lord. Really I'm the worst man in the world. You can't save me, I'm too bad."

Upon hearing this, Ma Taylor began to quietly talk to Mac, telling him that God loved him so much that He would save him and take away his sins. Ma Taylor remembered a testimony she had heard some weeks before, by a Mr. Crawford of the American Tract Society, on "Calvary Covers It All." And so she continued "Mac, Calvary covers it all — all the sin of your past life!" "Please say that again, Mrs. Taylor," asked Mac. Mrs. Taylor repeated, "Mac, Calvary covers it all." There was a moment of silence and then the reply, "Calvary does cover it all! My whole past of sin and shame! Oh! Mrs. Taylor, I'm so glad it's true and you told me."

That night, Walter MacDonald became a new creature in Christ — or as he liked to say it — "Jesus found me and made me all over at the Pacific Garden Mission."

Happy Mac, as he became known after his conversion, left the entertainment world and went on to become an Evangelist and outstanding soul-winner.

Something also happened to Ma Taylor that night. In her heart and mind a seed for a song had been planted. One afternoon that same week, she went into the mission chapel when no one was there and, in the quietness, sat down at the great Steinway piano and wrote, "Calvary Covers It All." As each phrase took form, there echoed and re-echoed in her ears and heart the response of Happy Mac, "Calvary does cover it all! My past with its sin and shame! Oh! Mrs. Taylor, I'm so glad you told me." ABS

Not Dreaming
GYPSY SMITH
E. EDWIN YOUNG
DUET
1. The world says I'm dreaming, but I know 'tis Je - sus Who saves me from
2. My home in the glo - ry is fair - er than morn-ing, And Je - sus my
3. Oh, let me fight on for Je - sus my Sav - ior, And tell of the
bond - age and sin's guilt - y stain; He is my Lov - er, my
Sav - ior will wel - come me there; No, I'm not dream-ing! I'm a-
love He so won-drous - ly gave; Preaching or sing - ing, or
Sav - ior, my Mas - ter, 'Tis He who has freed me from guilt and its pain.
wake, it is dawn-ing, His smile and His love I'll e - ter - nal - ly share.
liv - ing or dy - ing, In life or in death He is might - y to save.
CHORUS
Let me dream on, If I am dreaming; Let me dream on, My sins are gone;
Let me dream on, dream on; My sins are gone;
Night turns to dawn, Love's light is beaming, So if I'm dreaming, Let me dream on.
Night turns to dawn's bright beam-ing, Let me dream on, dream on.

NOT DREAMING

One of the outstanding and beloved evangelists of all times, was a man named Rev. Rodney Smith or better known as "Gypsy Smith." He had been born in a Gypsy camp in Epping Forest, on the outskirts of London, England. It was there also, that he had been saved. (See story — "I Have Never Lost The Wonder Of It All") He made many trips to America to preach, and on one of these, he wrote "Not Dreaming." I remember Gypsy telling the story as to how he had been led to write it. He began by saying:

"I was on my way to Atlanta, Georgia, to hold a citywide meeting. I was sitting in a chair in the parlor car of a pullman train, reading my Bible. A man seated across from me, kept looking over to see just what it was that I was reading and what held such an interest for me. At last he spoke, 'Say — what's that you're reading?' I replied, 'The Bible, Sir.' There was a silence for a short time and then the man asked, 'The Bible, heh? Do you believe it — all those stories about the apple and the flood and hell and sin — and 'bout gettin' to Heaven?' I replied, 'Why yes, Sir. I do, Sir — all of it, Sir.' With a look of distain, the man smirked 'You are worse off than I thought you were — why you're dreaming!' My reply was, 'sir, this is the book that told me that God loves me. This is the book that spoke peace and assurance to a poor barefoot and unlearned boy in a Gypsy camp and has sent him around the world many times telling the rich and the poor, the learned and the unlearned, that in this world wrapped in sin and despair there is hope Eternal in Jesus Christ. Sir, if I'm dreaming, let me dream on!'"

It was some days later, as Gypsy recalled the incident, that the Lord led him to write this lovely song "Not Dreaming." The beautiful musical setting was supplied by his pianist, E. E. Young. ABS

Saved By Grace

FANNY J. CROSBY

GEORGE C. STEBBINS

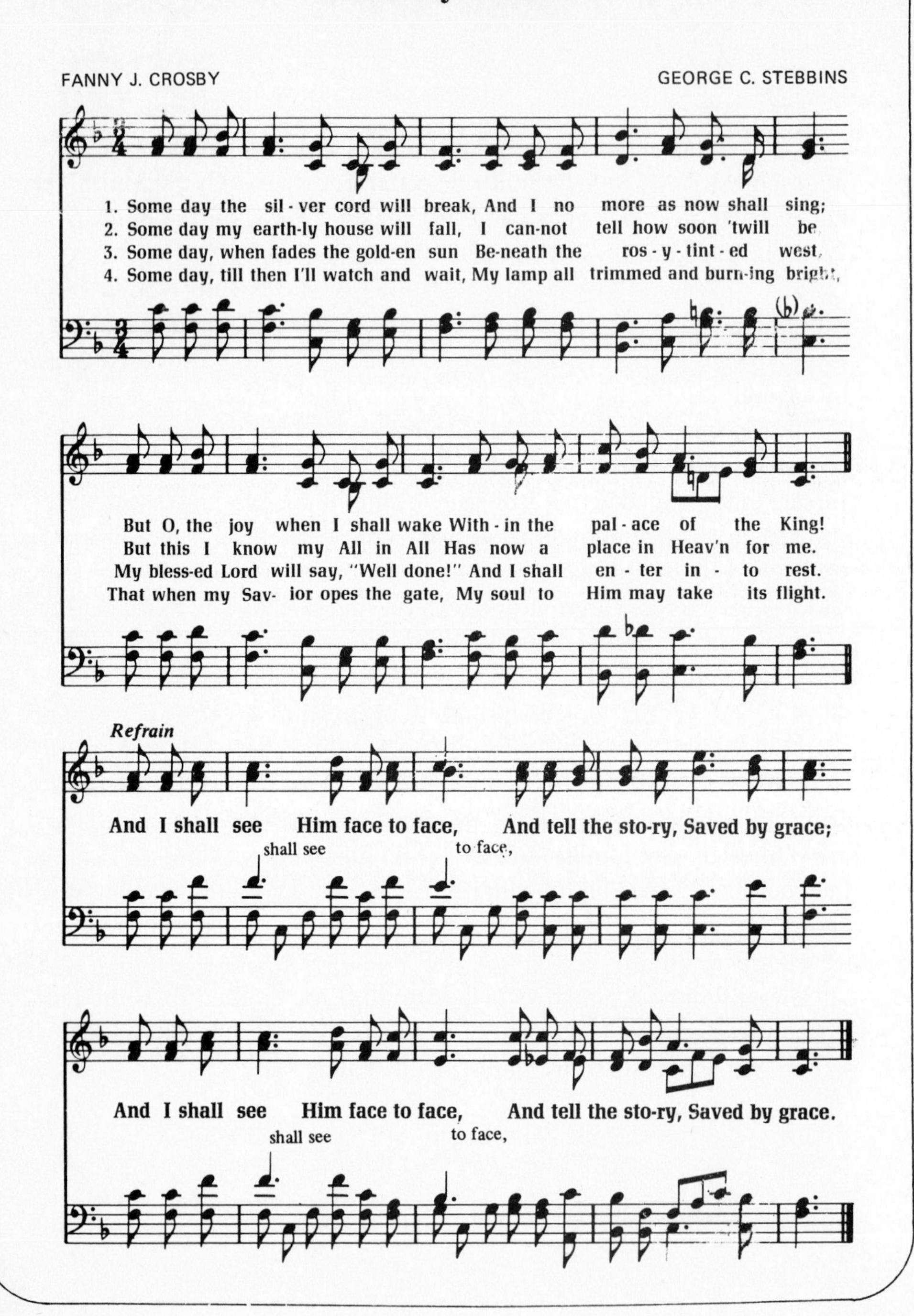

SAVED BY GRACE

Dr. L. W. Munhall, the great Methodist lay evangelist, was the principal speaker at the 1890 Poughkeepsie, New York, camp meeting. Also on the program was God's gift to the singing church — blind Fanny Crosby.

Early one evening as God began to paint the western sky with the galaxies of color as only He can do, Fanny and Dr. Munhall along with other guests were sitting on the porch of the hotel. As the colors began to intensify and form themselves into great shafts of colored light, Dr. Munhall began to describe to Fanny the brilliance and the glory of the setting. She hung on his every word as he used every colorful adjective he knew to paint mind's-eye pictures for her. When he had finished, Fanny thanked him for the strength it had given her for as he was describing it, her mind went back to the sunsets her grandma used to describe to her as a little girl and now through Dr. Munhall's description, she realized anew that God was still able to paint beautiful sunsets. As she arose to go into the hotel she said to the doctor, "Tho' I cannot now see the sunset, someday I'll see my Saviour face to face!"

It was two summers later that Fanny was attending D. L. Moody's Northfield Conference. Dr. A. T. Pierson was in charge of the afternoon meetings and he asked Fanny to take part. At first she refused, saying that she had really come to listen and laughingly said, "After all, aren't women supposed to keep silent in church?" But Dr. Pierson would not take no for an answer and so finally Fanny consented to give a little talk on Thursday afternoon.

Many were there to hear this blind saint. Fanny held their attention every minute as she gave a testimony of praise to the Lord for His blessing upon her life. She even thanked Him for the privilege of being blind, if this had been the only way He could have equipped her for the ministry He had given her. There was not a dry eye in the audience. In conclusion, Fanny quoted a poem which she had composed two years before while attending the camp meeting at Poughkeepsie.

Someday the silver cord will break,
And I no more as now shall sing;
But O the joy when I shall wake,
Within the palace of the King.

She then went on to recite the other verses concluding with,

Someday 'til then I'll watch and wait,
My lamp all trimmed and burning bright;
That when my Saviour op'es the gate,
My soul to Him may take it's flight . . .
And I shall see Him face to face,
And tell the story saved by grace.

George C. Stebbins, whom I had the privilege of knowing the last six of his one hundred years, was at that never-to-be-forgotten meeting. "If ever there was a touch from Heaven at Northfield, it was that Thursday afternoon," he told me. "Every eye was moist and every heart throbbing with expectation as Fanny lifted us into the heavenlies."

Mr. Stebbins also told me that after the meeting Ira D. Sankey had gone to Fanny and asked for the words. Her reply was that at least for a while she wanted to keep them just for herself. But her wish was not to be. In the audience that day, was a reporter from an English publication called "The Christian." He had transcribed all of the messages in the meetings and so had recorded Fanny's talk including the poem. There were published the following fall.

When word came, that this had been done, Ira Sankey again contacted Fanny about the possibility of writing the music for them. Tho' Mr. Sankey and Fanny were the closest of friends, she told him she hoped it wouldn't offend him but that she felt that in this particular case Mr. Stebbins should write the music. Characteristic of the wonderful way these men worked together, it was Mr. Sankey who delivered the words to Mr. Stebbins advising him that Fanny wanted him to write the music. "He did of course add," said Mr. Stebbins, "I see who has the inside track with our dear Fanny."

Of the over 8000 Gospel poems written by Fanny Crosby, this one certainly. would be near if not at the very top for usefulness and longevity.

ABS

At The End Of The Road

AT THE END OF THE ROAD

Nestled in the mountains of Northeastern Pennsylvania is a little hamlet called Springhill. It consists of a few homes, a small community hall, and a quaint, beautiful, little white Methodist Church with green shutters. The little church is much the same today as it was back in the 1880's when the Reverend Alfred H. Ackley was its pastor. Of course, Reverend Ackley isn't there anymore. Neither are his two sons, Alfred and Bentley, who are following the footsteps of their father, and also went into the Lord's work. But they were to gain worldwide fame, not as preachers, but as writers of Gospel songs. It was my privilege to know both of these sons very well and to spend many visits with them at the Winona Lake Bible Conference in Indiana.

It is around Alfred H. Ackley that this story centers. I'll pass it on just as it was told to me by Reverend Ackley, himself. "Al, I love to fish. In fact, one of the first things I ever did with my preacher father was to go fishing in the Wyalusing Creek which flows by Springhill. Some of these experiences are still fresh in my memory, particularly the time in the spring when we would get ready for trout season. During the winter, dad would show me how to make 'trout flies'; for you couldn't buy them in those days. When the spring thaws had passed, the trees had begun to bud, and the grass was beginning to weave a green carpet, we would go down to the creek to see if we had been successful in making our flies alluring enough to catch the speckled brook trout. It was at such times that dad would thrill me with stories of 'fishing for men.' He early instilled into my heart and mind the privileges and rewards of serving God. How that not all of the rewards are 'caught' here but that at the end of the road we would find that God had kept the account and would never sell us short.

"Years had gone by since those days and in my life there had developed a feeling that something was missing. This, in spite of the fact that I had a very successful church, and had achieved some recognition as a composer. What could it be? I decided that a return to the spot of my childhood might be the answer, and so a few days later found me back among the old familiar scenes. Things hadn't changed too much. There were still the beautiful Pennsylvania farms that surrounded the little town, the little white church still rang its bell of invitation and, as I looked down the valley, the Wyalusing Creek was still winding its way into the Susquehanna. I decided I'd go fishing. This time I had the best trout flies and fishing pole money could buy — I'd surely catch my fish now. But things weren't quite the same. The fish didn't seem to want to bite. Maybe my new store-bought flies were at fault — maybe I'd better try another spot — it could be the fish didn't haunt the old familiar 'holes' anymore. Whatever the cause, I caught nothing, or almost nothing; for when the day had ended, I had a grand total of three 'just-over-the-limit-size' trout. I don't have to tell you that this 'experienced' fisherman was very disappointed. After I dejectedly climbed my way back to my old Buick and had seated myself on the running board to rest, I began to think of the days of old — of my preacher father, the little homemade fishing pole and the handmade trout flies. In memory's eye, I heard him say, 'A. H., remember you won't always see your reward here but don't forget, God keeps the accounts and at the end of the road He won't forget you!'

"My seeming failure and disappointment that day had preached a sermon to me down the long, long road of memories. On my way back to Springhill, the words and melody of "At The End Of The Road" came to me like a cresting Wyalusing Creek. I hadn't caught many fish but I had caught the idea for a song." ABS

The Mercies Of God

THE MERCIES OF GOD

Of the many songs that I sing, "The Mercies of God" is one that has blessed hearts in an unusual way. It was after I found out the circumstances which led to its writing that I understood why.

For a number of years I had as a Christian friend and advisor, Jacob Stam, an attorney who lived in Paterson, New Jersey, and who is now in Glory. "Jake" was an active Christian layman and an ardent Gideon — having been at one time its International President.

One evening Jake and a fellow Gideon were going over the membership list of the New Jersey Camp, checking to see who had and had not paid their annual dues. In those days it was the great sum of $5.00 per year. In reviewing the list they would cross out the names of those, who after having received two notices, had not sent in their fee. Just as Gideon Stam was going to run his pen through one of the names, his fellow Gideon said, "Jake, do you know who that man is?" "T. O. Chisholm," pondered Jake. "No, I don't." "Why he's the fellow that wrote "Great Is Thy Faithfulness," that was your brother John's favorite hymn." (John Stam had been murdered in 1934 by communists in China along with his wife, Betty.) "Why that's also my favorite song," replied Jake, adding, "That sure is worth $5.00 — I'll pay the brother's dues for him!" And with that they both went on to finish the list. When they had finished it, Jake filed the list away and said good-night to his friend and went to bed.

But Jake had a hard time going to sleep for something kept telling him "Mr. Chisholm needs more than his membership dues." After wrestling with his conscience for awhile, Jake exclaimed, "All right, Lord, I know what you're trying to tell me — I'll send the dear brother a check in the morning." With this, he went soundly to sleep only to be awakened at 6:00 A.M. by a phone call from his fellow Gideon who said, "Jake, I've had a hard time sleeping last night. You know I couldn't get that fellow Chisholm out of my mind and Jake, knowing your schedule, I didn't know if you might already be on your way to the office or not so I have just posted a letter to you with a check for Brother Chisholm. I didn't have his address so would you be kind enough to send the money on to him?" Jake readily consented and told his friend of his experience also. Together they rejoiced feeling that God was in it.

On the next day, which was a Friday, Jacob Stam received the brother's check, took it out of the envelope and with his own check and a note, sent them off immediately in his own envelope to T. O. Chisholm in Vineland, New Jersey.

On Saturday Mr. Chisholm had gotten up to begin another day. His wife had been very ill for a long period of time and the day usually began with his giving her her medicine; but, as Mr. Chisholm lifted the bottle he remembered he had given his wife the last pill yesterday. He should have gotten the prescription refilled but he had had no money at the time and so had put if off, thinking in his mind that somehow he could get enough during the day to get it. But yesterday had turned out to be a day of emergencies and it had slipped his mind until now. He felt so sorry but reasoned, "Well, I'll prepare a little breakfast for her to make her feel comfortable and maybe somehow today I'll be able to get the prescription filled." But as he looked into the refrigerator he found it in almost the same condition as the medicine bottle — almost empty. There was nothing there that he could give his sick wife. What would he do?

He remembered that he had a few dollars coming in commissions and thought, "Maybe they're due today. I'll look at the calendar and see." But as he looked at it, his heart almost failed within him, for he found that their due date was a week away and added to that, there was a circle around today's date which meant — his rent was due. What could he do!

It seems but yesterday as Mr. Chisholm related this part of the story to me, as he said, "You know, Al Smith, we had really never had a lot of this world's goods. Ours had been a real "hand-to-mouth" life — but it was always God's hand — but never before had I faced a situation quite as hopeless. Being Saturday, I reasoned with myself, there'll be nothing at the post office which will help because the commissions aren't due for another week. But something inside seemed to say, 'Why don't you go?' And so I headed for the post office. When I got there and looked through the window, I just knew there would be nothing there and that piece of mail that I saw in my box just had to be an advertisement of some sort. In spite of my unbelief, I did go in, opened the box, and took out its contents. It was a letter and it was addressed to me! As I looked at the upper lefthand corner of the envelope I almost dropped it for fear. I read, Jacob Stam, Attorney at Law, Paterson, New Jersey. I said to myself, 'All of the trouble I'm in and now an attorney is after me!' As I opened the letter, I found a note which read, 'Dear Brother, we have never met you but we love you in the Lord. Thank you so much for "Great Is They Faithfulness." Enclosed is a little something the Lord told us to send you.'

Mr. Chisholm continued — "Along with the note there were two checks and as I looked at them I realized how faithful our God is, for they had been dated and sent before I was even aware of what my needs were to be that Saturday. Amidst the tears streaming down my cheeks, I saw the amount of the checks — there was enough for the medicine, the rent, and our good Lord had even put in enough for groceries."

Mr. Chisholm's eyes were again filled with tears as he recounted that wonderful day in which God had proven His faithfulness to the one who had years before written a song which set the Christian world to singing, "Great Is They Faithfulness."

After getting the medicine, paying the rent, and picking up some groceries at the corner store, T. O. Chisholm came home to have a time of praise and thanksgiving with his dear invalid wife. It was during this time that she said, "Thomas, you've written so beautifully about other things that have happened through the years, why don't you go into your study and write something about today, so that others too may share and rejoice in the goodness of God." Following her suggestion, Mr. Chisholm did go into the study. With a heart overflowing with love and gratitude, is it any wonder that he then wrote the song, "The Mercies of God"? ABS

The Old Rugged Cross

George Bennard George Bennard

THE OLD RUGGED CROSS

Although written almost 75 years ago, "The Old Rugged Cross" is still without a doubt, one of the most used and requested songs in Christian church music.

I had the privilege of singing at the famous "Mel Trotter Mission" in Grand Rapids, Michigan, in the 1940's. The evening meeting had closed and I had wandered over to Walgreen's drugstore to get a sandwich. After I had given my order, an elderly man with flowing snow white hair and very thick glasses came up to me and asked, "Are you Al Smith?" When I replied that I was, he introduced himself and shaking my hand said, "I'm George Bennard." God was answering "a desire of my heart" for I had often wished to meet the writer of "The Old Rugged Cross" and here he was — now I could get the story of its writing firsthand.

Here's how he told it to me that night.

"John 3:16 had always been a favorite verse of mine. The more I quoted it, instead of becoming worn and threadbare, it became more alive and seemed to take on a deeper meaning. But always there was with it a vision of a cross — not a beautiful gold-colored one but a rough and rugged one — a cross of shame stained with the blood of God's only begotten Son shed for me. One day as I was again reviewing this scene in my mind's eye, I began to compose a song. A complete melody really came in a matter of minutes but all I could get of the words was, "I'll Cherish the Old Rugged Cross" — nothing more.

"For the next several months I would take it out and work on it polishing the melody and words, but with it all I was not satisfied. I did by then have the completed chorus but the words of the stanzas did not seem to gel right.

"During this time I had meetings in several churches including the Friends Church in Sawyer, Wisconsin, and at the Methodist Church in a town called Pokogon located in the southwest part of Michigan. At both of these places I sang what I had completed of the song and the people seemed to respond favorably but I still was not satisfied.

"It was after my meetings in Pokogon that I took some evangelistic services in New York State. In these meetings I felt led to major on the theme of the cross. At each service many were coming to Christ claiming the finished work at Calvary as their right to Eternal life. More and more the Lord was showing me the true meaning of His love as shown at Calvary.

"The thrilling experiences of these meetings, so overwhelmed me with the importance of the cross, that when I returned to Albion, Michigan, I took the manuscript I had been trying to finish for those several months. I sat down at the kitchen table in the parsonage and immediately was able to rewrite the stanzas of the song without so much as one word failing to fall into place. I called in my wife, took out my guitar, and sang the completed song to her. She was thrilled!

"I then sent the manuscript to Charles H. Gabriel in Chicago, asking him to harmonize it so that I could have a music plate made and publish it. When Mr. Gabriel returned the finished manuscript he enclosed a note saying, 'You will hear from this song.' And when I played and sang it for some friends they too said, 'God has given you a song that will never die, it has moved our hearts as no other song ever has.' The kind remarks were appreciated very much but I realized then, as I do now, that I could take no credit for the song, for you see I really hadn't written it — I was merely the instrument that God used."

Dr. Bennard then excused himself saying, "I must get back to Albion tonight for it isn't good for a young fellow like me [he was then over 75] to be out too late after dark." ABS

I LOVE TO TELL THE STORY
and
TELL ME THE OLD, OLD STORY

In 1866 Katherine Hankey wrote a very long poem on the life of Christ. It had some fifty verses all told. The first half, which she wrote in January of that year, she entitled, "The Story Wanted." The second half written in November, she entitled, "The Story Told."

It is interesting to see how God often overrules in the ways of men, and this poem is a good example. First of all, it was of a size that would discourage any musician from attempting to set music to it and secondly, it had two separate themes. Yet, God let two men unknown to the other, take four stanzas from each part and send them on to become widely used Gospel songs.

It is also of interest to see that both the songs were written in the order in which Miss Hankey wrote the poem.

It was in 1867 while William Howard Doane was attending an international convention of the YMCA held in Montreal, Canada, that he heard Major-General Russell, a famous English General, recite the first part of Miss Hankey's poem from a crumpled sheet of paper. Tears were streaming down his bronzed cheeks as he read and soon there was not a dry eye in the whole meeting as those in attendance caught afresh the picture of God's amazing love.

When the meeting was over, Mr. Doane secured a copy of the poem and put it in his pocket.

A few weeks following, on a hot summer day, Mr. Doane was riding on a stagecoach from Glens Falls, New York, heading for the White Mountains. As he did, he was reading Miss Hankey's poem. Soon he began to relive his experience with the General in Canada and before the trip had ended, he had written music for it.

That evening at the Crawford House, the guests gathered in the parlors of the hotel and sang it for the first time.

It was a year later, 1868, that William G. Fisher, a well-known church musician of Philadelphia, who in 1876 would lead the choir for the great Moody-Sankey meetings in that city, wrote the music for the four stanzas taken from the second part of Miss Hankey's poem. Of the two songs, I feel safe in saying that "I Love To Tell The Story" is the most often used and is still a great favorite of young and old alike. ABS

I Love To Tell The Story
Katherine Hankey
William G. Fischer
1. I love to tell the sto - ry Of un - seen things a - bove, Of
2. I love to tell the sto - ry, More won - der - ful it seems Than
3. I love to tell the sto - ry, 'Tis pleas - ant to re - peat What
4. I love to tell the sto - ry, For those who know it best Seem
Je - sus and His glo - ry, Of Je - sus and His love. I love to
all the gold - en fan - cies Of all our gold - en dreams. I love to
seems, each time I tell it, More won - der - ful - ly sweet. I love to
hun - ger - ing and thirst - ing To hear it like the rest. And when, in
tell the sto - ry, Be - cause I know 'tis true; It sat - is - fies my
tell the sto - ry, It did so much for me; And that is just the
tell the sto - ry, For some have nev - er heard The mes - sage of sal-
scenes of glo - ry, I sing the new, new song, 'Twill be the old, old
long - ings As noth - ing else can do.
rea - son I tell it now to thee.
va - tion From God's own Ho - ly Word.
sto - ry That I have loved so long.
CHORUS
I love to tell the sto - ry, 'Twill
be my theme in glo - ry To tell the old, old sto - ry Of Je - sus and His love.

Tell Me The Old, Old Story

Mansion Over The Hilltop
IRA F. STANPHILL
IRA F. STANPHILL
1. I'm sat - is - fied with just a cot-tage be - low, A lit - tle
2. Tho oft - en tempt - ed, tor - ment-ed and test - ed And, like the
3. Don't think me poor or de - sert - ed or lone - ly— I'm not dis -
sil - ver and a lit - tle gold; But in that cit - y where the
proph-et, my pil-low a stone, And tho I find here no
cour-aged, I'm heav - en - bound; I'm just a pil - grim in
ran-somed will shine, I want a gold one that's sil - ver - lined.
per - ma - nent dwell-ing, I know He'll give me a man-sion my own.
search of a cit - y, I want a man-sion, a harp and a crown.
CHORUS
I've got a man - sion just o - ver the hill - top, In that bright
land where we'll nev - er grow old; And some-day yon - der we will
© Copyright Copyright 1949. Renewal 1977 by Ira Stanphill. Assigned to Singspiration, Division of the Zondervan Corporation.
All rights reserved. Used by permission.

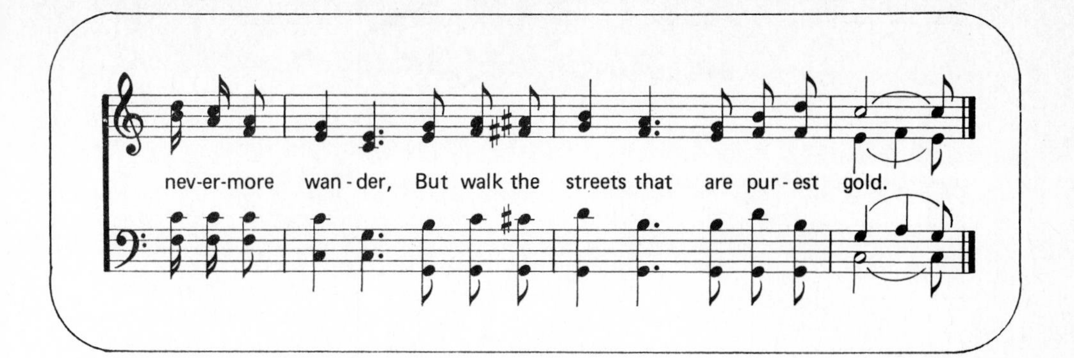

MANSION OVER THE HILLTOP

God had given many Gospel composers a unique style all their own. It is almost like a trademark. Ira C. Stanphill falls into this category. There is a freshness and originality in his writing that separates his songs from so many of the "run-of-the-mill" songs that are written today. Every composer has one song which seems to tower over the rest, and Mr. Stanphill's "Mansion Over The Hilltop" seems to be the one. The inspiration for writing "Mansion" came after hearing this story.

"A man of means was taking a trip through a part of our country marked by the fact that there were a lot of 'Po' folks living there. As he was driving through the area, he came to a part which was called 'the hollow.' Here he saw a house that was so badly in need of paint and repairs that he wondered how it could still be standing. Most of the windows had oiled paper to take the place of the glass which had been broken a long time ago. Parts of the roof and shingles were missing; in fact it looked as if much of the original house was missing. Playing out front of this ramshackled house was a little boy of about eight or nine. The traveler felt an urge to stop and chat with him. This he did and, during their conversation, he mentioned how sorry he was for the little fellow because he had to live in such poor surroundings. To this the little fellow replied, 'Oh, Mister, you don't understand. I won't have to live in this house forever, for you see, Mister, just over the hilltop up there, my dad has been building a new house for mother and us kids. I don't know when it will be done or when we'll move in but Mister, I won't have to live in this old house forever — no siree!" ABS

Lord, I'm Coming Home

LORD I'M COMING HOME

Professor William J. Kirkpatrick was leading the music for a Methodist Camp Meeting in one of the country areas surrounding Philadelphia.

Mr. Kirkpatrick had been writing Gospel music for some years before this incident happened in 1902. His life was one dedicated to serving the Lord, and with this had come a spiritual sensitivity and discernment. At this camp meeting, God had given him reason to question the salvation and sincerity of the special soloist who had been chosen to help him in the meeting. The soloist would never stay to listen to the messages after he had sung his solo, nor was he present for the times of Christian fellowship which played such an important part in the early camp meetings. With the situation as it was, Mr. Kirkpatrick began to pray for the singer.

Two days had gone by, and although the messages of the evangelists and preachers were bringing many to decide for Christ, they failed to move the singer. As Kirkpatrick continued to pray he questioned, "Will God ever hear my prayers?"

In later years Mr. Kirkpatrick would say, "I became very burdened for him and the Lord led me to use an unusual plan. He told me to write a special song of invitation just with the singer in mind and then I was to have him sing it. This I did, and the very evening that he sang it, God so spoke to his heart that he did not go out after singing but stayed to hear the message. Praise God! — he was the first to the altar letting Christ come into his heart. My new song had been the Lord's means of answering my prayer. It was 'Lord, I'm Coming Home.'"

Of added interest concerning Mr. Kirkpatrick, is this story of the last song he wrote on September 20, 1921. It was during the writing of a song that God called him home. Here is the story as it was told to me by George Sanville, who was a close friend of Mr. Kirkpatrick.

"Kirk was at his desk in his study working on a poem which he would later put to music. Mrs. Kirkpatrick was tired and had retired for the night. She awakened sometime later and seeing that the light was still on in her husband's study, she called to him, 'Professor, it's very late, don't you think you had better come to bed?' He replied, 'I'm all right, dear. I have a little work I want to finish. Go back to sleep, everything is all right.' Mrs. Kirkpatrick went to sleep, but when she awakened a second time and called, there was no response. She went to his study and found him sitting in his chair but leaning forward on his desk. Mr. Kirkpatrick had boarded the Heavenly Train for that continuing city of which he had so often written so beautifully."

The poem on which Mr. Kirkpatrick had been working was but a review of his dedicated life — a life, which like the apostle Paul's was lived for Christ. Here is the poem as Mrs. Kirkpatrick found it.

"Just as Thou wilt, Lord, this is my cry
Just as Thou wilt, to live or die
I am Thy servant, Thou knowest best,
Just as Thou wilt, Lord labor or rest."

The second verse was written in a hurried scrawl — lacking the usual neat, fine script — showing he felt the urge to hurry, as God's call was near. Note the second verse:

"Just as Thou wilt, Lord, which shall it be?
Life everlasting waiting for me —
Or shall I tarry, here at Thy feet?
Just as Thou wilt, Lord, whatever is meet."

That was all. He left this life quietly, in full obedience of a complete surrender to the Will of God. "I will receive you unto Myself, that where I am, ye may be also." ABS

My Saviour First Of All

MY SAVIOUR FIRST OF ALL

In the western section of New York state, near Lake Erie, lies Lake Chautauqua. Situated on its western shore is a Christian association that has been in existence for over 100 years, known as the Chatauqua Institute. It did more to shape, for the good, the cultural and religious climate in young America than any other institution.

It was for the special Bible classes and vesper meetings in 1877, that Mary Lathbury wrote "Break Thou The Bread Of Life" and "Day Is Dying In The West" — two songs that have become church standards. It was here, also, that William F. Sherwin, the famous composer of the day, held forth. He wrote the music for Miss Lathbury's songs and was the composer of many songs including "Sound The Battle Cry." From this alone, one can see the important part good Gospel music played in the Chautauqua program; therefore, it is no wonder that each summer for at least a week, Fanny Crosby, the blind Gospel poetess, could be found there.

Fanny often took part in the programs and Fanny's week at Chautauqua also proved an ideal time for musicians to meet and fellowship with this gifted and enjoyable person. On one such week, John R. Sweney of "More About Jesus" fame, was attending. He had written the music to several of Fanny's poems — two of which were "Tell Me The Story Of Jesus" and "Take The World But Give Me Jesus." He was hoping that sometime during his visit, Miss Crosby would be inspired to write some more poems for him to compose the music to.

One evening, after a very inspiring and blessed service, Mr. Sweney and Fanny were sitting on the porch of the hotel. They were discussing the blessing of being able to come aside from the care and turmoil of a busy world to a place such as this. It was the nearest thing to heaven a person could find on this earth.

It was then that John R. Sweney said, "Fanny, speaking of Heaven — I mean the real one that the Lord is preparing for His children — do you think we'll recognize each other?" She replied, "John, I think we will. In fact, I agree with Annie Herbert who wrote, 'We shall know each other better when the mists have rolled away.' But John, the question that is really on your mind is: 'Fanny, you're blind and you have never seen a human being before; therefore, how will you recognize your friends and especially the Lord?' To which I reply, John Sweney, I've thought about that quite often and I know that I will not have a bit of trouble recognizing my friends or my beautiful Saviour; however, contemplating that there might be a problem, I have this to offer. Mind you, I still believe I won't have any problem; but just in case I do, I'll go to the one whom I feel is my Saviour and will say, "May I please look at your hands?' John, I'll know it's my Saviour by the print of the nails in His hands."

For a moment John R. Sweney was speechless. The beauty and the force of Fanny's presentation had so overwhelmed him. When he could speak he exclaimed, "Oh Fanny, could you capture that picture in verse? It would bless many hearts if you could!" Fanny replied, "John, I'll make it a matter of prayer but right now it's quite a bit past my bedtime. I'll see you in the morning."

Early the next morning Fanny called for Mr. Sweney and, as she dictated, he began to write down a poem which Fanny entitled, "My Saviour First Of All." It began, "When my life work is ended and I cross the swelling tide ..." She went on until they had finished the first stanza. Then came the chorus, "I shall know Him, I shall know Him," until the last phrase, "by the print of the nails in His hand!" Fanny had captured the discussion of the previous evening and John R. Sweney had another of Fanny's gems for which to write the music. ABS

Brighten The Corner

BRIGHTEN THE CORNER

Shattered hopes, frustrations, cherished amibitions gone up in smoke — all of this and some folks had said that life could be beautiful.

As Ina Duley Ogdon faced the future much of what she had planned had been swept away by one happeing — her father had become an invalid and she was the only one to take care of him. Instead of the thousands, who she had planned would come to hear her speak on the Chautauqua Circuit, she now had an audience of one confined to a bedroom in her house. Yet from this "wit's-end corner" experience would come a song that would bless many more than she could have ever touched in person and would encourage untold thousands to be a blessing to others.

The transition from utter despair to quiet acceptance was something that took place rather quickly in the life of Mrs. Ogdon for she had learned early that God's ways are not always our ways but God's ways are always the best and so she did not wait for a chance to do some "great deed of greatness to shed her light abroad" but immediately began to do her deeds of kindness in the home and in her own neighborhood. Her household duties became a delight and a challenge as she took them as a calling from the Lord. She did it in such a way that her whole life became a homespun lilting lyric — a foreshadowing of the song she would eventually write.

The dreams of Chautauqua were behind her. Ina Duley Ogdon had found God's corner for her to brighten. Is it any wonder that one day as she reviewed all that had happened that she reasoned, "If God could do this with me He can do it with anybody. Lord help me get the message across" — the result was — "Brighten The Corner Where You Are."

That these words eventually came to the attention of composer Charles H. Gabriel was by no accident for it is his inspiring, catchy, and lilting melody that so wonderfully gave them wings.

Where Mrs. Ogdon might have reached thousands by way of the Chautauqua Circuit, by God's way she has literally reached millions for through the years more than twenty-five million copies of her song have been reproduced in books and on recordings. It is still heard on radio and television, even though it was written over 60 years ago. ABS

Then Jesus Came
Oswald J. Smith
Homer Rodeheaver
1. One sat a - lone be - side the high-way beg-ging, His eyes were blind, the
2. From home and friends the e - vil spir - its drove him, A-mong the tombs he
3. Un-clean! un-clean! the lep - er cried in tor-ment, The deaf, the dumb, in
4. So men to - day have found the Sav-iour a - ble, They could not con - quer
light he could not see; He clutched his rags and shivered in the shad-ows, Then Je-sus
dwelt in mis-er - y; He cut him-self as demon pow'rs possessed him, Then Jesus
helplessness stood near; The fev-er raged, disease had gripped its victim, Then Je-sus
pas-sion, lust and sin; Their broken hearts had left them sad and lonely, Then Je-sus
Refrain
came and bade his dark-ness flee.
came and set the cap - tive free.
came and cast out ev - 'ry fear.
came and dwelt Himself with - in.
When Je - sus comes the tempter's pow'r is
bro - ken; When Je - sus comes the tears are wiped a - way. He takes the
gloom and fills the life with glory, For all is changed when Jesus comes to stay.
© Copyright 1940 The Rodeheaver Co. Renewed 1968 The Rodeheaver Co. All rights reserved.
International copyright secured. Used by permission.

THEN JESUS CAME

He looked like a very distinguished and successful businessman. He could have passed as a banker or the president of a very successful corporation or perhaps you might even have taken him as an important professional man — say a lawyer or a doctor. With his pin-striped suit, his colorful choice of tie, and his folded handkerchief peeking out of his lapel pocket, this man seemed to breathe success. Why he must always have been successful. But as we are so often reminded, "It is not always that which meets the eye." So is the story of Mel Trotter.

Together, with Mel Trotter, I will try with words to paint a picture of defeat and despair only God could change and in the end bring glory out of gloom and through it cause the writing of a great Gospel song.

The date was sometime in the late 1930's. The place was the Winona Lake Bible Conference at Winona Lake, Indiana. A crowd of many thousands had assembled to fill the large Billy Sunday Tabernacle. The occasion was to hear Mel Trotter preach and give his account of the great meetings he had been privileged to conduct in the British Isles as he had retraced the steps of Moody and Sankey in their great revival meetings of 1873 through 1875.

The song service had finished. Homer Rodeheaver had motioned the great crowd to be seated after which, in his own warm and inimitable way, he introduced Mel Troter.

As Mel rose, a great wave of expectancy seemed to fill the tabernacle. The audience knew he was an interesting, entertaining, and inspiring speaker and what he had to say would more than make up for the extra effort they might have had to extend to be there that night. All of this would prove true.

Well, I think I'll let Mel carry on from here. "Friends, I do so appreciate being here tonight and I know most of you are here because it has been advertised that I would tell about the recent visit I have just made across the Atlantic. But as I looked over this wonderful crowd, I was impressed with the fact that there are so many young people here tonight. Young people just at the age I was many years ago when I began to make choices. Choices and decisions which at the time didn't seem too important, but in a few years were to lead to my complete ruination and almost lead to a disgraceful end — except for the grace of God. With your kind permission, and because the Lord has put it on my heart, I would ask that tonight instead of giving an account of the meetings which I could do at a later date, I will tell you a story I don't enjoy telling. I tell it only that it might be used to keep some boy, some girl, some man, some woman from making the horrible mistakes I made in my life.

"From the time I began going to school and playing ball with the boys on the sand lot in my little hometown, it was easy for me to make friends. Wherever I went I never lacked for a gang around me. This continued on through my young life and even on into the beginning of my married life. This, early, caught the eyes of the townfolk and they were heard to remark that I was a born leader and that someday I might even be President of the United States. Of course, I was unmindful of their remarks and expectations but some of the men were serious about it and began to "groom" me with political ambitions in mind, not only for me but for themselves and what they might gain with their own Mel in the office. Soon, what had started as rather innocent ball games and fellowships, began to be turned into social events including the social drink and all that goes with it. The old gang was soon forgotten — why I was heading for the big time! But you know, it wasn't long before the social drink was not reserved for the special occasions but it became a morning, noon, and night experience. The virtues I had been noted for began to disappear as steam does when it hits the cold air. My ambitious political friends were the first to leave. Why they couldn't have faith in a 'young lush' — even if they had been the ones who had started me drinking. It wasn't long until even the children began to give me a wide berth because I was anything but friendly when I would weave back from the corner saloon. I went from one job to another, from one place to another to live, and each time both the job and the living quarters became less desirable. Until one day it found me in Chicago living in a rat-infested cellar apartment in the worst section of the city. Why my wife and little child stayed with me only God knows, for the pain and suffering I caused them cannot be described.

"One day our little child was taken seriously ill. A faithful doctor came even though he knew that there would be no payment for his call. After diagnosing the case he reached into his own pocket, took out some money and thrust it into my hands shouting, 'Mel, run, don't walk, to the drugstore which is two blocks from here — here's the prescription, come right back — it may even now be too late — so hurry!'

"I climbed the stairs and was out onto the pavement. I looked to my left and sure enough I saw the drugstore about two blocks away, but then I looked to my right and saw that the saloon was only one-half block away. A sudden desire came over me — one that drove all thought of my little sick child out of my head. Even the fact that the money in my hand did not belong to me was erased as I blindly rushed to the saloon, threw the money on the bar, and shouted, 'Let's all drink — it's on me.' Soon the doctor's money was gone and then some other fool threw his money on the bar and we continued on and on through the day and into the night. When it was time to close I was so far gone that the saloonkeeper just threw me in a back room to 'sleep it off.' When he came back the next day, I was still there and it wan't until the night began to approach that I came enough to my senses to decide to go home.

"When I arrived back, I slowly descended the rickety stairs. I saw that someone was talking very quietly to my wife and they were crying. I still did not know why and was still too far gone to have understood. I then looked into another room. There had been no furniture before but now there was a little box on a stand. I wondered what it could be. As I went over and looked into the box I saw that it was the body of my little child but looking very different. Someone had put on clean, new clothes and somehow there was even a pair of brand-new little shoes. Still I didn't get the message. As I stood there that sudden urge came over me. I craved another drink. What I wouldn't do for another drink!

"My dear friends — as I think back on this next part my heart feels as if it were being ripped out, for I'm so ashamed. As the urge overwhelmed me, I hurriedly slipped the new shoes from the cold feet of my precious little child, rammed them into my pocket — as yet I had not attracted the attention of my wife and the woman with her — I stole out of the apartment and I sold those little shoes for a few pennies and bought another drink. I had gone so low that I have often said I had to reach up to touch bottom. With all of this, I was not awakened to reality, until one day after some more debauchery and drinking I decided to end it all. With me out of the way I reasoned the world would be a lot better off, particularly my wife. With this in mind, I headed for Lake Michigan to drown myself. It had gotten dark and cold and, as I wove my way down Clark Street heading for one of the streets which would take me east to the lake, I was suddenly given a push by someone who said, 'Why don't you go in there, Bud, it's nice and warm.' And as I went through an open door, someone sat me in a chair. It had all happened so quickly that it took my muddled brain a little while to realize that I was in a room filled with men, and a man was speaking. He was talking as if he knew all about me as he said, 'Perhaps, you've come in here tonight and you haven't even planned it — in fact you had decided that you're going to end it all — you feel no one understands you, no one cares, and there is no hope. My friend, I'm here to tell you that you are wrong, for there is someone who understands you, there is someone who cares for you, and I assure you that there is hope for you. You will find all of your answers when you come to Jesus Christ and receive Him as your personal Saviour. He not only wants to save you from your mess but wants to go with you for the rest of your life, to keep you from getting into any more trouble.' The speaker was Harry Monroe and the place was the Pacific Garden Mission. I became a different person that night. God saved me and made me a new man. My wife got a new husband — the part with its sin and stain was washed away and I found a brand-new tomorrow."

At the Billy Sunday Tabernacle that night, when the altar call was given, many people young and old alike responded to the invitation. It was a meeting many would never forget. God had led Mel Trotter to change his message but that's not all that happened that night. I'll let Homer Rodeheaver, himself, tell the rest of the story.

"The meeting with Mel Trotter will live in my memory for a long time. After it was over, a group of us gathered at my home, 'Rainbow Point,' for food and fellowship. The conversation that night centered around what had happened at the meeting and how wonderful it was that Mel had had such a remarkable change. Dr. Harry Rimmer remarked how everything changes when Jesus comes. He recounted the story of a dead Lazarus and a sorrowing household but "then Jesus came' and that changed everything. Someone remarked, 'Why doesn't somebody write a song about that?'

"'Then Jesus Came' — these words began ringing in my heart and mind. The next week I had to go to our office in Philadelphia. While there — who should come in but Oswald J. Smith. He was speaking in Philadelphia at the time and was staying at the China Inland Mission Headquarters. I immediately began to discuss with him the possibility of a set of words which would tell the story of 'Then Jesus Came' and for which I perhaps could write the music. He returned to his room and before the day had passed, was back with the words just as they appear today. A melody came immediately. I sang it for my music editor, C. Austin Miles, he put it in manuscript form and I sang it in a meeting that evening."

"Then Jesus Came" gained instant success and in a short time became the Rodeheaver Company's most requested song.

Isn't it amazing how great things are, so often, caused by little events. Who lovingly pushed Mel Trotter into the Pacific Garden Mission? What if that man hadn't been working for the Lord on Clark Street in Chicago that cold night but had preferred to stay home and keep warm in front of a big fireplace? ABS

Holy, Holy Is What The Angels Sing (THE ANGEL SONG)
JOHNSON OATMAN
JOHN R. SWENEY
1 There is sing-ing up in heav-en such as we have nev-er known,
2 But I hear an-oth-er an-them blend-ing voi-ces clear and strong,
3 Then the an-gels stand and list-en, for they can-not join that song
4 So, al-though I'm not an an-gel, yet I know that o-ver there
1 Where the an-gels sing the prais-es of the Lamb up-on the throne,
2 Un-to Him that hath re-deem'd us and hath bought us, is the song;
3 Like the sound of ma-ny wat-ers by that hap-py, blood-wash'd throng;
4 I will join a bless-ed cho-rus that the an-gels can-not share;
1 Their sweet harps are ev-er tune-ful and their voi-ces al-ways clear,
2 We have come thro' trib-u-la-tions to this land so fair and bright,
3 For they sing a-bout great tri-als, bat-tles fought and vic-t'ries won,
4 I will sing a-bout my Sav-iour who up-on dark Cal-va-ry
1 O that we might be more like them while we serve the Mas-ter here!
2 In the foun-tain free-ly flow-ing He hath made our gar-ments white.
3 And they praise their great Re-deem-er who hath said to them, Well done!
4 Free-ly par-don'd my trans-gres-sions, died to set a sin-ner free.
REFRAIN
Ho-ly, ho-ly, is what the an-gels sing, And I ex-

HOLY, HOLY IS WHAT THE ANGELS SAY

(The Angel Song)

Two names well known for Gospel songwriting in the latter part of the 1800's were Johnson Oatman, Jr. and John R. Sweeney. To them, writing songs was not an occupation but a calling from the Lord. As one studies what they wrote, one also discovers that they built upon important truths from the Word of God. I am sure it is because of this that so many of their songs have endured.

"The Angel Song," as it is often called, is delightful to sing. I have never forgotten the thrill as I heard it sung for the first time by F. Carlton Booth. Though some theologians may argue whether angels sing or not, it doesn't take away from the impact of its message. I have always felt that the most important part of a song is the message. When the Bible refers to the angels "saying" I really feel that it is emphasizing that the message that was given was of the utmost importance and not how beautifully the angels may have presented it.

To the Christian "redeemed" is a wonderful word. How our hearts thrill as we sing "Redeemed how I love to proclaim it — Redeemed by the blood of the Lamb." This is redemption's story.

One day Mr. Oatman and Mr. Sweeney were reading in the book of the Revelation, the thrilling word picture of a great choir which will assemble in Heaven to sing praises and exalt the Lamb that was slain — the Lord Jesus. As they discussed this thrilling event, they realized that this would be a different choir than ever was heard in Heaven before. This one was made up of the "Redeemed" who had washed their garments white in the blood of the Lamb and, of course, angels couldn't be in this particular choir for they had never experienced the thrill and joy that comes into the heart and life through salvation.

Catching the picture of this, Johnson Oatman left Mr. Sweeney's home, telling him that when he came back he hoped to have put into words that which they had experienced in their mind's eye as they read the Bible description.

When Mr. Oatman came the next day, he had with him the thrilling set of words. As Mr. Sweeney read them, a melody came immediately to mind. This he quickly jotted down and in a few minutes Mr. Oatman and Mr. Sweeney were singing the song which would, in the years to come, wend itself around the world and bless and thrill the hearts of unnumbered Christians. ABS

His Name Is Wonderful
AUDREY MIEIR
AUDREY MIEIR
His name is Won-der-ful, His name is Won-der-ful, His name is
He is the might-y King, Mas-ter of ev-'ry-thing, His name is
Won-der-ful, Je-sus, my Lord; Je-sus, my Lord.
He's the great Shep-herd, the Rock of all a-ges, Al-might-y
God is He; Bow down be-fore Him, Love and a-
dore Him, His name is Won-der-ful, Je-sus my Lord.
©Copyright 1959 by Manna Music, Inc. All rights reserved.

HIS NAME IS WONDERFUL

In the early part of the 1950's I took a trip to California to be the guest of Dr. Charles E. Fuller and his much-loved Old-Fashioned Revival Hour program. While there, I also had the privilege of fellowshipping with Phil Kerr and was thrilled to be invited to take part in his great youth work. Some of the time was spent in a recording studio recording the Phil Kerr Singers under the direction of a young lady named Audrey Mieir. How they could sing! It was an experience that has stayed with me through the years. I'll never forget the inspiration of this young lady and so it was no surprise to me, in later years, that the songs written by Audrey would become the top favorites in the Gospel field and particularly "His Name Is Wonderful." Who better could tell the story of how it was written than Audrey Mieir herself?

"Christmas came on Sunday that year and for once His birth seemed more important to everyone than toys and presents. Fragrant pine boughs perfumed the air in our little Bethel Union Church in Duarte, California. A kind of hushed expectancy filled the place as 'Silent Night, Holy Night' swelled from the organ. All heads were bowed, eyes were closed, and an occasional tear rolled down a wrinkled cheek — remembering 50, 60, even 70 other Christmases, thankful for the love of God and family, their presents and His presence! Little children sat impatiently anticipating the re-creation of the old, old story — their eyes sparkling, reflecting Christmas tree lights, not wanting to miss anything including the Christmas play, afterward the dinner and presents which were stacked and waiting.

"The curtain opened. There it was as it would be depicted countless times that day, the humble manger scene. Mary was a shy teenager, cheeks flushed with excitement, holding someone's baby doll close in her arms. A young Joseph hovered over her, his smooth face discreetly hidden in old drapery. A beautiful angel glittered and shone, out-brillianced only by the flashing smile for mom and dad in aisle two. Her halo had slipped precariously to one side. Eleven-year-old shepherds shuffled down the aisle with unmistakable reticence, their jeans peeking out from under dad's old robe.

"The procession halted and the choir sang, 'Sleep in heavenly peace.' Dr. Luther Mieir's voice filled the small church — 'His name is wonderful,' he said with his hands lifted heavenward. And I — I heard the familiar rustling of angel wings. I did not know at that strangely moving moment that a once-in-a-lifetime experience was about to happen. As I grabbed my old Bible and wrote in it, more than with any other of my songs, I felt as if I were only a channel, as if I were not otherwise involved.

"God blessed 'His Name Is Wonderful' and it seemed to capture people's hearts but one day I met Tim Spencer who said to me, 'Audrey, it's a good song but there just isn't enough of it. Maybe you could write a bridge for it." (At that time I didn't know a bridge was also a musical term.) He explained the word to me and showed me how I could extend the song and enlarge the blessing of its message. I was just on my way to lunch. After I had ordered my hamburger, I began to think of Tim's suggestion and so I opened my Bible there in the booth to the concordance and began to run my finger down the list of names given to Jesus in the Scripture. I wrote them down on my napkin. After I had returned to the office, I went to the piano and finished the song.

"At the moment, I did not foresee the ministry one little song of praise could have and that I would hear it sung all around the world. I heard it in Sweden, all through Korea, and the Philippines. Never shall I forget the thousands of students in Hong Kong lifting it heavenward from their roof top schools; nor hearing it sung in the Garden of Gethsemane — an experience that was truly 'joy unspeakable!'"

In conclusion, Audrey had this to say. "The song will outlive the chubby hand chosen to write a few black notes on the fives lines and four spaces of the music score, but it will never outlive the original composer — God the Father — who glories in His only begotten Son's name and rejoices in our praise of Him for His name is truly wonderful!"

To which we say, God bless you, Audrey Mieir, and thank you for the immortal "His Name Is Wonderful!" ABS

Does Jesus Care?

DOES JESUS CARE?

Did you ever have the feeling of being abandoned? That you were all alone with your cares and problems?

Rev. Frank Graeff went through such a deep and heartbreaking experience. He was to say later that his "Whole attitude had become one of despair and defeat" and that in turn produced a life which was anything but happy and victorious. He had lost sight of the One who cares — the One who knows about our heartaches and griefs — the One who is the burden-bearer and has promised never to leave us in such times.

Each day saw him slipping, as did Bunyon's Pilgrim, deeper into the "slough of despair" until one day when he felt he could stand it no longer and had come to the end of the road — in this extremity, he began to sing a song that had been born out of just such an experience that he was going through. It had been written by Joseph Scriven 75 years before —

What a friend we have in Jesus,
All our sins and griefs to bear
What a privilege to carry,
Everything to God in prayer —
Oh, what peace we often forfeit,
Oh, what needless pain we bear ....

Frank Graeff could go no further. He dropped to his knees and began to pour out his heavy heart to the one who cared. The peace he had forfeited came flooding through his soul and with it a "joy unspeakable and full of glory." "I know He cares! I know My Saviour cares!" shouted the reclaimed preacher.

Is it any wonder that shortly after this experience there flowed from his happy and revived heart the song "Does Jesus Care?" that has blessed and encouraged so many thousands from the time it was written in 1900?

Rev. Graeff went on to become one of the leading pastors in the Philadelphia area where he became known as "The Sunshine Minister."

ABS

Take My Life And Let It Be

TAKE MY LIFE AND LET IT BE

She was a Hebrew and Greek scholar and was skilled in the use of several modern languages. She was the author of many helpful books. She was also a brilliant singer an pianist, and a glittering secular career was open to her. But Frances Ridley Havergal considered all her talents to be only loans from the Lord, to be used in His service. She would not even sing, except it was sacred music, and that only for the purpose of blessing or winning souls. She lived a life so earnest and devoted that all of the things she did had a deeper influence over the hearts of Christians than perhaps any other woman of her day.

It is no wonder that from a life so dedicated there would flow forth so beautiful a hymn of consecration that is considered the outstanding hymn of its kind in the Christian church.

It was in February, 1874, that Miss Havergal was a guest in a home where there were ten persons.Some of them were not converted and those who were converted did not seem to be very happy in their faith. A great longing came over Miss Havergal that all ten of them might, before she left, come to know her Saviour as joyfully and as assuredly as she had just come to know Him. She began to diligently pray to that end and God answered her prayers. For when the last evening of her stay arrived, all ten had either come to Christ for salvation or had entered into the joy of their salvation. That night she was too happy to sleep and spent it in writing this hymn ending with the triumphant declaration, "Ever, only, all for Thee!"

ABS

Oh, That Will Be Glory (THE GLORY SONG)
CHARLES H. GABRIEL
CHARLES H. GABRIEL
1. When all my la-bors and tri-als are o'er And I am safe on that beau-ti-ful shore, Just to be near the dear Lord I a-dore
2. When, by the gift of His in-fi-nite grace, I am ac-cord-ed in heav-en a place, Just to be there and to look on His face
3. Friends will be there I have loved long a-go, Joy like a riv-er a-round me will flow; Yet, just a smile from my Sav-ior, I know,
Will thru the a-ges be glo-ry for me.
CHORUS
O that will be glo-ry for me, Glo-ry for me, glo-ry for me; When by His grace
O that will be glo-ry for me, Glo-ry for me, glo-ry for me;
I shall look on His face, That will be glo-ry, be glo-ry for me!
rit.

OH, THAT WILL BE GLORY

(The Glory Song)

The year was 1899. A Gospel song composer had just finished writing eleven songs which he hastily put into an envelope with a letter to Mr. E. O. Excell, a publisher in Chicago. The songwriter's plight was that he needed money and Mr. Excell had often bought songs from him for prices ranging from $1 to $3 a piece. (This was not too bad a sum when one realizes that a week's wages in those days was often only $5.) To make sure that more than one song would tempt Mr. Excell, Gabriel had offered him the whole lot for $1 each. Upon receiving the songs, Mr. Excell gave them a "quick look-over" as he said later. He chose 10 of the songs but decided that #11 was unusable for it just seemed to have too many "black notes."

Mr. Excell took this remaining song and, with a $10 check, sent it back to the writer who in turn was so pleased with the $10 check that he sent the song back to the publisher free of charge. History does not tell us the names of the 10 songs which Mr. Excell had kept but the Christian church around the world has echoed and re-echoed the strains of #11, for who hasn't sung "The Glory Song" or "Oh, That Will Be Glory For Me," written by Mr. Charles H. Gabriel.

In later years, Mr. Gabriel would often relate the story of the man who had given him inspiration for the song. The man's name was Ed Card, who ran the Sunshine Rescue Mission in St. Louis. Ed's life had been dramatically changed when he met Christ. From a sullen, dull, vindictive individual, his life had become one radiating the love and power of the Gospel. Along the way, friends took his new radiant face and the word "Glory" which had become such an important part of his vocabulary — put them together and from then on Ed Card was known as "Old Glory Face."

Ed Card lived long enough to see the song, that he had inspired, become the most popular Gospel song of its day, and Charles Gabriel went on to become one of the outstanding Gospel song composers of all time. Favorites to his credit include: "His Eye Is On The Sparrow," "Since Jesus Came Into My Heart," "The Way Of The Cross Leads Home," and a host of others. ABS

The Unveiled Christ
N. B. H.
N. B. Herrell
mf
1. Once our bless-ed Christ of beau - ty Was veiled off from hu-man view;
2. Yes, He is with God, the Fa - ther, In - ter-ced-ing there for you;
3. Ho - ly an-gels bow be-fore Him, Men of earth give prais-es due;
4. Throughout time and end-less a - ges, Heights and depths of love so true;
But thro' suff'ring death and sor - row He has rent the veil in two.
For He is the might-y conq - 'ror, Since He rent the veil in two.
For He is the well be-lov - ed, Since He rent the veil in two.
He a-lone can be the giv - er, Since He rent the veil in two.
Chorus
f
crescendo
ff
O be-hold the man of sor-rows, O be-hold Him in plain view,
ff
p
Lo! He is the might-y con-q'ror, Since He rent the veil in two,
ff
p
rit.
Lo! He is the might-y con-q'ror, Since He rent the veil in two.

THE UNVEILED CHRIST

Rev. N. B. Herrell, the author of this song, wrote, "At the time we were living in Olivet, Illinois. I was pastoring a church at a nearby village called Georgetown. The year was 1916 and as a family we were traversing the deep valley of sorrow,' for our five-year-old son, William, had died. Those were difficult and heartbreaking days. It was then that I began to realize more fully what our Heavenly Father had gone through in giving His Son to die on the cross. It was a fearful and fateful day when the creature crucified his Creator. Even nature trembled and refused to look upon that dread scene enacted on Golgatha; I heard the cry, 'It is finished!' and in my mind's eye I saw Him bow His head and die. But it was not in vain, for within the sacred sanctuary the Temple an unseen hand tore in two, the veil which had separated the Holy Of Holies from the Holy Place. Before that moment no one could enter the Holy Of Holies except the high priest and he could only do it once a year and that 'not without blood.' But now the blood of the Paschal Lamb had been shed, once for all, opening the way to all who would enter through the merits of that blood. Now God's children could come boldly before the throne of grace to make their requests known and find help in time of need because the veil of separation had been rent in two.

"The truth so took hold of me, that had I been an artist, I would have painted a picture; but I used the talent God had given me and wrote 'The Unveiled Chirst.'" ABS

Have I Done My Best For Jesus?

HAVE I DONE MY BEST FOR JESUS?

Ed Spencer was attending Northwestern University at Evanston, Illinois. Ed was a rather well-known athlete of his day, for he was one of the first to win a gold medal for the United States in the Olympics.

The campus of Northwestern is boardered on one side by Lake Michigan. One evening, Ed was doing his studies in the library. Outside, a storm was raging. All of a sudden some fellows came in excitedly exclaiming, "Ed, the Lady Elgin has just been thrown upon the rocks and is sinking. There are a lot of people onboard who will drown unless we do something right away."

Ed ran from the library out to the lake and saw that the situation was indeed serious. The storm had calmed somewhat but it was still dangerous. Without a minute's hesitation, he rid himself of any extra clothing which might hinder him and dived into the rolling, chopping waves. He was able to reach the wreck and, fighting his way back, he brought the first person to safety. He had repeated this heroic effort several more times when those on shore said, "Ed, you've done all you can. You'll surely kill yourself if you try it anymore." Ed's reply was, "I've got to do my best," and again he plunged in and brought another to safety and then another and another and this he continued until he had rescued some 17 souls who had been destined to perish! He could go on no further but fell unconscious on the shore. All through the night, as he lay in the infirmary, he kept repeating, "Have I done my best, fellows? Fellows, have I done my best?" Ed Spencer had done his best but this experience had cost him his health. In the years that followed, Ed Spencer no longer won gold medals for athletic skill but lived the life of a semi-invalid.

Some years after this heroic night, a man taking a trip westward happened to stop in Phoenix, Arizona. He had heard of Ed Spencer and found by accident that he was living there and so decided he would pay the hero a visit. He was directed to a small humble cottage near the edge of town. Here he found the former Olympic champion — no longer a robust athlete but just a shadow of his former self. In the course of their conversation, the visitor said to him, "Ed, that was certainly a great thing you did that night many years ago. I know it has cost you a lot of health and wealth and I wouldn't call this cottage any substitute for what you could have gained had you kept your health. But humble as your life is, I'm sure that those you rescued haven't forgotten and they do remember you with some help from time to time." There was a long moment of silence and then slowly, with tears running down his cheeks, Ed replied, "Not one ever came back and even said thank you."

It was the relating of this story that led Ensign Edwin Young to write "Have I Done My Best For Jesus?". ABS

FOR GOD SO LOVED THE WORLD

The year was 1938 and I was on my way to meet, for the first time, George C. Stebbins, the Gospel song composer. Mr. Stebbins had been a friend and associate of D. L. Moody, Ira Sankey, P. P. Bliss, Fanny Crosby and many others of the early evangelists and song writers. Now in his 94th year, he was the only one left. As the mileage on the signs pointing to Catskill, New York became less, the anticipation of meeting him grew greater; for I was going to meet the man who could tell me about the early pioneers of the faith from personal experience. No doubt he could tell me much about them that had never been written and I was sure he would also give me some interesting stories of how his and many of the other Gospel songs were written. I could hardly wait!

At long last I arrived at Catskill and, after stopping for information as to where Mr. Stebbins lived, I found that his address most appropriately was on High Street. In a few minutes I had found a quaint little brick house. My search was over and I was about to meet the man who would do much to inspire and encourage me to dedicate my life to the ministry of music. In fact, it was this first visit which would provide the inspiration for writing the most widely known and used song I have been permitted to write. Here is how it happened.

My visit had come to a close and I was on my way, to a meeting in Oneonta, New York. Mr. Stebbins had drawn back the curtain of the past and for 3 hours he had introduced me to men and women who before had been only names to me, but as we traveled memory's lane it seemed that they again were alive and I could hear them speak and sing. Why, at times I even thought I heard the happy and contagious laugh of Fanny Crosby as she, though blind, shed abroad her sunshine of joy and cheerfulness! We chuckled as Mr. Stebbins told of Mr. Moody singing on one note and how he thought the pump organ had developed a cipher. Tears had filled our eyes as he told of his last good-bye to P. P. Bliss, who a few days later was killed in the great train wreck at Ashtabula, Ohio. On and on we traveled, and each step gave testimony that these great saints had counted it a privilege and an honor to serve the King of Kings. Humbly, but convincingly, Mr. Stebbins told me of God's working in his life and how the inspiration had come to him to write so many of his songs. Then, the time had come to pull "memory's curtain." I was to have more of these visits, for Mr. Stebbins lived to be 99 years old; but at the time I felt that this could be the last. I had been on the mountaintop and the inspiration and blessing of the three hours would never leave me!

As I continued toward Oneonta, there arose within me a desire that has often been repeated through the years — a desire to be used of God like He used these dedicated men and women of yesterday — not to be blessed so much personally, but to be a blessing to others.

I began to review the great songs that God had permitted Mr. Stebbins to write. Would there be room for one more song, even though small, that I might write that could sing its way along with the songs of Stebbins, Crosby, Bliss, and others?

As I drove along, I began to hum a melody. And soon words with a familiar theme began to fall into place. By the time I reached Oneonta I had completed all but one phrase. The meeting was to begin in a few minutes and so all I had time to do was to jot down the melody and the words that I had. I left these on the piano, and then rushed to church.

At the time, I was a guest in the Townsend home. In the family were two sisters, Grace and Frances. Grace was an invalid, and Frances an English teacher. While I was at the meeting that night Grace, who was crippled, said to Frances, "I wonder what song Al has put on the piano?" She and Frances had then gone over to investigate. They read my scribbled words, "For God so loved the world He gave His only Son — To die on Calvary's tree from sin to set me free — someday He's coming back — the next phrase was blank and then I had concluded with "Wonderful His love to me." As they looked at the not-too-neat copy, Frances exclaimed to Grace, "Al has left out a phrase," and with that she took the pencil I had left on the piano, and wrote in the words, "What glory that will be." God had used her to finish the song.

When the song was published I made sure that the name Frances Townsend was included; for had it not been for her, I feel sure that I would have put the song aside and perhaps never gotten around to finish it.

ABS

Let The Lower Lights Be Burning
PHILIP P. BLISS
PHILIP P. BLISS
1. Bright-ly beams our Fa-ther's mer-cy From His light-house ev-er-more,
2. Dark the night of sin has set-tled, Loud the an-gry bil-lows roar;
3. Trim your fee-ble lamp, my broth-er! Some poor sail-or tem-pest-tossed,
But to us He gives the keep-ing Of the lights a-long the shore.
Ea-ger eyes are watch-ing, long-ing, For the lights a-long the shore.
Try-ing now to make the har-bor, In the dark-ness may be lost.
CHORUS
Let the low-er lights be burn-ing! Send a gleam a-cross the wave!
Some poor faint-ing, strug-gling sea-man You may res-cue, you may save.

LET THE LOWER LIGHTS BE BURNING

"On a dark, stormy night, when the waves rolled like mountains and not a star was to be seen, a boat rocking and plunging, neared the Lorraine Harbor at Cleveland. 'Are you sure this is Cleveland,' asked the captain, seeing the light from the lighthouse. 'Quite sure, Sir,' replied the pilot. 'But where are the lower lights?' 'They're out, Sir.' 'Can you make it?' 'We must or we'll perish, Sir!' With a strong hand and a brave heart, the old pilot turned the wheel; but alas, in the darkness he missed the channel, and with a crash upon the rocks, the boat was slivered and many lives were lost in a watery grave." It was D. L. Moody preaching and using, as an illustration, this story that had first appeared in the Chicago papers. It was an actual account by the captain who had been one of the few fortunate enough to escape death.

Behind the tragedy of that night was a story — by then known to most of those in the audience — a story of careless negligence not intended to cause a tragedy, yet it did. Let me tell it to you as it was relayed by George C. Stebbins, a close friend and associate of both D. L. Moody and P. P. Bliss.

"It was around the time that I had arrived in Chicago, which was 1869, that there appeared in the papers an account of a ship being wrecked on the shores of Lake Erie near Cleveland, Ohio. The account told of a place called Lorraine, which is situated on the lake shore west of Cleveland. There was built a special harbor for relief of the ships that would most certainly be wrecked if they tried to ride out some of the intense and dangerous storms that can hit our large inland lakes. This harbor had a channel running from Lake Erie into a large basin — an inner harbor. Once ships reached this, they were safe. At the entrance to this channel were rows of lights which were lit at night and would show the ships where to enter. At the inner harbor there was placed a large lighthouse. This was to help the ships which were far out. It seems that on the very day the tragedy happened, the man who had the job of lighting the lower lights and keeping the lighthouse, said to himself, 'I've been on this job for several years and to date, not one ship has had to find the harbor at night. I just don't feel up to it today, to go out and refill the oil reservoir of the lamps along the shoreline. I think I'll forget about them, just for today. I'll feel better tomorrow and anyway, I just know that no one will need those lights tonight.' And so when night came, he went to bed — little dreaming that in a matter of a few short hours his unconcern would cost many lives and burden his conscience for the remainder of his life with something he would never forget. For that very night a turbulent and destructive storm swept across Lake Erie. Some of the ships were able to ride out the storm, some were not. But none so tragic as the one, that Mr. Moody described in his sermon, which was so close to safety and yet wrecked because of one man's neglect.

"Mr. Bliss was in the audience that night and, as Mr. Stebbins later told me, Mr. Bliss said to him, 'You know, George, I had read the newspaper account and I must admit I was shaken by the fact that one man's negligence could be so costly. But it was when I heard Mr. Moody use it as an illustration in his message that night I cried out in my heart, 'Bliss, you are just as guilty as the man in the story. As a Christian, you are to be one of the lower lights shining brightly so that some pour soul tossed about on the sea of life may find safety and everlasting life in the haven that God has prepared.' George, I couldn't dismiss the thought from my heart, neither from my mind. It so overwhelmed me that the very next week I wrote the song 'Lower Lights.'"

In conclusion, Mr. Stebbins remarked, "Bliss was a very unusual man, a very gifted man. He had a special ability to take a story from life or from the Bible and make it live through a song." ABS

No Night There

John R. Clements | Hart P. Danks

1. In the land of fade - less day Lies the "cit - y four - square,"
2. All the gates of pearl are made, In the "cit - y four - square,"
3. And the gates shall nev - er close To the "cit - y four - square,"
4. There they need no sun - shine bright, In that "cit - y four - square,"

It shall nev - er pass a - way, And there is "no night there."
All the streets with gold are laid, And there is "no night there."
There life's crys - tal riv - er flows, And there is "no night there."
For the Lamb is all the light, And there is "no night there."

CHORUS

mf

God shall "wipe a-way all tears;" There's no death, no pain, nor fears;
God shall "wipe a - way all tears;" There's no death, no pain, nor fears;

f *dim.* *mf*

And they count not time by years, For there is "no night there."
And they count not time by years, by years, For there is "no night... there."

NO NIGHT THERE

"Young man, if coming to Christ for you is a cross, put your shoulder under it and carry it forward as you come to Him. Do not try to creep under it; do not try to climb over it; do not try to go around it. He says, 'Take up thy cross and follow me.' Take it up! Just take it up! There is no other way."

It was this challenge given by D. L. Moody in a meeting in Binghamton, New York, that proved to be the turning point in the life of John R. Clements, a young Irishman, who had come to Mr. Moody's meeting at the invitation of his Christian employer, J. Ely Mills.

From that night on, the life of Mr. Clements changed. His training had been in business and, in the years that followed, he proved of great assistance in helping Christian organizations such as The Practical Bible Training School in Johnson City, New York, and the Montrose Bible Conference in Montrose, Pennsylvania. The latter was founded by Dr. R. A. Torrey in 1908, with Mr. Clements as its first president. Both of these organizations are still going strong. But Mr. Clements also had another talent — he was a gifted poet and wrote over 2000 poems, some of which were put to music. Two became exceptionally popular — "Somebody Did A Golden Deed" and "No Night There." Of the latter, Mr. Clements had this to say: "It was in the late 1890's that I had the privilege of traveling to California. As the train headed westward, each mile was a new revelation to me of the wonderful country in which we live and the Creator who made it all. The spacious skies, the amber waves of grain, the mountain majesties — all united in a praise hymn to the great God of wonders. But of all the marvels I experienced, one stands out above them all. It was a sunset witnessed at California's Golden Gate, a scene I will never forget! A sky, riot with every hue in the spectrum of color. So majestic, that I was afraid to move for fear of it disappearing — it actually took my breath away! And then came the thought — darkness will soon follow this great spectacle; but someday I'll be in the land where there is no night but eternal day, and with it no pain, no death nor fears. Just one great glorious day that will never end, in a place that Jesus has gone to prepare for us.

"I was so overwhelmed that I could not dismiss the glory from my mind and that evening I wrote 'No Night There.'" ABS

I'll Go Where You Want Me To Go

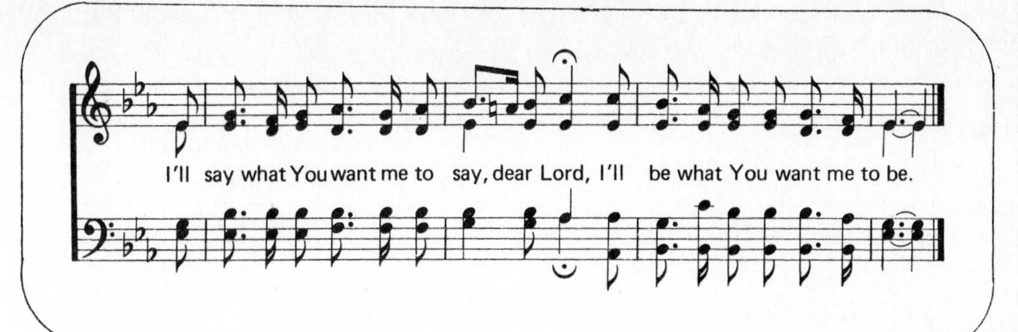

I'LL GO WHERE YOU WANT ME TO GO

Not too much is known about the writers of this wonderful song of dedication. We do know that Mary Brown lived in Jewett City, Connecticut, not far from the New York State line where Fanny Crosby lived; and that it was Fanny's song, "Rescue the Perishing," which played such a great influence on her life. This eventually led her to write "I'll Go Where You Want Me to Go, Dear Lord." Mary Brown's original song had only one stanza and the chorus and had as its title, "I'll Go Where Thou Wouldst I Should Go." Charles E. Prior, a banker, church organist, and composer, who also lived in Jewett City, wrote the rest of the stanzas. But it was a humble woman evangelist whom God used to rewrite the wings of melody which have carried them to almost every town and hamlet in the Christian world. Her name was Carrie Ester Rounsefell, who spent her time traveling around New England singing the Gospel and accompanying herself on an auto-harp. It was while in the vicinity of Jewett City that a copy of Mary Brown's words and melody were given to her. They expressed the deep, deep desire of her heart, and taking her auto-harp, she began to sing them to a new tune she composed as she sang. When she finished, "I'll Go Where You Want Me To Go, Dear Lord" had a new melody and a bright future. For years Carrie Rounsefell used it as her theme song and sang it wherever she traveled. But the song could not be confined to Carrie Rounsefell's limited ministry and soon it had found its way around the world.

Only eternity will reveal the full extent to which this song had touched hearts and lives. We do know that it was this song which influenced two young men to leave the mountains of East Tennessee to go wherever the Lord would send them. One was Charles M. Alexander, who became the warmhearted and inspiring musical associate of Dr. R. A. Torrey. The other was Homer A. Rodeheaver, who played such an important role as the songleader in the great Billy Sunday meetings.

It was my privilege to know Dr. Rodeheaver and one day he passed on this interesting story to me. "Al, some years ago it was my privilege to play golf at Palm Beach, Florida, with John D. Rockefeller, Sr. Just as we were about to tee off, Mr. Rockefeller asked me to sing his favorite song before we played our round of golf. It was 'I'll Go Where You Want Me To Go, Dear Lord.' And so, surrounded by perfectly kept greens, rainbows of flowers, stately palm trees, singing birds, and a beautiful blue sun-filled Florida sky, I sang the song for him — a man, who at that time, had amassed the greatest personal fortune in the history of our country. Al, it was an experience. I'll never forget it. Here was a man who realized that there was something more important than wealth and power or in even playing a game of golf. As I stood there after finishing the song, I heard him say, 'Homer, we have only one life — how soon it is passed. Only that done for Christ will last!' And with this he said, 'Now let's play golf.'" ABS

A Child Of The King
BINGHAMTON 10 11 11 11 Ref.
Harriett E. Buell, 1877
John B. Sumner, 1877
1. My Fa - ther is rich in hous - es and lands, He hold - eth the
2. My Fa - ther's own Son, the Sav - ior of men, Once wan - dered on
3. I once was an out - cast stran - ger on earth, A sin - ner by
4. A tent or a cot - tage, why should I care? They're build-ing a
wealth of the world in His hands! Of ru - bies and dia - monds, of
earth as the poor - est of them; But now He is reign - ing for
choice, and an al - ien by birth; But I've been a - dopt - ed, my
pal - ace for me o - ver there; Though ex - iled from home, yet
sil - ver and gold, His cof - fers are full, He has rich - es un - told.
ev - er on high, And will give me a home in heav'n by and by.
name's writ - ten down, An heir to a man-sion, a robe, and a crown.
still I may sing: All glo - ry to God, I'm a child of the King.
Refrain
I'm a child of the King, A child of the King:
With Je - sus my Sav - ior, I'm a child of the King.

A CHILD OF THE KING

This song, sometimes titled, "The Child Of The King" and at other times, "A Child Of The King" is one of the Gospel songs that has really endured the test of time and is still a favorite wherever it is sung.

Hattie Buell, the writer of the words, received her inspiration while attending an early Methodist camp meeting. I'll let her tell it in her own words.

"As I left my hometown of Cazenovia, New York, bound for the 1876 camp meeting held at the Thousand Island Park in upper New York State, my heart was hungering for the spiritual food I knew would be awaiting me there. It was an occasion I looked forward to each year, for God seemed to speak to peoples' hearts, and especially to mine, in an unusual way at that hallowed spot. I will never forget the opening Sunday morning service. Beginning with the doxology and through each hymn and scripture, it all served to remind me of the greatness of a God who had made the earth, the skies, and the great universe, and yet loved and cared for us, His children. The speaker, that morning, chose as his topic, our relationship to God through His Son, Jesus Christ. How man, as a sinner, was alienated and far from God; but how he became an heir of God and a joint-heir with Jesus Christ through faith in His finished work on the cross. In the course of the message, the speaker could control himself no longer and shouted, 'Christian friends, we are the children of a King! Our Heavenly Father's a King! Poor ones, take heart, you'll have a palace someday built for you by Jesus, Himself!' I don't have to tell you that I felt as if I were walking on air as I left that service and as I walked toward my cottage, the complete set of words had come to me. I entitled them, "The Child Of A King."

The simple, but forceful, musical setting of this song has had much to do with the song's acceptance and its continued use; and so I feel a word about John Sumner, who wrote this very fitting musical setting is in order.

Rev. John Sumner was a young Methodist pastor in the town of Wyalusing, Pennsylvania (about 20 miles from the town of Montrose, where I am writing this book). Before becoming a preacher, Sumner had been a singing school teacher. He and his wife, Alma, with their melodian in the back of their wagon, drove up and down the Susquehanna Valley teaching old and young alike to sing from a three-foot-high book which he had designed. This made it possible for those in the back of the room to see the notes clearly. It was while thus engaged that he met P. P. Bliss. It was in December of 1876 that the shocking news came to him of the terrible train disaster at Ashtabula, Ohio, in which the great writer of Gospel songs, P. P. Bliss, had been killed. Young Sumner was heartbroken, for Bliss had been a real friend to the young preacher. It was while on his knees in prayer for the loved ones who had been left that the longing came over him; and he prayed that in some way he might carry on for his departed friend. This desire stayed with him, and the following February, as he was looking through the Northern Christian Advocate magazine, he read Miss Buell's poem. Immediately he knew he must put it to music. This he did, and in a matter of a few short months, people over the length and breadth of the land were singing, "I'm a child of the King, with Jesus, my Saviour, I'm a child of the King." John Sumner did not go on to become a prolific composer like Bliss, but God did answer his prayer. For "A Child Of The King" has found its way alongside the songs of P. P. Bliss as a song that must be included in a Gospel hymnbook, if it is really to be considered complete.

OF ADDED INTEREST –

I had often wondered how in the days before radio, recordings, and television a song became widely used and well known. It was while reading a story by the late Dr. Daniel Polling, about his mother, that he told of at least one way in which it was done.

His mother as a young woman was a member of *The National Quartet*. This quartet appeared at many of the then popular camp meetings, Methodist conventions and also toured the Chautauqua circuit, which had a great influence upon the educational and spiritual climate of America in the late 1800's.

While in Binghamton, New York, she was given a copy of the song "A Child Of The King." She was so taken by the song that she adopted it as her theme song and wherever she went featured it. The travels with the quartet took her back and forth across our nation into large cities as well as small hamlets and soon the song had become a favorite of the Christian public also. In fact it was so well known that when wounded President Garfield was taken to Long Branch, New Jersey in hopes that the medicinal effect of the ocean air would help in his recovery he requested that the young lady, who later became Dr. Polling's mother, come from the great Methodist Conference at Ocean Grove where she was appearing and sing the comforting and encouraging song to him. It proved to be the last song he was to hear before his death. ABS

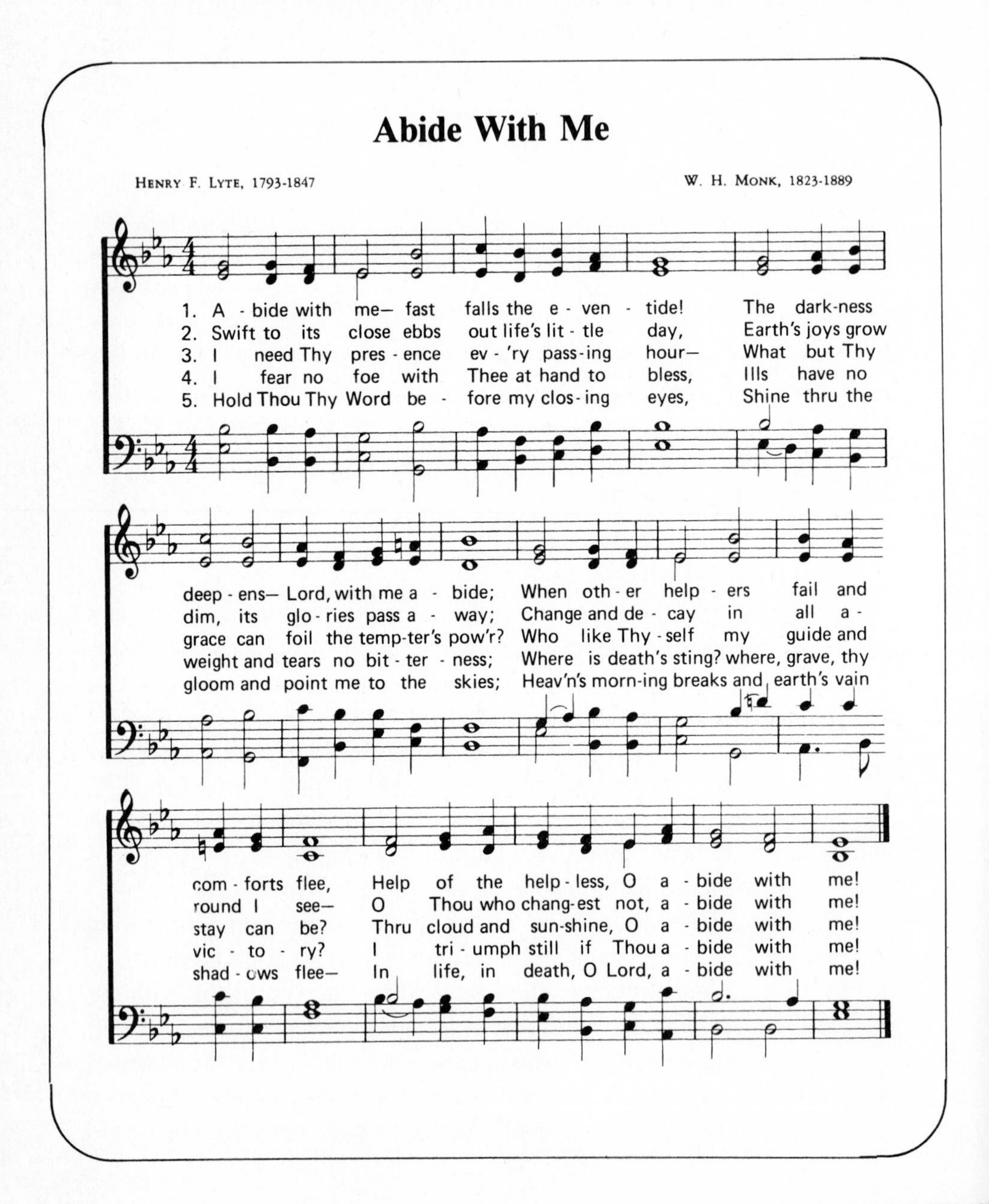

ABIDE WITH ME

"Few swan songs in all earth's history have been so honored by God and man." So wrote Amos R. Wells regarding "Abide With Me."

Henry Francis Lyte, the author of this, one of the greatest of all hymns was delicate in health all of his life yet in spite of this he toiled some 24 years as the pastor of rough seafaring men in a church on the seashore at Devonshire, England. The real change in Lyte's life had come when a fellow pastor, on his deathbed, had sent for Lyte to come and give him spiritual light and encouragement. To the grief of both of them they found they had been "blind, leaders of the blind." Together they prayed for God's forgiveness and for the assurance of salvation. Lyte emerged from that sick room a new man.

In 1847, Lyte had reached the end of his strength. He could go on no longer and had been advised by his physician to go to Southern France where the climate would be less severe. Just as he was about to leave England for this purpose, he was seized with an irresistable desire to preach to his people one more time. This he did against the protest of amazed friends. "Oh Brethren," he said, as he entered the familiar pulpit for the last time, "I stand here before you today, as alive from the dead, if I may hope to impress upon you, and get you to prepare for that solemn hour which must come to all. I plead with you to become acquainted with the changeless Christ and His death." He then closed the service by administering communion to his weeping church family.

That evening he wrote "Abide With Me," his last and greatest hymn and handed it to an adopted daughter that very night. Setting out the next day for France, he reached Nice where he had a seizure and passed away with the words, "Joy! Peace!" upon his lips. Heaven's morning had broken and earth's vain shadows had flown for Henry Francis Lyte. ABS

Softly And Tenderly

SOFTLY AND TENDERLY

Will Lamartine Thompson began publishing his own songs, when a publisher in New York offered him only 25 dollars from four popular songs he had written. In a short time millions of copies were being sold and soon he became known as "The Lord Of Ohio" and "The Millionaire Song-writer." With all this fame and fortune, Will Thompson felt that something was missing and as he was to say later, "I was grateful for all that had happened but one day God spoke to my heart through meeting D. L. Moody. He told me, 'Will, they are good songs you wrote but why not write some songs that will bless people's hearts and lives and bring them to Christ?' From that day on I have written only sacred songs and it's a decision I have never regretted."

Not much is known as to what led to the writing of this song, but the incident which I am about to relate, I am sure you will agree, merits its being included in our book.

In December of 1899 the news carried the story that the world-famous evangelist, D. L. Moody, had suffered a heart attack and was not expected to live. Upon hearing the news, Will Thompson left his home in East Liverpool, Ohio, for Northfield, Massachusetts, where Mr. Moody lived. He felt constrained to make this trip because of what Mr. Moody meant to him. It was Mr. Moody who had put before him the challenge of giving his talents over entirely to writing and publishing Gospel songs.

Upon arriving at Northfield, Mr. Thompson found that all visitors were barred from the sickroom because of the seriousness of Mr. Moody's condition; but when Mr. Moody heard that Will Thompson was there, he demanded that they admit his friend.

As the two men saw each other — the one, the great preacher who had heralded the Gospel around the world — the other, one who had set the world to singing the Gospel in song — Will took the feeble trembling hand of Moody in his own and thanked him for all he had meant to him through the years. Moody, with the little strength he had, squeezed his friend's hand and said, "Will, I would rather have written 'Softly and Tenderly Jesus Is Calling' than anything I have been able to do in the world." ABS

Some Golden Daybreak

C. A. Blackmore   Carl Blackmore

SOME GOLDEN DAYBREAK

"My friend, we have a glorious hope, the Bible calls it a blessed hope for Christians. The Bible also tells us that one day the trumpet will sound and Jesus will come back to take his children home! Dear friend, all your suffering and pain will be over, you'll have a new body, arms and legs that are missing will be replaced — friend, we'll be like Jesus! You'll have a glorified body someday, some golden daybreak when Jesus comes back." The Reverend C. A. Blackmore, one of America's pioneer radio preachers, was giving a message on Christ's second coming or the Rapture as it is called theologically.

A few days later, Reverend Blackmore received a letter from a woman listener who had been bed-ridden for many years. She wrote, "Rev. Blackmore, the message you gave on Jesus coming was such a blessing to me, I've been an invalid for almost 25 years and sometimes I get so discouraged, I can hardly wait for the Lord to come — to think I'll be able to walk again and there'll be no heartaches there. Thank you so much for your sermon."

This dear woman was not the only one that had been touched with the message. Rev. Blackmore's son had. Carl was the pianist and soloist for his father's broadcast and the message that day struck a chord of reality in his heart — what a day that will be! Remembering the words of his father, "Some Golden Daybreak," he began to compose a Gospel chorus with that theme and soon he had it completed.

Some golden daybreak, Jesus will come,
Some golden daybreak battles all won.
He'll shout the victory, break through the blue.
Some golden daybreak, for me, for you!

He played it over but it seemed to call for more than just a chorus and so he composed a suitable musical setting for some verses. It gave a complete feeling to the song, but who would write the verses? This was settled when Carl asked his dad if he would. He consented saying, "I'm not much of a poet but with the Lord's help, I'll give it a try." The Lord did help him, for sometime later he handed his son the completed verses. The song was then published in a special leaflet. It became popular immediately and soon young and old alike were singing the glorious truth — "Some golden daybreak, Jesus will come." ABS

Let Jesus Come Into Your Heart
Mrs. C. H. Morris
Mrs. C. H. Morris
1. If you are tired of the load of your sin, Let Je - sus come
2. If 'tis for pu - ri - ty now that you sigh, Let Je - sus come
3. If there's a tem - pest your voice can - not still, Let Je - sus come
4. If you would join the glad songs of the blest, Let Je - sus come
in - to your heart; If you de - sire a new life to be - gin,
in - to your heart; Foun - tains for cleans - ing are flow - ing near by,
in - to your heart; If there's a void this world nev - er can fill,
in - to your heart; If you would en - ter the man - sions of rest,
Let Je - sus come in - to your heart.
CHORUS
Just now, your doubt - ings give o'er; Just now, re - ject Him no more; Just now, throw
o - pen the door; Let Je - sus come in - to your heart.

LET JESUS COME INTO YOUR HEART

The Methodist Camp Meeting played a very important part in the life and growth of the early Methodist church and its people. They ranged all the way from the small Brush Arbor meeting of a few local churches to the huge Ocean Grove, New Jersey, camp meeting community with its auditorium seating several thousand. But large or small, God worked his miracle work of grace in all of them.

One Sunday morning Mountain Lake Park, a Methodist camp meeting ground in Maryland, was the scene of a soul-stirring and deeply moving service. Evangelist L. H. Baker had brought a searching message on "Repentance." Among the many who had responded to the invitation was a woman whose dress and manner evidenced refinement. Mrs. C. H. Morris, well-known Gospel song composer, was present at the meeting and upon observing that the woman was having difficulty, began to talk with her. She found that her problem was one of fearing that God would not receive her. Putting her arm around her, Mrs. Morris exclaimed, "Now, just now your doubtings give o'er." The songleader, Dr. H. L. Gilman, who had witnessed the struggle and had also gotten on his knees by the woman, added, "Just now reject Him no more." Evangelist Baker, who also by this time had gathered in the circle surrounding them replied, "Just now throw open the door," and Mrs. Morris added a last appeal with, "Let Jesus come into your heart."

That morning in a most unusual way, the woman let Jesus come into her heart and gained the assurance of salvation. That morning, also in a most unusual way, was born the chorus of an invitation song that has been the means of winning thousands to Christ.

Before the close of the camp meeting that week, Mrs. Morris had written a complete set of four stanzas and had also written the music for "Let Jesus Come Into Your Heart." God had worked in a "mysterious way" His wonders to perform. ABS

My Wonderful Lord
H. L.
Haldor Lillenas
1. I have found a deep peace that I nev - er had known And a joy this world
2. I de - sire that my life shall be or-dered by Thee, That my will be in
3. All the tal - ents I have I have laid at Thy feet, Thy ap-prov - al shall
4. Thou art fair - er to me than the fair-est of earth, Thou om-ni - po - tent,
could not af - ford, . . Since I yield-ed con-trol of my bod - y and soul
per - fect ac - cord; . . With Thine own sov'reign will Thy de-sires to ful - fill,
be my re - ward; . . Be my store great or small, I sur - ren - der it all
life - giv-ing Word: . . O Thou An-cient of Days, Thou art wor-thy all praise,
To my won - der - ful, won - der - ful Lord.
My won - der - ful, won - der - ful Lord.
To my won - der - ful, won - der - ful Lord.
My won - der - ful, won - der - ful Lord!
CHORUS
My won - der - ful Lord, my
won - der - ful Lord, By an - gels and ser-aphs in heav - en a - dored; I
bow at Thy shrine, my Sav-ior di - vine, My won-der - ful, won-der-ful Lord.

MY WONDERFUL LORD

I can still hear his voice as he talked with me. I was a guest of Dr. Haldor Lillenas and he was telling me how he had come to write "My Wonderful Lord."

"You know, Al Smith, there are not many straight, level stretches on the highway of life. Much of it is a winding road, we often climb rugged mountains or go down into deep valleys. Not often can we see very far ahead. I was driving down the Paseo Boulevard in Kansas City, on my way to the office early one morning. It was a gray day, chilly, with some fog and smoke in the air. Both of our children had married and left home. My wife was very ill, and it was with a heavy heart that I had left home that morning. I recalled brighter days, when we were busy in our much-loved pastorates and when we had the children at home. Now I was busy writing songs, compiling and editing books, doing what I felt God had called me to do; but I sometimes wondered how many of them would be sung. Suddenly as I drove along the avenue, it seemed that Someone quietly opened the car door and sat down beside me. I could feel the warmth of His sacred presence and I began to sing quietly.

My wonderful Lord, my wonderful Lord,
By angels and seraphs in heaven adored!
I bow at Thy shrine, my Saviour divine,
My wonderful, wonderful Lord.

"Al, I've had the opportunity to hear great congregations pour out their love and adoration as they sing this song to the same wonderful Lord for which I sang it that day, and as I listen, I seem to again hear Someone come in quietly and sit down beside me." ABS

JESUS, SAVIOUR, PILOT ME

Rev. Edward Hopper, the author of this very beloved hymn, was born in New York City in 1818. On his mother's side, he was a descendant of the heroic Huguenots, that gallant group who suffered martyrdom and persecution for their faith in Christ.

For eleven years, Rev. Hopper was pastor of a Presbyterian church in Sag Harbor, Long Island, and then became pastor of the Church of Sea and Land, which was located in the New York harbor. Here he had opportunity to meet seamen from all of the countries of the world and not one of them ever left without the plea of God for their souls.

Rev. Hopper was an educated man, having graduated from New York University and Union Theological Seminary. He had also received the degree of Doctor of Divinity from Lafayette College, yet with it all, he was a very humble man even to the extent of not signing his name to the songs that he wrote. These he wrote particularly for his seafaring family. They were in the language and themes that they could understand best, such as "Wrecked and Struggling In Mid-Ocean" and "They Pray Best Who Pray and Watch."

"Jesus, Saviour, Pilot Me" is an experience song, and is without a doubt the best that he wrote, and is still today considered one of the most plaintive and heart-touching Gospel hymns ever written. It was the culmination of a life in which the majority of years had been devoted to ministering to seafaring men.

If Brother Hopper had been working among railroad men, he would, I am sure, have used terms familiar to railroading. Space does not permit me to go into every line, but each one is a movement in itself. A composer could write a symphony built upon the moods and word pictures presented. There is a feeling of power and grandeur and yet it has a quiet tenderness. Rev. Hopper, who never claimed to be a poet, captured in this song the feeling that every great poet has strived for. It was first published anonymously in "Spiritual Songs" in 1878. Some 10 years afterward he acknowledged that he was the author. In 1888 Rev. Hopper was found dead in his study chair; he had just written some lines on "Heaven" and his pencil still lay on the manuscript. He, at last, had come near the shore and had heard the wondrous Sovereign of the Sea say, "Fear not, I will pilot thee!" ABS

Surely Goodness And Mercy
Based on Psalm 23
JOHN W. PETERSON
and ALFRED B. SMITH
ALFRED B. SMITH
and JOHN W. PETERSON
1. A pil - grim was I, and a - wan-d'ring— In the cold night of sin I did roam When Je - sus the kind Shepherd found me— And now I am on my way home.
2. He re - stor - eth my soul when I'm wea - ry, He giv - eth me strength day by day; He leads me be - side the still wa - ters, He guards me each step of the way.
3. When I walk thru the dark lone-some val - ley, My Sav - ior will walk with me there; And safe - ly His great hand will lead me To the man - sions He's gone to pre - pare.
CHORUS
Sure - ly good - ness and mer - cy shall fol - low me All the days, all the days of my life; Sure - ly good - ness and mer - cy shall
© Copyright 1958 by Singspiration, Inc. All rights reserved. Used by permission.

(opt. D.C.)
fol - low me All the days, all the days of my life.
May be omitted until final chorus
And I shall dwell in the house of the Lord for - ev - er, And I shall
feast at the ta - ble spread for me; Sure - ly good - ness
and mer - cy shall fol - low me All the days, all the days of
my life, All the days, all the days of my life.

SURELY GOODNESS AND MERCY

Rome, Pennsylvania, is a little town situated some 25 miles West of Montrose, where I am writing this book. It is still about the same size that it was when three of our well-known songwriters lived there over a hundred years ago. These men were Daniel B. Towner, James McGranahan, and Philip P. Bliss. Quite a reputation for such a small village. In the cemetery is a large marble shaft with the inscription: *"In memory of Philip P. Bliss author of 'Hold the Fort.'"*

This monument was bought and erected by D. L. Moody with pennies which were given by the Sunday schools of both England and the United States. It has been said that no man won the hearts of the boys and girls as did P. P. Bliss with his Gospel songs.

Some of the descendants of Bliss still live in the vicinity and one day I received a note from one of them. It read:

> *Dear Mr. Smith —*
>
> *Here's a little true and quaint story about Uncle Phil which you might enjoy having. Uncle Phil, when he was a barefoot boy about six years of age, went to the little one-room country schoolhouse for the first time. As he entered the school room his heart skipped a beat when he saw the teacher. She was very petite, less than five feet tall, and red hair, blue-green eyes and her name was Miss Murphy. To little Bliss, he had never beheld anything quite so beautiful and needless to say he fell in love with his teacher. She must have been a wonderful teacher, Dr. Smith, for the first thing she did with the class was to take her own Bible and from it teach the class to memorize the 23rd Psalm. As the class progressed in the Psalm and they came to "Surely goodness and mercy shall follow me all the days of my life," little Bliss, who of course couldn't read as yet, thought for sure that it said, "Surely good Miss Murphy shall follow me all the days of my life!" What a joyous prospect for his little heart — of course it wasn't long before he found that it didn't say that at all.*

The recalling of this incident gave us the seed-thought for a song.

I remarked to John W. Peterson, who was working for me at the time, "John, that would make a good title for a song — not 'Surely good Miss Murphy' but 'Surely Goodness and Mercy'." He agreed and before the day was out, together, we had written a song.

Only Eternity will reveal the full extent of how Gospel songs have affected the lives of people. One incident regarding this song will long be remembered.

Some I am sure will remember the tragedy in Atlanta, Georgia, when

Mrs. Martin Luther King, Sr. was murdered in her own church during a service. A man with a gun had come into the church and in a matter of moments, Mrs. King, who was church organist and choirleader, and an usher were dead.

Mrs. King, who was a devoted Christian, had left instructions for when the time came for her funeral. In them she had asked that her choir sing "Surely Goodness And Mercy." Of course, I was unaware of this. On the evening newscast on the day of her funeral the announcer said, "There was a tragedy in Atlanta some days ago and Mrs. Martin Luther King, Sr. was killed by a gunman. Today was her funeral, and there were many there to pay their last respects to a woman who was admired and respected. It was a service that will be long remembered and particularly the part played by her choir which she had so long directed. The television camera then focused on the choir just as they were singing, "And I shall dwell in the house of the Lord forever."

Tears filled my eyes as I realized that this had really come about all because of a barefoot boy in Pennsylvania and a teacher named Miss Murphy. ABS

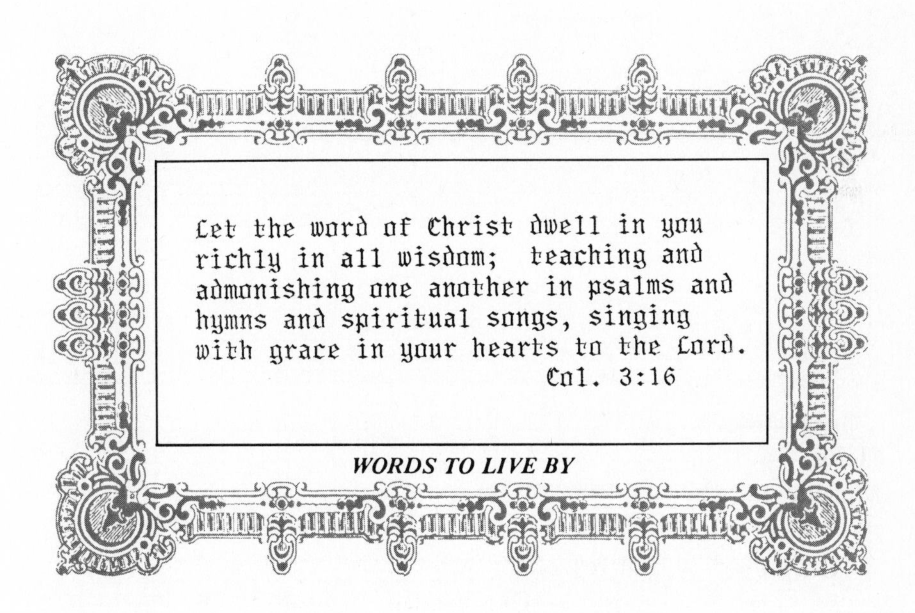

My Redeemer
PHILIP P. BLISS
JAMES McGRANAHAN
1. I will sing of my Re-deem-er, And His won - drous love to me;
2. I will tell the won-drous sto-ry, How my lost es - tate to save,
3. I will praise my dear Re-deem-er, His tri - um - phant power I'll tell,
4. I will sing of my Re-deem-er, And His heaven - ly love to me;
On the cru - el cross He suf-fered, From the curse to set me free.
In His bound-less love and mer - cy, He the ran - som free - ly gave.
How the vic - to - ry He giv - eth O - ver sin, and death, and hell.
He from death to life hath brought me, Son of God, with Him to be.
Sing, oh, sing . . . . of my Re - deem - er,
of my Re - deem - er, Sing, oh, sing of my Re - deem- er,
With His blood . . . . He pur - chased me, ...
He pur-chased me, With His blood He pur-chased me,
On the cross . . . . He sealed my par - don,
He sealed my par - don, On the cross He sealed my par-don,

MY REDEEMER

Christmastime, 1876, for Mr. & Mrs. P. P. Bliss, had proved a most enjoyable time. They had been able to rejoin their two small sons who had been staying with friends; and also spend some time with friends and relatives while back home at Rome, Pennsylvania. They were due back in Chicago after the first of the year when they would join Mr. Moody and his associates in a great evangelistic campaign. It had been not only a rewarding trip, as far as fellowship was concerned, but Mr. Bliss had also had time to work on some new Gospel songs. He had decided that he would write only the words and later when back in Chicago, he would attempt to write the music for them.

The time for farewells had arrived and the Bliss' again had to say good-bye to Phil and George, their two small sons, as well as relatives and friends. Once more they were leaving the boys behind because the coming Chicago Campaign would require more of their time. There were tears in the eyes of everyone as the Erie train pulled out, headed for Chicago. The Bliss' were due to arrive in Chicago early the next day but as the train approached Hornell, New York, it blew a piston. This meant that the train must stop for repairs at the trainyard at Hornell before going on. This would take several hours and so the passengers were housed in a local hotel overnight. (While a student at Moody Bible Institute, I remember seeing the framed page of the Hornell Hotel registry with the names Mr. & Mrs. P. P. Bliss on it.)

The next day the Bliss' were able to continue on their way, but they would never reach Chicago, for as the train approached Ashtabula, Ohio, it had to cross a wooden and steel bridge built across a ravine which was some 80 to 100 feet deep. The bridge moorings, which had been weakened by the winter weather, gave way and the train plunged into the abyss below. There was an immediate fire as the smashed wooden coaches were ignited by the bursting pot-bellied stoves which had been used to warm the cars. When it was over some eighty persons had lost their lives including Mr. and Mrs. Bliss. The fire had been so thorough in its devastation that none of the eighty persons could be identified. Major D. W. Whittle and songwriter James McGranahan, both close friends of the Bliss', had both been sent to find the bodies of Mr. & Mrs. Bliss, but had to return without them. After all efforts of identification had failed, the remains of these people were buried in a communal grave in Ashtabula.

It was thought at the time, that all of the baggage belonging to the Bliss' had also perished in the fire, but some days later, a large trunk was found. It had somehow been transferred to another train. In it were some of their personal effects, including unfinished manuscripts of Gospel songs — among them a set of words entitled "My Redeemer," which Mr. Bliss had written during the Christmas stay at Rome, Pennsylvania.

These words were given to Mr. James McGranahan who put them to music. It is interesting to note that Mr. McGranahan was one of P. P. Bliss's closest friends. He it was, who also took Bliss's place as an associate of D. L. Moody and Major Whittle, and it seems so appropriate that he would write the music for this — one of P. P. Bliss's last works. ABS

O Little Town Of Bethlehem

O LITTLE TOWN OF BETHLEHEM

The morning after the writer of this beautiful carol was called "Home," the mother of a little girl of five, who had been one of his special favorites, entered the room where the child was playing. Holding the little face between her hands, she said tearfully, "Bishop Brooks has gone to Heaven." "Oh, Mama!" was the reply, "How happy the angels will be!"

This little true story paints but a part of the story of Phillips Brooks — preacher extraordinare, lover of children, gifted orator, poet, and above all, a believer — with all his soul — in the divine Son of God of whom he preached and for whom he lived.

The idea for this song had been simmering in the heart of Phillips Brooks since 1865 when, on a trip abroad, he was able to spend Christmas in Bethlehem. This for his day, was unusual and was an experience he would never forget. On Sunday, December 24, he rode on horseback from Jerusalem to Bethlehem, and as twilight was falling, he went out to the field where tradition says the shepherds saw the glory of the Lord. As he looked toward the little town of Bethlehem, with the moon acting as the illuminator and the stars shining in the sky, he witnessed a scene much the same as the shepherds had witnessed almost 2000 years before. Except for the absence of the great light and the shepherds, nothing had changed very much. Instead of a candle to light their way, some who were traveling through the quiet streets were using lamps. There also were no angels present, yet the aura of the occasion lent a holy hush to the surroundings. Speaking of this experience in a letter to his Sunday school in Philadelphia, Phillips Brooks wrote, "Again and again it seemed I could hear voices telling each other of the 'Wonderful Night' of the Saviour's birth."

All this while the words of a new carol were singing in his heart, but it would not be until he came home to America that he would write them down. This would not happen until just a short while before Christmas 1868. He was preparing the Christmas service for the Sunday school and as he began to review the music he would use, there flooded through his soul a re-echo of the Christmas Eve he had spent in the shepherd fields overlooking Bethlehem, and the carol that had been singing in his heart since that time. He could contain it no longer, and as it burst forth, he began to write —

O little town of Bethlehem,
How still we see thee lie!
Above thy deep and dreamless sleep,
The silent stars go by.

On and on it flowed until, as a river reaches the sea, so his inspired words too reached the zenith of what Christmas is all about as he exclaims, "O come to us, abide with us, Our Lord, Emmanuel!"

Phillips Brooks then hurriedly left his study and walked to the home of Mr. Lewis Redner, who was the organist of the church. Upon showing him his poem, Mr. Redner consented to try his hand at writing an appropriate melody. His effort proved successful, and today in all of hymnology there can be found no tune which so greatly enhances a set of words as does this one.

There were many very happy children that Christmas in the Sunday school of The Church of the Holy Trinity in Philadelphia as they sang, for the first time, the carol that their own pastor had written for them. In the years to come, it would be an important part of each of their Christmas celebrations but it would take more than twenty years before it would receive general recognition and be sung around the world. ABS

Be Thou Exalted

BE THOU EXALTED

As far as I know this beautiful and praiseworthy hymn does not have any special story connected with its writing but the more I study it the more I feel that it was the Doxology of a life which had unstintingly dedicated its love and talents to serving a wonderful God. It was Fanny Crosby's way of saying Praise Father, Son, and Holy Ghost.

I'd like to take this space which would normally be taken to tell a hymn story and use it instead to introduce you to Fanny Crosby — a vessel for the master's use.

It was a Grandmother who said, "Well, if this means Fanny will be blind all of her life, then I will be her eyes." The news had just been received that the wrong medication applied to the eyes of the infant Fanny Crosby had done its destroying work and she would be blind permanently. In those days it meant being destined to a life of uselessness, seclusion, and dependence upon others. But Fanny had a grandmother. Thank the Lord for Christian grandmothers!

From that day on it was Fanny's grandmother who would describe to little Fanny the beautiful sunrises and the breathtaking sunsets that a great and powerful God painted in the sky. It is said that she did such a good job that Fanny could describe a sunrise and sunset better than a person with normal sight.

Grandmother Crosby did not stop there. But sitting in her rocking chair with her little granddaughter on her lap she began to patiently teach her God's Word — the Bible. First it was a verse at a time, then two verses, then whole chapters and eventually Fanny could quote entire books in the Bible.

Grandmother didn't realize it at the time but God was using her to equip a life with the knowledge of His Word and because of it this life would bless untold millions around the world. That Fanny enjoyed these times is evidenced with a poem she wrote in later years entitled;

"GRANDMA'S ROCKING-CHAIR"

I am thinking of a cottage, In a quiet, country dell,
And a brook that ran beside it, That I used to love so well;
I have sat for hours and listened, While it rippled at my feet,
And I thought no other music In the world was half so sweet.

There are forms that pass before me; Those are times I yet recall;
But the voice of gentle Grandma I remember best of all;
In her loving arms she held me, And beneath her patient care
I was borne away to dreamland, In her dear old rocking-chair.

I am thinking of a promise That I made when last we met;
'Twas a rosy summer twilight That I never shall forget;
"Grandma's going home," she whispered, And the time is drawing nigh;
Tell me, darling, will you meet her In Our Father's house on high?"

She was looking down upon me; For a moment all was still;
Then I answered with emotion; "By the grace of God, I will."
How she clasped me to her bosom! And we bowed our heads in prayer
Where so oft we knelt together, By her dear old rocking-chair.

She has passed the vale of shadows, She has crossed the narrow sea,
And beyond the shining river She is waiting now for me:
But in fancy I recall her, And again we kneel in prayer,
While my heart renews its promise By her dear old rocking-chair.

From Grandmother's rocking chair Fanny graduated and became one of the first students of the then-brand-new New York Institute for the Blind. Here she established a reputation as an unusual scholar and later became a member of the faculty. Her reputation also as a poet began to spread and in time she was even visited by newly elected President Polk who credited much of his victory to a poem Fanny had written heralding him as the man to elect. In fact, Fanny Crosby was the first woman ever to speak from the floor of the Senate in Washington, D.C.

But with all of this success and acclaim something was lacking in her life. She found out what it was while attending some evangelistic meetings in a little Methodist church in New York City. As Fanny was to say later, "I found out that even though I had heard the message often and could quote from memory whole books of the Bible yet I did not know the author in a real and personal way and so during those meetings I made sure and gave my heart and life to Christ." She would later write commemorating that happy day, "Blessed assurance, Jesus is mine, O what a fortaste of glory divine."

Fanny was 31 at the time and for the next 64 years there would flow from her dedicated life somewhere between 8 and 9 thousand Gospel songs and hymns.

During the first 31 years of her life Fanny's mind had developed into a wonderful memory bank. One in which she could store things and withdraw them any time she wished. This became a great asset over the years for writing songs. Often someone would assign some 15 different subjects for which she was to supply song poems. Fanny would formulate all of the 15 poems in her mind, then call a stenographer and dictate the whole fifteen, one after the other.

I am sure Fanny never made a mistake but I feel that sometimes the stenographer would have some trouble in transcribing the shorthand when he or she was at about poem number 12 or 13 and would inadvertently put in words that Fanny had not said.

One such poem I feel was sent by Fanny to Edmund S. Lorenz who was the founder of the Lorenz Publishing Co. I later obtained this poem and found that it did have lines which needed fixing and rewriting. As I looked at the poem I began to view it as I felt Fanny would have, had she had her sight to see where it needed correcting. Immediately the new words and phrases began to fall into place. I then wrote a chorus and as quickly as I could write the melody began to take form. In a matter of minutes it was completed.

I like to feel that God permitted this poem to lie dormant for some 70 or 75 years so that I might have the privilege of giving wings to this marvelous hymn poem that Fanny Crosby had written. A message of praise which is one of the best she ever wrote both for style and Scriptural content. ABS

JESUS NEVER FAILS

This was one of the first "new" Gospel songs I learned as a young Christian, first as a chorus and then later on as a complete song. I am always blessed as I sing or hear it. In later years, it was one of the first copyrights I owned. I purchased the renewal rights from its author, Rev. Arthur A. Luther, who at the time was the pastor of a little church in North Collins, New York.

At the time of the writing of "Jesus Never Fails," Art Luther was playing the piano for an evangelistic team. They had received an invitation to a church in a very remote area in the Kentucky mountains. It was in a little community, literally at the end of the line. For most of the year, it was accessible from the outside only by a mountain railroad which came up the mountain once a week.

The team had just arrived and had had opportunity for only a day or two of meetings, when word was received over the railroad's telegraph line that Art's young son had been taken seriously ill and had been rushed to the hospital. As Art Luther told me himself, "Al, when I received that word, my world seemed to stop, for I felt so helpless. There I was so many miles away from home and in a place where I would either have to walk the many dangerous miles down the mountain or wait some four or five days before the train could take me out. At that moment I realized how limited man can be in the extremities of life. In the little Kentucky home where I was staying I began to collect my thoughts and to talk to the Lord, for I knew He alone had the answer to my dilemma. Perhaps from force of habit, I sat down at the piano and soon found myself playing a new melody to a truth that came flashing into my mind — 'Jesus Never Fails!' I repeated the phrase and then came 'Heaven and earth may pass away but Jesus Never Fails.' I sang the completed chorus and from there wrote a verse to it — 'Tho' the sky be dark and drear, fierce and strong the gale, just remember He is near and He will not fail.' This eventually became the second verse of the completed song which I wrote that very afternoon. When I finished, a peace had settled over my anxious heart. I knew the God who never fails would find the answer and He did, for just then there was a knock at the door and someone came with the news — word had just been received over the telegraph wire that my son had passed the crisis and all was well!"

The Lord had used Art Luther's hour of extremity to give to the world the beautiful song of assurance and trust, "Jesus Never Fails."

Just recently a daughter of Art Luther handed me a little pamphlet that he had written in answer to the many requests that had come in for the story of "Jesus Never Fails." Even though a few details may be repeated I am adding it in its entirety for your blessing and enjoyment just as Art himself wrote it.

So many requests have come in for the story of this song that I am preparing it in this form so that any who may be interested may have it. During the last twenty years this simple song has literally gone round the world on its Mission and stories still come in telling of its blessing and helpfulness. As a school boy Christian I had a burning desire to be a foreign missionary. That was not to be. Later I had an urge to write a song that everyone would sing. I tried a popular song but it was a dismal failure, yet God, in His own time and way, granted my wish and "Jesus Never Fails" has reached to the uttermost of mission fields and the multitudes have sung it. The song was written at Somerset, Kentucky, while I was there with the Dr. O. E. Williams Evangelistic Party. I received some very disturbing news from my family some 600 miles away. Worried and homesick, I sat down at the old square piano in the "Old Kentucky Home" where we were staying and as my "fingers wandered idly," a simple melody developed beneath them which seemed to sing, "Jesus Never Fails." Then and there the words and music of the Chorus were born. I accepted this as the answer to my heart's prayer and I thank Him that it proved true. Reassuring news came from home. He did not fail me. However, the others in the party insisted on using the song that I selfishly thought was just for me. Evangelists all over the land began using it and soon it spread to every quarter of the globe. Scores of testimonies have come from Missionaries, Evangelists, and others, of the blessing that this simple three-word message has been to them. It has been translated into ten European languages and into Chinese.

The missionaries on the torpedoed Zam Zam sang it while floating in the shark-infested waters of the South Atlantic. It was carried into the concentration camps of Germany by these same faithful witnesses and we may be sure that God used it there to His Glory. No one will ever know in how many ways this message has appeared on mottoes, plaques, etc. Dr. Philpot tells how a Motto was slipped into the casket at the funeral of a Jewish newsboy who had become a Christian. His pals who did it reported, "It went to Heaven with Bonnie." Mrs. Williams tells me of a man who heard the Chorus as he was on his way to drown himself. He tarried to hear the Gospel Message, was gloriously saved, and is now preaching the wonderful Grace of The Jesus Who Never Fails. "Jesus Never Fails" has become a sort of musical slogan of Bible-believing Christians everywhere. Men sang it at the battlefront as they girded themselves for the fray. On the homefront, Saints sing it as they do battle with the forces of sin, in true confidence that the Captain of their Salvation fails not. I surely have ever reason to praise God for this Song that He gave me in the hour of my need and which has gone on to bless the entire world with its message of triumph. God has indeed permitted me to be a Missionary and hosts of His Children are singing the Song He put in my Soul.

During World War II, Dr. William Ashby of London, England, tells of a church in that blitz-torn city which had "Jesus Never Fails" painted on the front of the building. For a long time the church was spared all except minor damage. One night the pastor, who had been staying in the basement, went to spend a few hours with his family, who had been sent to a safer area. That night a bomb fell that wrecked all but the front wall of the building. The motto stood with its silent testimony until the war ended and it was torn down. That church became known as "The Church Where Jesus Never Fails."

Some have asked why I wrote "May pass away" instead of "Shall pass away." The thought is to bring the truth of the song into the present tense. Let heaven and earth pass away at this moment if it be His Will. He fails not and the future is secure. Let come what may, He is with us NOW! "Therefore will not we fear, though the earth be removed . . . "

Yours in His Precious Name,
A. A. Luther
North Collins, New York
September 1, 1947

ABS

God Will Take Care Of You
CIVILLA D. MARTIN
W. STILLMAN MARTIN
1. Be not dis-mayed what - e'er be - tide, God will take care of you;
2. Thru days of toil when heart doth fail, God will take care of you;
3. All you may need He will pro-vide, God will take care of you;
4. No mat-ter what may be the test, God will take care of you;
Be - neath His wings of love a - bide, God will take care of you.
When dan-gers fierce your path as - sail, God will take care of you.
Noth-ing you ask will be de - nied, God will take care of you.
Lean, wea-ry one, up - on His breast, God will take care of you.
CHORUS
God will take care of you, Thru ev - 'ry day, o'er all the way;
He will take care of you, God will take care of you.
take care of you.

GOD WILL TAKE CARE OF YOU

Dr. and Mrs. William Stillman Martin and daughter were guests at the Practical Bible Training School in Lestershire, now Johnson City, New York. The year was 1904 and Dr. Martin was traveling in the area as an Evangelist. One Sunday, he was scheduled to speak in a church some distance from Johnson City, but when Mrs. Martin awakened that morning she felt ill; in fact, to Dr. Martin she seemed ill enough for him to cancel his engagement. This thought he voiced to his wife but before she could answer her husband, their young daughter, perhaps 7 or 8 years of age replied, "Oh, Daddy, you don't have to stay home because of mother — God will take care of us." Taking this as a voice from the Lord and having his wife's full approval, he boarded the Erie train and went on to his meeting. When he arrived at the church, there was word awaiting him. It was from his wife saying, "All is well — God did take care of us."

When Dr. Martin arrived back at the school he was met by his wife who was now fully recovered. As she greeted him, she handed him a paper with some verses written on it. In the hour of extremity, God had given the confidence needed — and all through the little child the Lord had given them. The poem was entitled, "God Will Take Care Of You." Soon, Dr. Martin had taken these words and while seated at the piano in the apartment wrote the melody which through the years has proven to be one of the most perfect and singable musical settings ever composed for a Gospel song.

Free From The Law
PHILIP P. BLISS
PHILIP P. BLISS
1. Free from the law— O hap-py con - di - tion! Je - sus has bled,
2. Now we are free—there's no con-dem - na - tion! Je - sus pro - vides
3. Chil-dren of God— O glo - ri - ous call - ing! Sure-ly His grace
and there is re - mis - sion; Cursed by the law and bruised by the fall,
a per - fect sal - va - tion; "Come un - to Me—" O hear His sweet call!
will keep us from fall - ing; Pass - ing from death to life at His call,
Grace has re - deemed us once for all.
Come—and He saves us once for all.
Bless - ed sal - va - tion—once for all.
CHORUS
Once for all— O sin-ner, re-
ceive it! Once for all— O broth - er, be - lieve it! Cling to the
cross, the bur-den will fall— Christ has re - deemed us once for all!

FREE FROM THE LAW

(Once For All)

This was the first solo sung by Ira D. Sankey as he and D. L. Moody started what was to be a history-making visit to England in 1872. Knowing that there would be opposition by many to any music other than the Psalms, yet realizing the wonderful power of the Gospel song to "Preach the Gospel" in a new way, Mr. Sankey, led by the Holy Spirit, asked the audience to bow with him in prayer asking God to bless the song and its message to the hearts of all who listened. With such an introduction, who could voice opposition — at least outwardly? God did bless the singer and the song, and soon all over the British Isles folks were buying and singing from the Moody and Sankey "Gospel Hymns" leaflets.

"Free From The Law" was the result of a birthday present given to P. P. Bliss by his wife. It was a bound copy of the book *Things New And Old* by C. H. M. (C. H. McIntosch), who also wrote *Notes On the Pentetuch.* In it, Mr. Bliss read the blessed fact of the believer's deliverance from the penalty of the Law by the death of Christ on the cross.

The thrill of realizing that Christ had fulfilled for the believer all that the Law had required, was to Mr. Bliss something every Christian should know; and how better to spread the message than through song? It has been over 110 years since Mr. Bliss wrote this stirring song, but its simple, yet vivid, teaching of an important Bible truth has kept it as fresh as if it had been written yesterday.

Mr. George Stebbins, an associate of Moody and Sankey, had this to say about the song, "'Free From The Law' is conceded to be the clearest statement of the doctrine of grace, in distinction from the Law, to be found in hymnology." ABS

Dedicated to my Father and Mother

J. C. M. | JAS. C. MOORE

WHERE WE'LL NEVER GROW OLD

Young Jim Moore was coming home at last and was to preach in the old home church. His father, C. R. Moore, had waited many years for this occasion. Jim had been away for several years — first working to get enough for college and then attending Mercer University in Macon, Georgia. Now his dad's wish was finally coming true. He'd directed the music in the little Baptist church for oh, so many years both for pastors and special speakers but now he would be leading it for his very own son.

That Sunday morning as young Jim looked over the congregation, he searched for certain faces but they were gone. Some had died, others had moved away and so many of the familiar faces, which were still there, showed they were growing old. Even his nine brothers and sisters had all grown up since he had gone away.

But the thing that touched him most, was to listen to his dad's singing. C. R. Moore had been known as one of the finest singers in Georgia. He had had as his teacher, Mr. A. J. Showalter, an outstanding voice teacher and composer of "Leaning On The Everlasting Arms," but now his father's voice was breaking — something Jim had never heard before. He was to say many years later, "I felt so sorry for him. He would lose his pitch and his voice would break — in my heart I knew I would not hear him sing much longer."

When James C. Moore went back for graduate work at Macon, he carried with him a new awareness in his heart of the "change and decay" that the hymnwriter wrote about so many years before. But with this also came the assurance of the place that our blessed Lord had promised to prepare — a land where no one ever grows old. With this truth burning deep in his heart, he wrote both the words and music of the beautiful song "The Land Where We'll Never Grow Old." ABS

Stand Up, Stand Up For Jesus
GEORGE DUFFIELD
GEORGE J. WEBB
1. Stand up, stand up for Je - sus, Ye sol - diers of the cross!
2. Stand up, stand up for Je - sus, The trum - pet call o - bey;
3. Stand up, stand up for Je - sus, Stand in His strength a - lone;
4. Stand up, stand up for Je - sus, The strife will not be long;
Lift high His roy - al ban - ner— It must not suf - fer loss.
Forth to the might - y con - flict In this His glo - rious day.
The arm of flesh will fail you— Ye dare not trust your own.
This day the noise of bat - tle— The next, the vic - tor's song.
From vic - t'ry un - to vic - t'ry His ar - my shall He lead,
Ye that are men now serve Him A - gainst un - num-bered foes;
Put on the gos - pel ar - mor, Each piece put on with prayer;
To Him that o - ver - com - eth A crown of life shall be:
Till ev - 'ry foe is van - quished And Christ is Lord in - deed.
Let cour - age rise with dan - ger, And strength to strength op - pose.
Where du - ty calls, or dan - ger, Be nev - er want - ing there.
He with the King of glo - ry Shall reign e - ter - nal - ly.

STAND UP, STAND UP FOR JESUS

During the great revival of 1858, "Stand up for Jesus" was the dying message of the Reverend Dudley Tyng to the Philadelphia Young Men's Christian Association and the ministers associated with them in the noon-day prayer meeting usually known as the "Work of God in Philadelphia." On Sunday, Rev. Tyng had spoken to over 5000 men gathered in Janes Hall. Of these 5000 men, over 1000 responded to the invitation. The following Wednesday, Dr. Tyng was at home on his farm and decided he would go out to the barn where they were shelling corn. While there, the sleeve of the silk study jacket he was wearing caught in the cogs of a wheel as a mule was turning the corn sheller. Dr. Tyng's arm was pulled into the sheller and literally pulled out at the roots and within a few hours Dr. Tyng would be dead. But not before he had given those stirring words in answer to a question from his father who asked, "Dudley, hundreds of your friends and co-workers are waiting for news from you. What should I tell them?" His answer was, "Father, tell them to stand up for Jesus." These were his last words. At the funeral service the following Sunday, Dr. George Duffield, a well-known Presbyterian pastor, gave the message. At the conclusion he quoted a poem that he had written based upon the last words of Dudley Tyng. This has become our well-known and beloved Gospel song, "Stand Up, Stand Up For Jesus." ABS

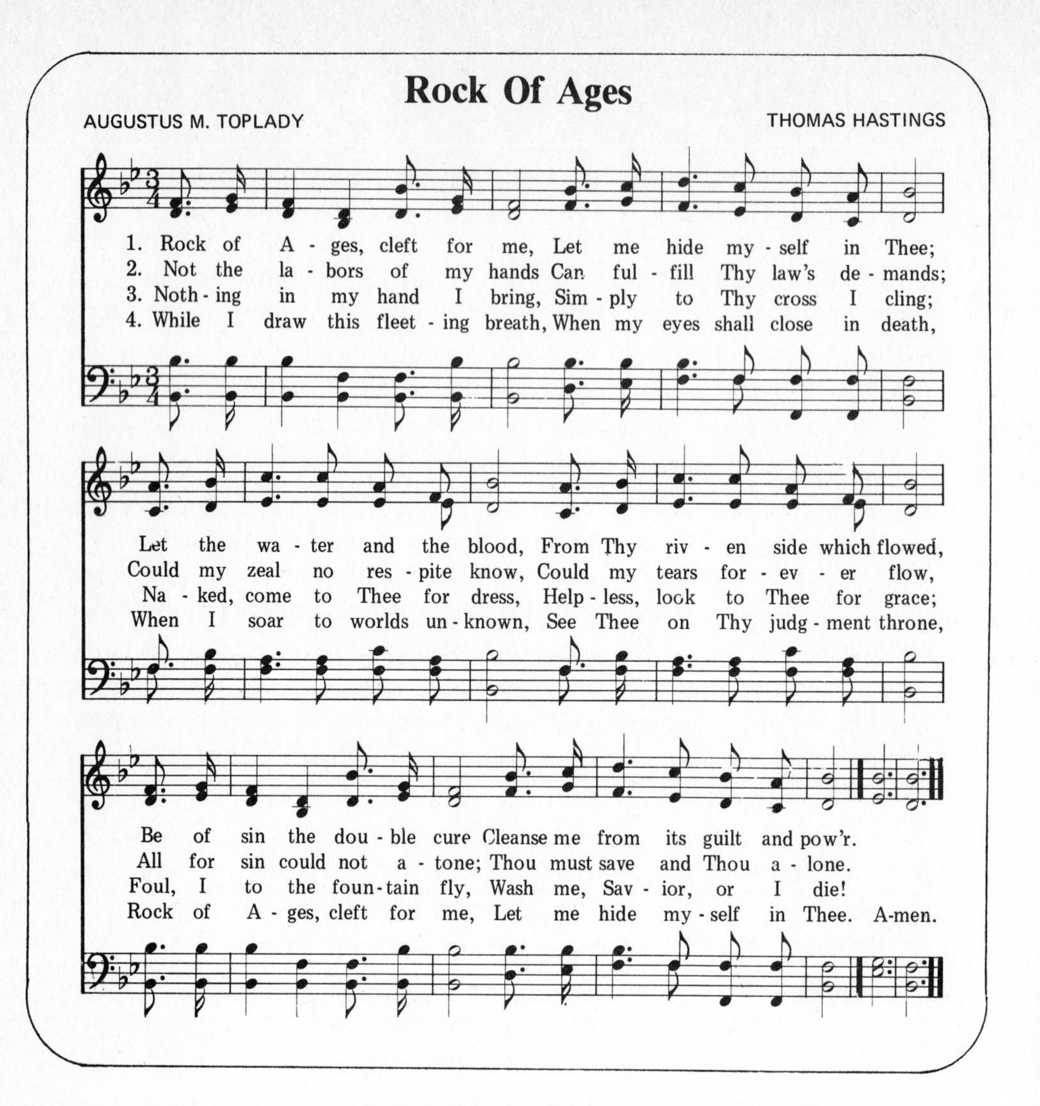

ROCK OF AGES

This rare gem of Christian hymnody, often called the most popular of the hymns, was a favorite of my father. The original four stanzas first appeared in 1776, in the March issue of the evangelistic publication, "The Gospel Magazine." It was placed at the conclusion of an article by its author, Augustus Toplady, who was writing on the impossibility of man to pay for his own sins. In the article, Toplady calculated that if a man lived to be 80 he would have the opportunity of committing over two and one-half billion sins, making it impossible to save himself. He needed a Saviour!

As is so often the case with these older hymns, more than one story exists as to the writing of "Rock Of Ages." Often it is an impossible task to ferret out the right one, but after years of carefully researching this great hymn, I have come to the conclusion that not one but two separate incidents were involved. The first one was a sermon by a Dr. Daniel Brevint in which he said, "Let not my heart burn with less zeal to follow and serve Thee now when this bread is broken at this table, than did the hearts of Thy disciples when Thou didst break it at Emmaus, O Rock of Israel, Rock of Salvation, Rock struck and cleft for me. Let those two streams of blood and water which once gushed out of Thy side . . . let not my soul less thirst after them at this distance, than if I stood upon Horeb, whence sprang this water and near the very cleft of rock, and the very wounds of my Saviour whence gushed out this sacred blood." According to his own words, Toplady was so stirred by these word pictures that he could not shake them from his memory.

The second incident occurred one day while Toplady was taking a walk through Barrington Coombs. He was caught in a thunderstorm. His church was too far away to offer protection so he took shelter in the cleft of a large rock on the Coombs. As the storm raged about him, Toplady was securely sheltered and protected in the cleft of the rock. It was while going through this experience that the soul-stirring sermon of Brevint's again came into his mind. Was this experience, in a small way, depicting what Christ had done at Calvary?

The storm subsided. Toplady went on his way to his study at the church and before time could erase the happenings of the day from his heart and mind he wrote, "Rock of Ages cleft for me, let me hide myself in Thee ..."

It was my privilege to stand at the Harrington Coombs rock and in memory's eye relive, in a small way, that which transpired there over 200 years ago. ABS

What A Friend We Have In Jesus

WHAT A FRIEND WE HAVE IN JESUS

But for a chance perusal of a little Sunday school song leaflet by Ira D. Sankey, this song might have been lost to the Christian church and literally millions of people would have missed the encouragement and blessing that it brings. I'll let Mr. Sankey tell the story.

"Returning from England in 1875, I soon became associated with P. P. Bliss in the publication of what would become known as *Gospel Hymns #1.* After we had given the completed compilation to our publishers, I chanced to pick up a small paper-covered pamphlet of Sunday school hymns just published at Richmond, Virginia. I discovered this song and sang it through, and determined to have it appear in *Gospel Hymns.* Since the composer of the music was my friend, C. C. Converse, I took the liberty to withdraw one of his other compositions from the collection and substituted for it, 'What A Friend We Have In Jesus.' Thus, the last hymn that went into the book became one of the first in favor.

"As published in the small Richmond hymnal, the authorship of the words was erroneously attributed to the great Scottish preacher and hymnwriter, Dr. Horatious Bonar. We were in error, also, in assigning the words to him. Some time later Dr. Bonar informed us that he was not the author and that he did now know who wrote it. It was not until some seven or eight years after the hymn first appeared in our collection that we learned who the author really was."

Joseph Scrivin was born in Dublin, Ireland, in 1820. After graduating from Dublin's Trinity College, he had great expectations and plans. He would marry his beautiful Irish sweetheart and together they would begin a Christian home. He would put to use the fine training he had been getting at the college in starting a business. But this would never materialize, for tragedy struck. His bride-to-be was accidentally drowned the day before the wedding, and when Joseph Scriven saw her body as it was taken from the water, he suffered a shock which was to stay with him for the remainder of his life.

In the hope of forgetting, which he never did, Scrivin went to Canada where he spent his life helping the less fortunate in the towns of Lake Rice and Port Hope. Some thought him rather strange and eccentric but to the many he helped, he was God's answer to their prayers.

After being in Canada some ten years, Joseph Scrivin received word that his mother was going through a time of testing and grief. To comfort her, he wrote a poem which he called, "A Friend Who Understands" and sent a copy of it to her in Ireland. That was in 1855. Years were to pass and during that time a hymn would appear titled "What A Friend We Have In Jesus." The music was attributed to C. C. Converse but the author of the words was unknown. It was not until around 1880 that the mystery was solved — "What A Friend" was the poem Joseph Scrivin had sent to his mother. This came to light when a neighbor of Mr. Scrivin's found the original manuscript in Mr. Scrivin's bedroom while he was taking care of him during an illness. When faced with the discovery, the Irishman admitted that it was his but insisted that he and the Lord had really written it "between" them.

As to how the words first got into print no one knows, but it is a good conjecture that Joseph's mother was so blessed and pleased with them that she spread them abroad and, in so doing, someone sent a copy to some Christian periodical where it was found by Mr. Charles C. Converse who wrote the perfect musical setting for it. ABS

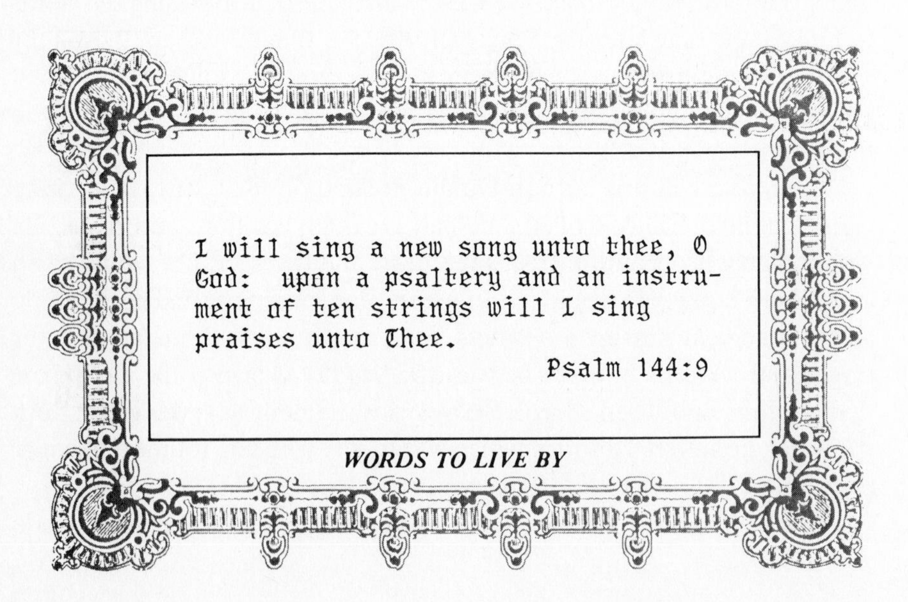

When The Roll Is Called Up Yonder

WHEN THE ROLL IS CALLED UP YONDER

"I think I'll cut through this alley to save some time." So thought James M. Black as he headed towards the Williamsport, Pennsylvania, Post Office. He had never used the alley before and so was not aware of the poverty and misery it contained. Neither was he aware of the effect that this spur-of-the-moment decision he was making would have upon his own life and that of others.

As he walked through the alley, he saw a young girl sweeping the porch of a ramshackled house. She was dressed oh, so poor, and in her young face were already the traces of worry and neglect. "Young lady," asked Jim Black, "Do you go to Sunday school?" "No, Sir, I'd like to but I don't have anything fit to wear; but Sir, how I'd love to go!" was her reply.

Soon Jim's wife and some friends had delivered clothing and all of the things that would be needed to make a young girl happy and feel wanted and "fit" for church.

Thus began a faithful attendance record for both the Sunday school and the Epworth league. Bessie didn't miss a meeting. Each time there was a roll call she was there to respond until one day when her name was called there was no reply. Again James Black repeated her name and still no reply. Troubled thoughts went through his mind. Maybe her drunken father had forbidden her to come or perhaps he had taken to beating her again. After church, Black hurriedly made his way to Bessie's house, for he had a feeling that all was not well. When he arrived, he found a very sick girl. Realizing that it was serious, he summoned his own doctor who diagnosed it as a case of advanced pneumonia.

In walking back to his house, Black had not yet been able to throw off the feeling that had come over him when Bessie had failed to respond to the roll call that morning. The thought kept coming back to him. Someday there will be a roll call in Heaven and oh, the sadness there will be for those whose names are not written in the Lamb's Book Of Life. That morning he had tried to find a suitable song to sing which he could use to impress this truth upon the hearts of his young people, but could not find any. This was a great disappointment to him. Black, who was also a songleader of exceptional ability, closed the meeting feeling that a great opportunity had passed and in his heart a voice said, "Why don't you write one?" He was to say later, "I put away the thought but as I opened the gate and walked up the path to my house, the same thought came again so strongly that tears filled my eyes. I went into the house and sat down at the piano. Without any effort at all the words seemed to tumble from my mind.

When the trumpet of the Lord shall sound,
And time shall be no more;
And the morning breaks Eternal, bright and fair,
When the saved of earth shall gather over on the other shore,
And the roll is called up yonder I'll be there.

After the complete set of words had come, the tune then came in the same manner. I felt that I was only the transcriber — I dared not change a note or word. In a few days I more fully understood why, for our beloved Bessie went home to Heaven to await that glorious day.

"This song was first sung publicly at her funeral and before singing it, I related the circumstances which led to its writing. Never will I forget the effect it had upon the large audience of friends who had come. The Lord had taken little Bessie home, but in her place He had given a song to keep reminding all of us to be ready for that great roll-call day."

"When The Roll Is Called Up Yonder" was first published in an Epworth League songbook in 1892. It perhaps would have gone unnoticed, unpublished, and unknown but for the fact that Mr. Black wrote his manuscript in green ink which attracted the attention of Mr. Charles Gabriel who was editing the book. He later said, "The composer's name was not familiar to me, but the green ink had made the song stand out. It was a new thought. I played it over, liked it, and published it — the rest is history." ABS

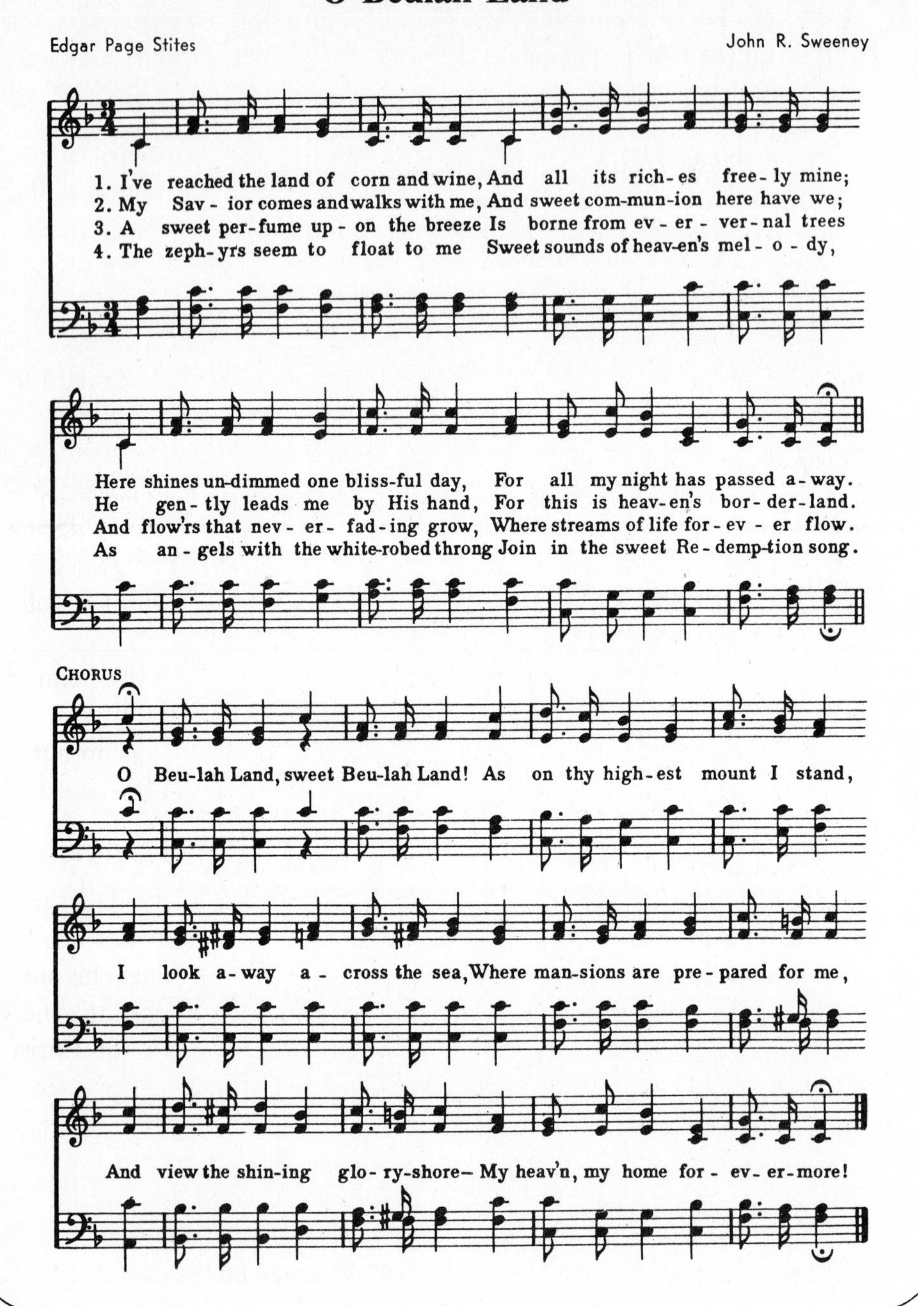
O Beulah Land
Edgar Page Stites
John R. Sweeney
1. I've reached the land of corn and wine, And all its rich-es free-ly mine;
2. My Sav-ior comes and walks with me, And sweet com-mun-ion here have we;
3. A sweet per-fume up-on the breeze Is borne from ev-er-ver-nal trees
4. The zeph-yrs seem to float to me Sweet sounds of heav-en's mel-o-dy,
Here shines un-dimmed one bliss-ful day, For all my night has passed a-way.
He gen-tly leads me by His hand, For this is heav-en's bor-der-land.
And flow'rs that nev-er-fad-ing grow, Where streams of life for-ev-er flow.
As an-gels with the white-robed throng Join in the sweet Re-demp-tion song.
CHORUS
O Beu-lah Land, sweet Beu-lah Land! As on thy high-est mount I stand,
I look a-way a-cross the sea, Where man-sions are pre-pared for me,
And view the shin-ing glo-ry-shore– My heav'n, my home for-ev-er-more!

O BEULAH LAND

"Few songs are better known or more extensively used than 'Beulah Land,'" so wrote Dr. Haldor Lillenas in the year 1950. The inspiration for its writing came because of a very unusual place. Let me tell you about it.

Among some of the earliest memories of my youth are the visits taken to the Methodist Camp Meeting Community of Ocean Grove, located on the Atlantic coast in New Jersey. To my young mind it was hard to comprehend there was a building as large as the Grove Tabernacle. It seated around 7500. And the huge organ! Why it made thunder and lightening as Klarence Kohman played "The Storm"! A very unique experience also was to suddenly see the cars, which were so prevalent during the week all disappear on Saturday night and not reappear again until Monday. This regulation has now been done away with by protest vote, not by the camp meeting people but by unsympathetic people who through the years moved into the area. I am very sorry about this because it was a wonderful reminder that Sunday was different — it was the Lord's day. Families walked together to church and there was no hurry to leave the service. In fact the great auditorium was the focal point of activity and the spiritual banquet served there far surpassed anything the world could afford. It was here that we heard and sang for the first time many of the Gospel songs which today are our everyday favorites.

It was here also that I met personally and heard great missionaries and preachers. I first heard Gypsy Smith preach and introduce his song "Not Dreaming" at Ocean Grove. It was here that I first heard the energetic former baseball champion who became a champion for Christ. His name? Billy Sunday! At the time I was not aware of a man named Edgar Page Stites but at the "Grove" we sang "Beulah Land" often. It would be years later before I found out who he was and that he was the author of this song.

Edgar Page Stites' ancestors had come over on the Mayflower and had eventually settled at Cape May, New Jersey, where he was born in 1836.

The first twenty years of his life had been rather uneventful but in 1857 something wonderful happened — he was saved in the great revival which started in Philadelphia and swept across America. It is often called the awakening of 1857 and '58. Stites immediately became involved in service for the Lord, joined the Methodist Church of Cape May and became a local "lay pastor." Eventually he became a home missionary starting new churches in the South Jersey area. Around the year 1870 Stites along with other Methodist ministers and laymen founded the "Ocean Grove Camp Meeting Association." The Association had acquired a considerable amount of acreage on the ocean shore and felt it could be developed into a summer spiritual retreat for the people of the many Methodist districts surrounding the Philadelphia and New York City areas. This it proved to be and far beyond their expectations. By 1875 it was already developing into a city of its own with its many tents, neat summer cabins, and even homes of a permanent nature. To many, including Stites, it had become a little foretaste of Heaven.

From its beginning, music played an important part of the services at the Grove. Because of this it attracted as regular attendants such names as Kirkpatrick, Sweney, Fanny Crosby, Hewit, and others, all known as writers of Gospel hymns. It was the means also of encouraging others to try their God-given talents in writing new songs. Edgar Page Stites was one of these. He wrote his first set of words in the summer of 1874. This was sent by a religious editor at the camp meeting to a newspaper in Chicago. It was published in the spring of 1876. They were in turn given to Ira D. Sankey who then wrote the music for "Trusting Jesus, That Is All."

The "Grove Summers" as he called them had become the highlight of the year for Stites and this he enthusiastically proclaimed throughout the year, wherever he went, inviting others to share in this experience which was so much like Heaven words could not really describe it.

It is no wonder then that to Stites the train seemed to be almost standing still as it chugged its way from Cape May toward the Grove, a distance in those days of at least 150 miles of travel. The meetings of 1874 had been mountaintop experiences and what did 1875 hold? Stites could hardly wait.

It was after the first day of meetings and he was back in his cottage that Edgar Page Stites, with a full heart, could contain his thoughts no longer. “All this and Heaven too!” he exclaimed! He then began to write — aided by the light of a kerosene lamp — I'VE REACHED THE LAND OF CORN AND WINE AND ALL ITS RICHES FULLY MINE; HERE SHINES UNDIMMED ONE BLISSFUL DAY FOR ALL MY NIGHT HAS PASSED AWAY.

O BEULAH LAND, SWEET BEULAH LAND! Higher and higher he soared — Far above the mundane things of the world — he was seated in the Heavenlies!

For years Mr. Stites' songs were published using only his first two names — that is Edgar Page. It was done at his request for he felt if he were known as a songwriter it would dim his work as a preacher. This request was honored until after his death in 1921. ABS

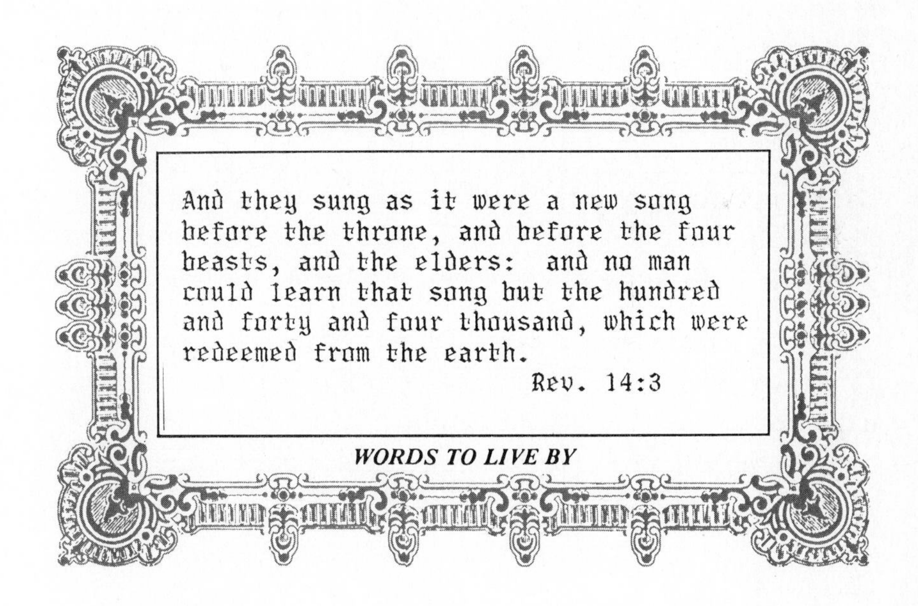

He Keeps Me Singing

LUTHER B. BRIDGERS
LUTHER B. BRIDGERS
1. There's with-in my heart a mel - o - dy— Je - sus whis-pers sweet and low,
2. All my life was wrecked by sin and strife, Dis-cord filled my heart with pain;
3. Feast-ing on the rich - es of His grace, Rest-ing 'neath His shelt'ring wing,
4. Tho sometimes He leads thru wa - ters deep, Tri - als fall a - cross the way,
5. Soon He's com-ing back to wel-come me Far be - yond the star - ry sky;
"Fear not, I am with thee—peace, be still," In all of life's ebb and flow.
Je - sus swept a - cross the bro - ken strings, Stirr'd the slumb'ring chords again.
Al - ways look-ing on His smil - ing face— That is why I shout and sing.
Tho some-times the path seems rough and steep, See His foot-prints all the way.
I shall wing my flight to worlds un-known, I shall reign with Him on high.
CHORUS
Je - sus, Je - sus, Je - sus— Sweet - est name I know,
Fills my ev - 'ry long - ing, Keeps me sing - ing as I go.

HE KEEPS ME SINGING

(JESUS, SWEETEST NAME I KNOW)

Luther Bridgers began preaching at the age of seventeen, while he was a student at Asbury College in Kentucky. After graduation, he went on to become a Methodist pastor and became widely known for his sincerity and evangelistic zeal. In 1910, the future looked bright for this young 26-year-old preacher. He had a lovely wife, three energetic young ones, and a growing demand for his preaching services. Then tragedy struck.

The Bridgers were visiting Mrs. Bridgers' parents at Harrodsburg, Kentucky. It had been a happy time of reunion for the families and they had retired rather late. The late hour, plus the rigors of the trip over the rough Kentucky roads of that day, assured them that they would have no trouble getting a sound sleep. Within minutes after retiring, all were fast asleep and then, like a thief in the night, the tragedy happened. A neighbor, spending a restless night, glanced out of his window and saw that Mrs. Bridgers' parent's home was a mass of flames. As quickly as he could, he ran to give the alarm; but by the time he got there it had become a raging inferno. He was able to arouse only Mrs. Bridgers' parents and Luther Bridgers. After getting out of the house and realizing that his wife and boys were still inside, Luther Bridgers tried to go back in after them, but had to be restrained. By this time, the house was a complete mass of flames and had begun to fall. When the carnage was over, Luther Bridgers' young wife and three sons were dead. What had started as a joyous reunion, had turned into a tragedy of tears. What would the young preacher do? In the days that followed, as the deep waters of sorrow were flooding over him and the darkness of night surrounded him, he remembered the Lord had promised "Songs in the Night" and that He also would never leave or forsake him.

It was during this period of heart-searching and sorrow that he wrote:

There's within my heart a melody,
Jesus whispers sweet and low.
Fear not, I am with thee, peace be still
In all of life's ebb and flow.

In the fourth stanza Luther Bridgers alludes to the floods of sorrow as he writes:

> **Tho' sometimes He leads through waters deep,**
> **Trials fall across the way ...**

Thus we see that a tragedy has given the world a song which will continue to bless and encourage Christians around the world for years to come. ABS

AMERICA

On an afternoon in February, over a century and a half ago, gray clouds were hovering over Andover Hill, site of the Theological Seminary at Andover, Massachusetts. The wind was moaning through the trees, nature was in a sullen mood. In a drab-looking frame house on the northerly slope of the hill, just below the summit, a young theological student sat in a meagerly furnished room. He was oblivious to the weather. The table in front of him was strewn with papers. In his hand was an open book — a book of German songs. The student glanced from page to page. The music printed with one of the songs, simply done but stately, attracted his attention. Hurriedly translating the German words, he saw that this was a patriotic hymn. Thoughts of his own country flooded over him. They demanded expression. Why should he not write a hymn for America and fit it to this tune? He picked up his quill pen, seized the first scrap of paper that came to his hand, and began with these words, "My Country 'tis of thee, sweet land of liberty, of thee I sing." Darkness was falling as the student laid aside his pen and tucked the paper into his portfolio. Thus did Samuel Francis Smith, a youth of 23 years, write the hymn that came to be known to the world as "America."

Many years afterward he said, "I did not propose to write a national hymn. I did not know I had done so." In fact, the press of his studies soon drove all thought of the verses from his mind; but the paper which bore them found its way into a sheaf of poems — some original and some translated from the German which the student sent to Lowell Mason. It was Mason, pioneer in the introduction of music into the schools of Boston, who had sent him the book of German songs and had asked him to translate some of them. Five months later, on July 4, 1832, greatly to the surprise of young Smith, his patriotic hymn was first sung in public by a chorus of children under Mason's direction in the Park Street Church. It was enthusiastically received. Schools, Sunday Schools, gatherings of all kinds, gradually picked it up. In a few years it was being sung all over the country. ABS

The Love Of God
FREDERICK M. LEHMAN
FREDERICK M. LEHMAN
1. The love of God is great-er far Than tongue or pen can ev - er
2. When years of time shall pass a - way And earth-ly thrones and kingdoms
3. Could we with ink the o - cean fill And were the skies of parch-ment
tell, It goes be - yond the high-est star And reach-es to the low-est
fall, When men, who here re-fuse to pray, On rocks and hills and mountains
made, Were ev-'ry stalk on earth a quill And ev-'ry man a scribe by
hell; The guilt-y pair, bowed down with care, God gave His Son to
call, God's love so sure shall still en-dure, All mea-sure-less and
trade, To write the love of God a - bove Would drain the o - cean
win: His err-ing child He rec-on-ciled And par-doned from his sin.
strong: Re-deem-ing grace to Ad-am's race— The saints' and an - gels' song.
dry, Nor could the scroll con-tain the whole Tho stretched from sky to sky.
CHORUS
O love of God, how rich and pure! How mea-sure-less and strong!

THE LOVE OF GOD

F. M. Lehman lived in California and worked in a Pasadena packing house. Through business reverses, he had lost everything and was now spending his time in hard manual labor lifting, and moving, as much as thirty tons of lemons and oranges a day which then were packed into crates for shipment. From all outward appearances, this certainly would not be a place conducive to doing anything artistic and especially writing songs. But as is so often said, "the exception proves the rule" and "The Love Of God" is one of the exceptions.

Mr. Lehman was a Christian who rejoiced in his salvation. Therefore, it is no wonder that on Sunday evening after hearing a heart-warming sermon on God's love, he could hardly contain himself — in fact, so much so that he found it hard to go to sleep. The next morning as he was having breakfast, the thrill of the previous evening had not left him and on his way to work he began to compose a song, with God's love as the theme.

In those days the oranges and lemons were packed in crates made of the thin wooden slats with solid wood ends. Often some pieces of the slats would break off and I can invision that from time to time Lehman would pick up one of these and jot down his song ideas on them. On through the day the song expanded and by the end of the day I'm sure he had collected quite a few of these important pieces of wood. He could hardly wait to get home to put his new song ideas on paper.

On arriving home he hurriedly went to the old upright piano and with the help of his day's collection of ideas, he began to transcribe the song on paper. Soon he had a finished melody with two stanzas and a chorus but in those days a song had to have at least three stanzas to be complete. Someone has said that today a song is complete when it has just three words. As he tried to write the third stanza, he found that the words just wouldn't fall into place. What would he do? Some time before, he had heard a poem about the love of God and had been given a copy of it printed on a card. He reasoned, "If I could only find that poem — for it so wonderfully pictured the vastness of God's love — maybe I could get an idea upon which to build this last stanza. His search was rewarded for he soon found the card. He had used it as a bookmark. As Lehman read the words, his heart was again thrilled as it had been when first he had read them.

He noticed that at the bottom of the card some smaller but heavier printing gave this story. "These words were found written on a cell wall in a prison some 200 years ago. It is not known why the prisoner was incarserated; neither is it known if the words were original or if he had heard them somewhere and had decided to put them in a place where he could be reminded of the greatness of God's love — whatever the circumstances, he wrote them on the wall of his prison cell. In due time, he died and the men who had the job of repainting his cell were impressed by the words. Before their paint brushes had obliterated them, one of the men jotted them down and thus they were preserved." With poem in hand, Lehman went to the piano. On the spur of the moment he began to voice the words to the melody. They fitted perfectly. It was a miracle! Lehman's song was then published with these words as the last stanza.

It is within recent years that I have become acquainted with facts that make the writing of this song an even greater miracle. I have found that the original third stanza was written in Hebrew around the year 1000 by Meir Ben Isaac Nehoria, a Jewish Rabbi. I like to feel that God knowing that Lehman was going to write a song also realized that Lehman would have trouble writing a third stanza and so He chose this Rabbi, who though not accepting Christ as the Messiah did possess the skills to graphically paint a picture of God's love in words. He would preserve these words and then hundreds of years later He would have them translated by this prisoner into a language that did not as yet exist namely English. And to think that He did it in the exact metre to fit Lehman's melody! ABS

He Lives

A. H. A.
Rev. A. H. Ackley
1. I serve a ris-en Sav-iour, He's in the world to-day; I know that He is liv-ing, what-
2. In all the world a-round me I see His lov-ing care, And tho' my heart grows weary I
3. Rejoice, rejoice, O Chris-tian, lift up your voice and sing E-ter-nal hal-le-lu-jahs to
ev-er men may say; I see His hand of mer-cy, I hear His voice of cheer, And
nev-er will de-spair; I know that He is lead-ing, thro' all the storm-y blast, The
Je-sus Christ the King! The Hope of all who seek Him, the Help of all who find, None
just the time I need Him He's al-ways near.
day of His ap-pear-ing will come at last.
oth-er is so lov-ing, so good and kind.
REFRAIN Spirited
He lives, He lives, Christ Jesus lives to-
He lives, He lives,
day! He walks with me and talks with me along life's narrow way. He lives, He lives, sal-
He lives, He lives,
rit. ff
va-tion to im-part! You ask me how I know He lives? He lives with-in my heart.

HE LIVES

It was Easter Sunday morning and the Rev. Alfred H. Ackley was getting ready for the service at his Presbyterian church in California. The year was 1932 and radio was the great communicator. Rev. Ackley had tuned in and was listening to the various local programs when suddenly the announcer said, "We now join the complete red and blue networks (N. B. C. and A. B. C. they are called today) for a special program originating in New York City."

The speaker introduced was a well-known preacher from New York City who was known for his liberal thinking, and this morning he greeted the radio audience with, "Good morning — it's Easter! You know, folks, it really doesn't make any difference to me if Christ be risen or not. As far as I am concerned His body could be as dust in some Palestinian tomb. The main thing is, His truth goes marching on!"

"It's a lie!" exclaimed Rev. Ackley — forgetting that the speaker on the radio couldn't hear him and also oblivious to the fact that he was shaving with a straight razor and could cut himself. But Mrs. Ackley did hear and asked him, "Why are you shouting so early in the morning?" Mr. Ackley chuckled as he told me the story. "Didn't you hear what that good-for-nothing preacher said?" he replied. "He said it didn't matter whether Christ be risen or not!"

That morning Mr. Ackley told me he preached as he had never quite preached before. For several weeks he had been talking to a young Jew who had asked, "Why should I worship a dead Jew?" Rev. Ackley had replied, "That's the whole point. He isn't dead — He's alive!" And now this preacher had dared, with one fell swoop, to try to destroy that which had given the early church it's power and for which many had given their lives to proclaim — a resurrected, living Saviour!

"When Sunday evening came around," said Mr. Ackley, "I gave them the second barrel. And when that service was over and I had gotten home I still hadn't said all I had planned to say. My wife sized up the situation and said, 'Listen here, Alfred Ackley, it's time you did that which you can do best. Why don't you write a song about it and then maybe you'll feel better. Then you'll have something that will go on telling the story.'

"Heeding her advice," said Ackley, "I went into my study. I once again turned to the resurrection story as found in Mark 16:6 and reread the words 'He is risen; He is not here!' A thrill filled my soul — a glorious experience I will never forget. As I thought of the reality of His ever-living presence right there in the room with me, I could hold back no longer and began to write.

I serve a risen Saviour,
He's in the world today.
I know that He is living,
Whatever men may say.

"On and On I wrote until within a comparatively short time, all the stanza lines and thoughts had fallen into place. Then as I sat down at the piano, the words and melody of the chorus followed immediately — just as they are today." ABS

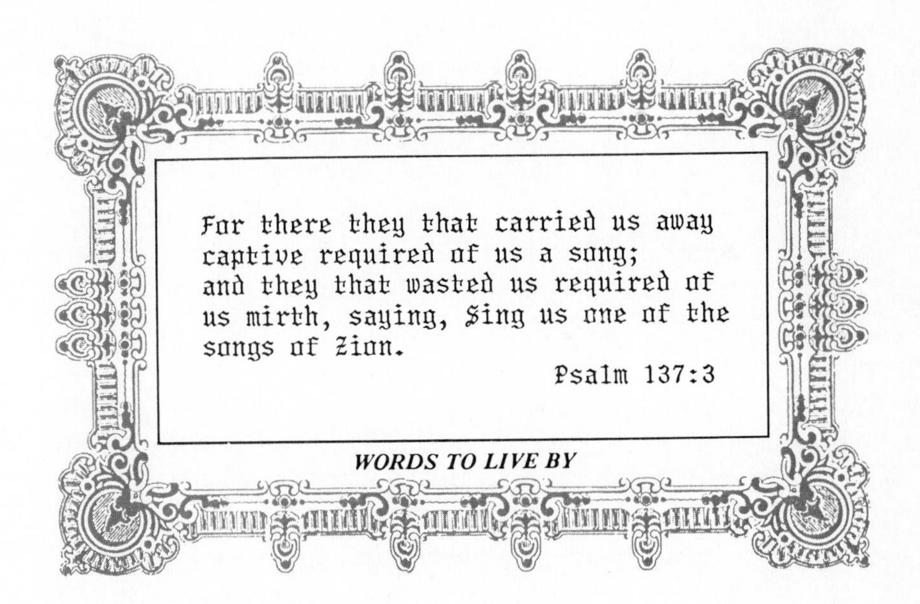

Overshadowed
H. A. Ironside
George S. Schuler
1. How des - o-late my life would be, How dark and drear my nights and days,
2. With burdened heart I wandered long, By grief and un - be - lief dis - tressed;
3. Now judgment fears no more a-larm, I dread not death, nor Sa-tan's pow'r;
If Je - sus' face I did not see To bright- en all earth's wea- ry ways.
But now I sing faith's hap- py song, In Christ my Sav-ior I am blest.
The world for me has lost its charm, God's grace sustains me ev - 'ry hour.
Chorus
I'm o - ver-shadowed by His might-y love, Love e- ter-nal, changeless, pure,
O - ver-shadowed by His might - y love, Rest is mine, se-rene, se- cure;
He died to ransom me from sin, He lives to keep me day by day.......
rit.

OVERSHADOWED

Two men who had great influence upon my early Christian life and work are involved in the writing of this beautiful song. The manner in which it was written is nothing short of a miracle and a proof that God often can use our extremities for His opportunities.

The two men are Dr. H. A. Ironside, world-renowned Bible expositor, who was pastor of the famous Moody Memorial Church in Chicago for many years and Dr. George S. Schuler, who was a teacher in the music department at the Moody Bible Institute, also in Chicago.

It was my privilege to work with both of these men as a soloist and songleader and also as a student of Professor Schuler. This story is exactly how they told it to me.

One day, as George Schuler was improvising at the piano the thought of God's nearness began to impress itself upon him in a new and deeper way. In his mind's eye he began to relive many of the experiences of the past. Through them he could not help but see the guiding hand of God. At the moment he could almost feel the presence of God with the same protecting power he had experienced all through life.

During all of this retrospection he had kept on "doodling" at the piano as he later told me. Soon a distinct melody began to take form and with it words which said, "I'm overshadowed by His mighty love, love eternal, changeless, pure. I'm overshadowed by His mighty love."

The melody kept flowing but the needed source of words had seemingly dried up so Schuler finished the melody of the chorus, then wrote what he thought would be an appropriate musical setting for some verses. As be began to review that which he had written he was still overwhelmed with the thought but try as he would he could write no further. In the midst of this dilemma there flashed into his mind the name of Dr. Ironside, who was then pastor of the world-famous Moody Church. Something seemed to say, "Why not ask him to complete the words?" Picking up the phone, Mr. Schuler found that Dr. Ironside was in his study at the church. This in itself was very unusual for ordinarily during the week Dr. Ironside was off speaking in some distant city. Mr. Schuler explained his call and his need and Dr. Ironside said he would be glad to see him, but warned that he was not noted as a poet.

After writing a second copy of the melody and the existing words on a piece of manuscript paper, Mr. Schuler hurriedly took them to Dr. Ironside and left them with the promise that as soon as he had time he would try his hand at completing the words. He would then call Mr. Schuler. Mr. Schuler left with the impression that perhaps in a few days the song would be completed but this was not to be — in fact, a whole year went by and one day as Mr. Schuler was going over some of his unpublished manuscripts he came across the unfinished song — he would give Dr. Ironside a call. Unable to contact him he told Dr. Ironside's secretary that he would be at the church the next day at which time he hoped to pick up the finished song for he was sure Dr. Ironside had just forgotten to send it. It was a surprised Dr. Ironside the next morning when his secretary greeted him with the news that Mr. Schuler would be in that day to pick up the song. With his busy schedule he had put Mr. Schuler's song aside planning to get to it within a few days but somehow he had entirely forgotten about it. Hurriedly he found the misplaced manuscript, sat down at his desk, and in a matter of less than 30 minutes, he was able to write the stanzas and complete the unfinished chorus. The song was always an amazement to Dr. Ironside for his life's habits usually were marked with diligent schedules and not "on-the-spur-of-the-moment" decisions. This was "the exception that proved the rule." God did it! With which the countless thousands who have heard it sung and have been blessed by it's truth agree — for such a song had to have been inspired by God.

ABS

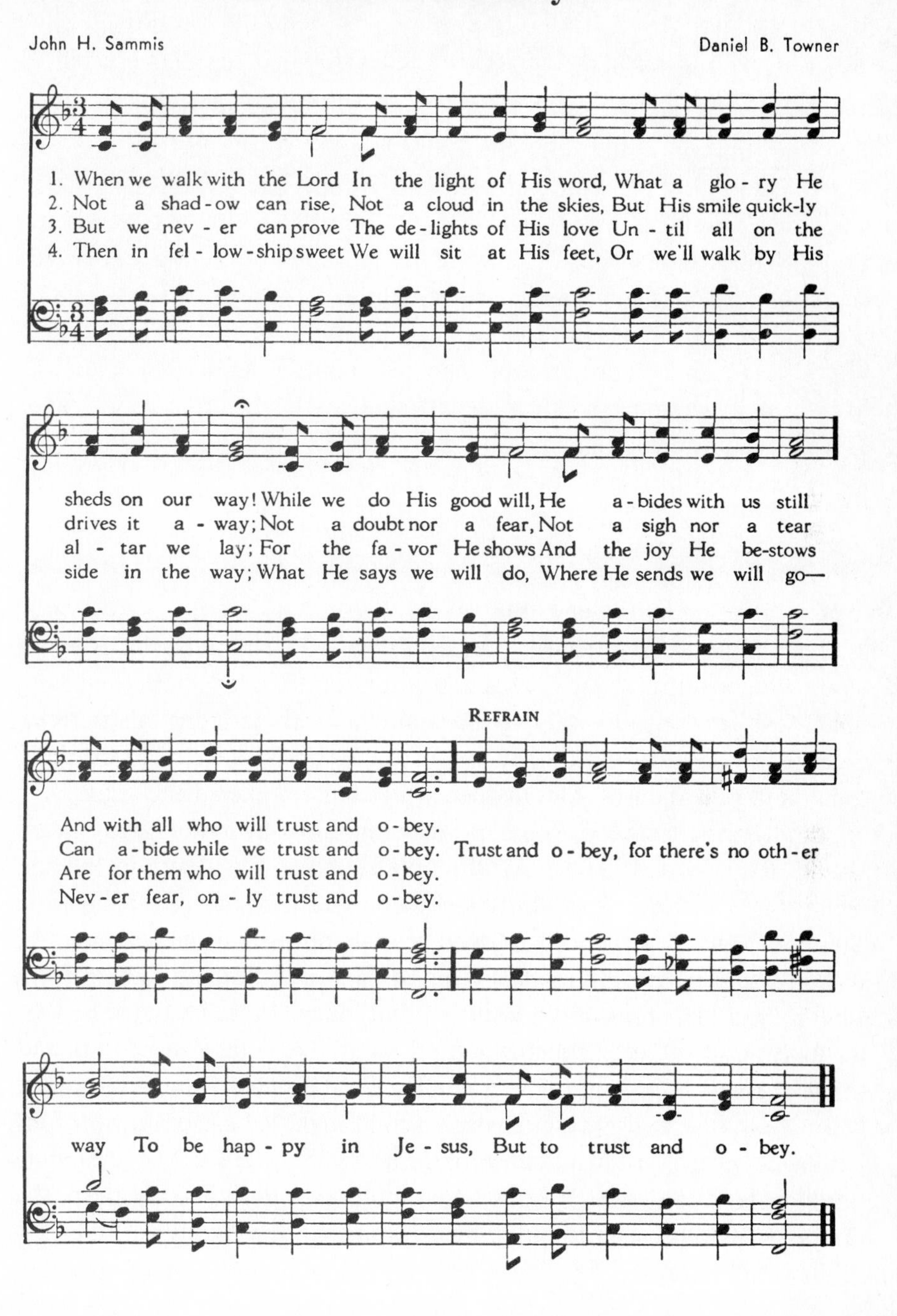
Trust And Obey
John H. Sammis
Daniel B. Towner
1. When we walk with the Lord In the light of His word, What a glo - ry He
2. Not a shad - ow can rise, Not a cloud in the skies, But His smile quick-ly
3. But we nev - er can prove The de - lights of His love Un - til all on the
4. Then in fel - low - ship sweet We will sit at His feet, Or we'll walk by His
sheds on our way! While we do His good will, He a - bides with us still
drives it a - way; Not a doubt nor a fear, Not a sigh nor a tear
al - tar we lay; For the fa - vor He shows And the joy He be-stows
side in the way; What He says we will do, Where He sends we will go—
Refrain
And with all who will trust and o - bey.
Can a - bide while we trust and o - bey. Trust and o - bey, for there's no oth - er
Are for them who will trust and o - bey.
Nev - er fear, on - ly trust and o - bey.
way To be hap - py in Je - sus, But to trust and o - bey.

TRUST AND OBEY

"I am not quite sure how, but I am going to trust and I am going to obey." These were the words of testimony from a young man who was in a meeting conducted by Dwight L. Moody in Brockton, Massachusetts, in 1887. His heart had been stirred by Mr. Moody's preaching and he had come forward to give himself unreservedly to the Lord.

Leading the singing in this meeting, substituting for Ira D. Sankey, was Dr. Daniel B. Towner, who had just become associated with Mr. Moody in developing a music department at the Institute in Chicago. The words of the young man impressed themselves upon Dr. Towner who immediately, in his mind, formed the chorus,

Trust and obey,
For there's no other way
To be happy in Jesus
But to trust and obey.

Dr. Towner then jotted the phrase, "Trust and Obey" on a slip of paper along with his idea for the chorus and with the little story about the young man, sent it to the Rev. J. H. Sammis, a Presbyterian minister. Rev. Sammis, upon receiving the letter, wrote the verses as we still sing them today and sent them to Dr. Towner, who then completed the song.

Dr. George Schuler, musician and composer, who for many years taught at the Moody Bible Institute, passed on to me a very interesting incident concerning "Trust and Obey," one which could have resulted in "Trust and Obey not being published, at least not with its present melody. It seems that when Dr. Towner received the words for the stanzas from Rev. Sammis, he took them home so that he might finish the song that night. He was not at all satisfied with the way the melody turned out and threw the manuscript into the waste basket. Perhaps it was because the half note in the third phrase seemed to call for more beats than two. This has always been a problem with congregations as I have led them in singing this song thru the years. I usually put a hold over the note. Whatever the reason, he had crushed the manuscript and thrown it away.

The next day as Mrs. Towner was straightening and dusting Dr.

Towner's study, she saw the crumpled paper in the basket and, out of curiosity, took it out and read the words of the first stanza which Dr. Towner had written on the paper with the proposed melody. As she sang it over, she felt compelled to leave it on the organ. When Dr. Towner came home and found it on the organ he called to his wife, "Dear, I thought I had thrown this away." To which she replied, "I know you did, Daniel, but I feel that the melody you have written is just what is needed to carry the message." Dr. Towner took his wife's advise, with the result that the popularity of "Trust and Obey" was immediate and has continued as a favorite to this day, proving that Mrs. Towner was so right. ABS

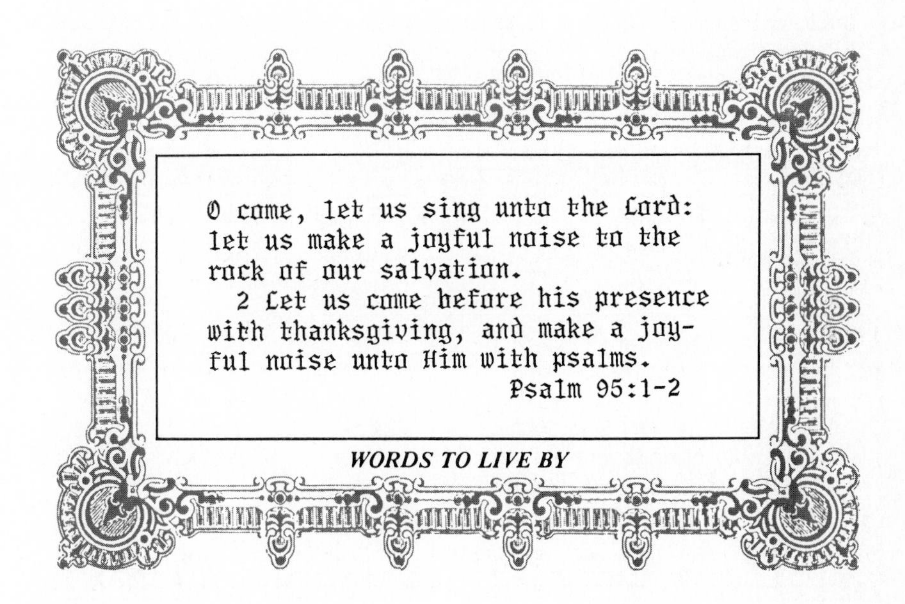

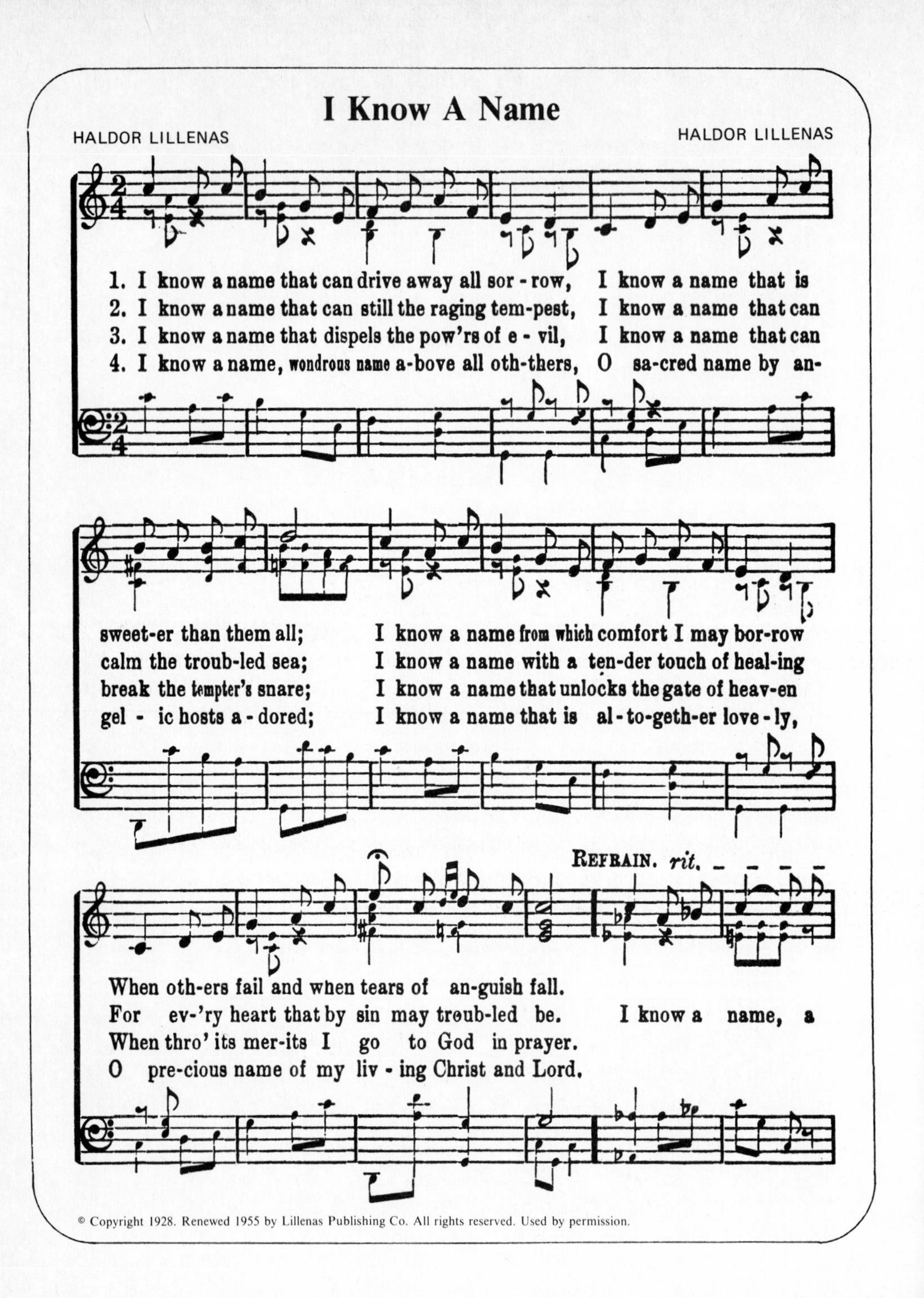
I Know A Name
HALDOR LILLENAS
HALDOR LILLENAS
1. I know a name that can drive away all sor - row, I know a name that is
2. I know a name that can still the raging tem-pest, I know a name that can
3. I know a name that dispels the pow'rs of e - vil, I know a name that can
4. I know a name, wondrous name a-bove all oth-thers, O sa-cred name by an-
sweet-er than them all; I know a name from which comfort I may bor-row
calm the troub-led sea; I know a name with a ten-der touch of heal-ing
break the tempter's snare; I know a name that unlocks the gate of heav-en
gel - ic hosts a - dored; I know a name that is al - to-geth-er love - ly,
REFRAIN. rit.
When oth-ers fail and when tears of an-guish fall.
For ev-'ry heart that by sin may troub-led be.
When thro' its mer-its I go to God in prayer.
O pre-cious name of my liv - ing Christ and Lord.
I know a name, a

I KNOW A NAME

It was while visiting with Haldor Lillenas, the writer of this lovely Gospel song, that he told me the story of its writing.

"We had taken delivery of a new grand piano in our home in Indianapolis, Indiana. I sat down to try the instrument and as I played, I began to find new chord combinations of which there seemed to be no end. With these chords there came a new melody singing its way, a melody which took form and which clamored for words to express its meaning. It is customary to write the words of a song, then the music; but in this instance the music was written first.

"This melody stayed wordless with me for several months. I could think of no appropriate theme or words to fit it.

"It was while I was in a revival meeting in Denver, Colorado — Mrs. Lillenas was with me — that the song was completed. God had to use a rather humbling, yet in some ways amusing, incident to bring it about. The church we were in had lost its pastor and so the running of the meeting was left entirely in my hands. Mrs. Lillenas and I had been placed in a small housekeeping apartment and were expected to provide our own meals. One day our cash reserves had been exhausted and when I took a personal check to the local bank they refused to cash it. The fact that we were conducting an evangelistic campaign in the area failed to impress the banker. In our apartment building lived a secondhand furniture dealer who was kind enough to endorse my check. This he carelessly did with a stub pencil held in a grimy hand. I went back to the same bank and this time had no further difficulty in securing the cash. I had the right signature on the check — one known to the banker. As I held out my hand and the cashier began to count out the money, this blessed truth came flooding over me. Every name has a meaning, some are powerful because of the owner's reputation, others are a liability because of the ill fame of those who have them. There is a name that far exceeds any earthly name. It weaves a magic spell over life's pathway. Its music is more thrilling than any symphony. Its melody brings into accord all the dissonants of earth. Its mention dispels the deepest shadows and puts sunshine in the soul. That name is Jesus!

"It was then that words began to weave themselves around the melody I had been carrying with me for several months and before we left Denver the next week, they had formed a musical mosaic about 'the sweetest name on mortal tongue,' 'I know a name, a wonderful name. That wonderful name is Jesus.'" ABS

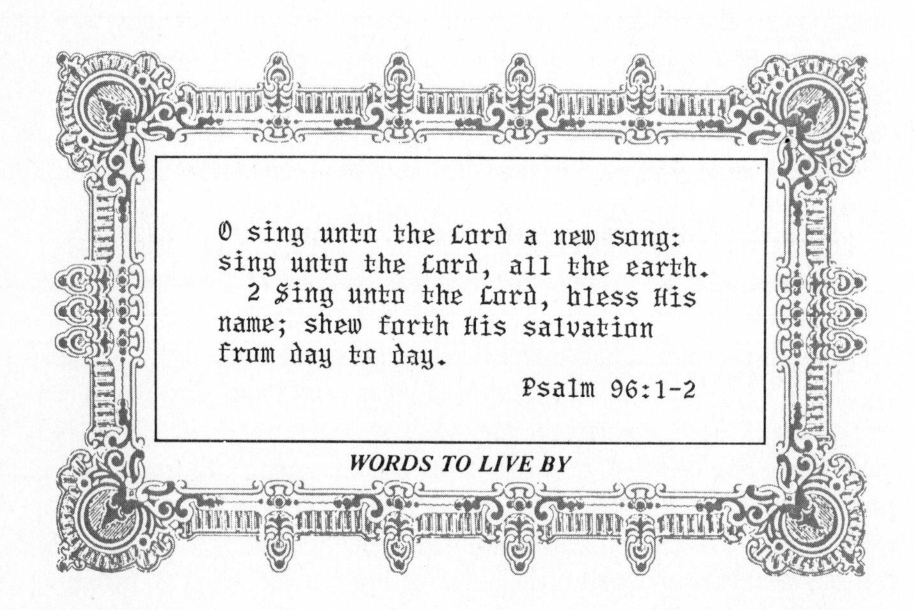

The Glory Of His Presence

OSWALD J. SMITH | BENTLEY D. ACKLEY

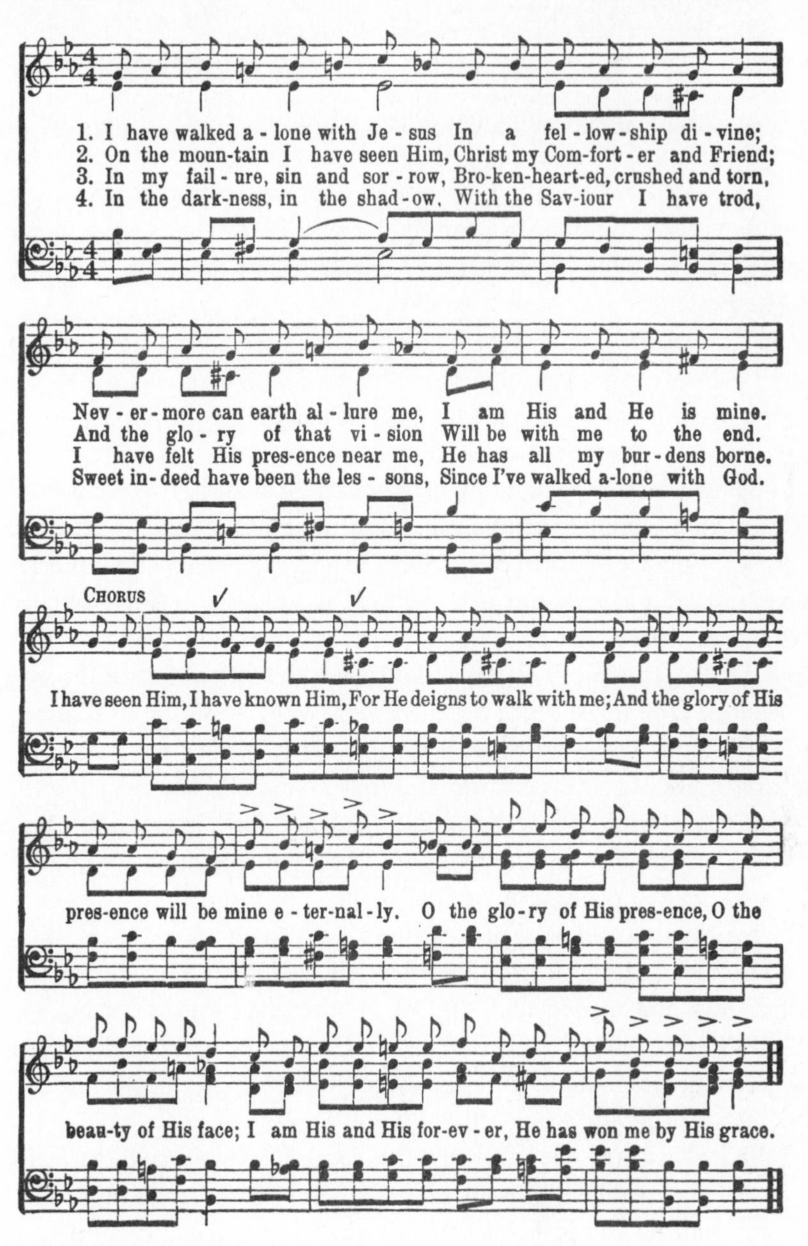

THE GLORY OF HIS PRESENCE

"No lovelier Gospel song has appeared in twenty years than this gem. It probes the depths of my being with emotion and holy desire every time I hear it or sing it. It stands out like a giant Sequoia among the many Gospel lyrics you have written." So wrote the well-known Gospel songwriter, A. H. Ackley, to his friend, Dr. Oswald J. Smith, regarding "The Glory Of His Presence." The year was 1946.

I first met Dr. Smith back in 1942 when we were both the guests of the well-known physician and soul-winner, Dr. Walter A. Wilson, at his great church in Kansas City, Missouri. I have been with Dr. Smith many times since that memorable occasion and each time it has been a blessing and a delight. Among the many qualities of Dr. Smith, two seem to stand out most in my mind. The one is his sincerity and the other is the urgency of his life. He never seemed content just to sit still but even in a motel room he had the habit of walking back and forth as he spoke to you. This characteristic, you will see, is very evident as I pass on to you the writing of "The Glory Of His Presence" as it was told me by Dr. Paul Smith, his son.

"One of the earliest things I remember about Dad was his walking back and forth in his bedroom which was next to my brother's and mine in the parsonage. Very early every morning, that is when he was not somewhere in meetings, I would hear Dad pacing back and forth in his room. No one had said anything to us children about this but somehow we knew that Dad was spending the time talking to the Lord and making important plans for the day and we knew he should not be disturbed.

"This one particular morning, Mother had come down early to the kitchen and had made breakfast. We children had joined her but Dad's daily walk was taking longer than usual. Could it be because the demands had been greater lately with the wider outreach in the 'World Wide Missionary Program.'

"Whatever it was, we still knew that Dad should not be disturbed and so we began breakfast without him. Sometime later he came down, his face was smiling and in his hand he held a large piece of cardboard that had come from one of his laundered shirts which he had gotten on one of his trips. After he had sat down at the breakfast table, he said, 'I have had quite a time of testing lately. There have been some heartaches and disappointments, but this morning God in a wonderful way has made Himself real to me and as I was walking in the bedroom, the vision of His glory flooded all of my soul. It was so wonderful that I had to write about it.' From the piece of cardboard he began to read, 'I have walked alone with Jesus in a fellowship divine . . .' Dad later sent these words to Mr. B. D. Ackley who put the beautiful music setting to them." ABS

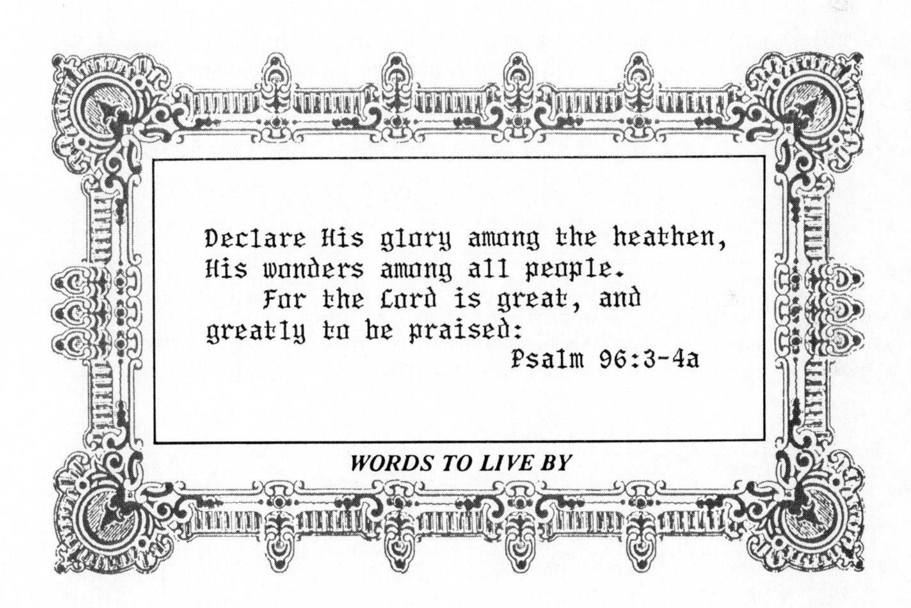

His Eye Is On The Sparrow (THE SPARROW SONG)

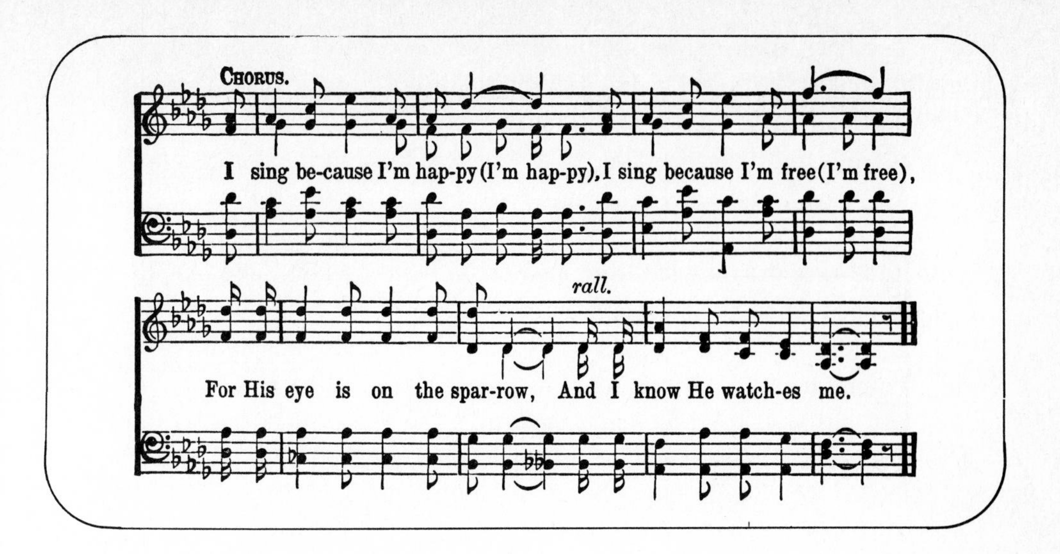

HIS EYE IS ON THE SPARROW

(The Sparrow Song)

Mrs. Civilla D. Martin was born in Canada. She had been educated in the public and state schools of Nova Scotia and was, for a number of years, a successful teacher. After her marriage to Dr. William Martin, she joined her husband in evangelistic work. She loved to write poetry, but had never aspired to have any of it published. It was only after she had written the poem, "God Will Take Care Of You" for her husband, who put it to music, that she began to give any serious thought to the possibility that her endeavors could be used to bless people's hearts.

The Martins were living at a Bible School in Johnson City, New York. The year was 1904, the same year that "God Will Take Care Of You" was written. Mrs. Martin had heard of a dear woman who was an invalid and who lived in Elmira, New York. She decided that she would visit the poor woman to cheer her up and so she boarded the Erie train bound for Elmira which was located some 50 miles west of Binghamton. This was quite a long trip for that day but the burden had been on Mrs. Martin's heart for days and she knew she must visit the woman. In later years she would reflect upon the journey and realize that it was one of the most important decisions of her life, the results of which only Eternity would reveal. I'll let Mrs. Martin tell it herself.

"I wrote the song 'His Eye Is On The Sparrow' in the company of a bedridden saint in the city of Elmira, New York. I was reading and singing to her and during our conversation, I chanced to ask her if she did not sometimes get discouraged. She answered, 'Mrs. Martin, how can I be discouraged when my Heavenly Father watches over each little sparrow and I know He loves and cares for me?' Procuring paper and pencil, in a few moments I had written 'His Eye Is On The Sparrow.'

My husband tried his hand at writing the music for it but was not satisfied with the results so a short time later he mailed it to Mr. Charles H. Gabriel who wrote the present music and sent it to Mr. Charles M. Alexander in England. The song was first sung in Royal Albert Hall, during the great Torrey-Alexander revival in 1905. From there it has gone all over the world." ABS

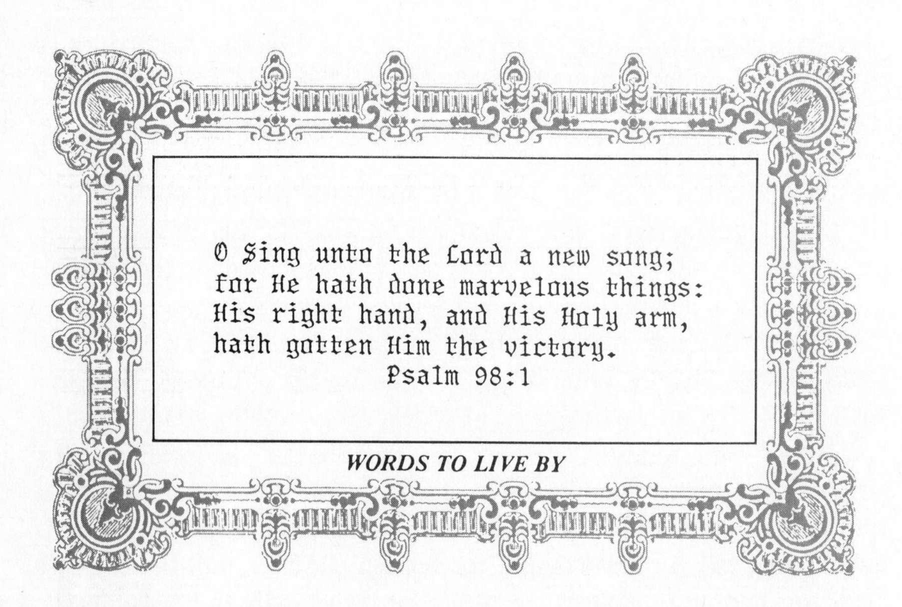

Jesus Is The Sweetest Name I Know
Lela Long
Lela Long
1. There have been names that I have loved to hear, But nev - er has there
2. There is no name in earth or heav'n a-bove, That we should give such
3. And some day I shall see Him face to face To thank and praise Him
been a name so dear To this heart of mine, as the name di-vine, The
hon - or and such love, As the bless-ed name, let us all ac-claim, That
for His won-drous grace, Which He gave to me, when He made me free, The
pre-cious, pre-cious name of Je - sus.
wondrous, glo-rious name of Je - sus.
bless - ed Son of God called Je - sus.
Chorus
Je - sus is the sweet-est name I
know, And He's just the same as His love - ly name, And that's the rea-son
rall.
why I love Him so; Oh, Je - sus is the sweet-est name I know.

JESUS IS THE SWEETEST NAME I KNOW

The story of this lovely song really had its beginning in a hotel room in the city of Chicago, Illinois. I'll let the late Dr. P. W. Philpot, well-known pastor and evangelist, tell the story as he told it to me.

"It was while I was pastor of Moody Church in Chicago that I received a frantic phone call. It was about 2 o'clock in the morning and came from the Stephens, now the Hilton Hotel. The voice on the other end of the line pleaded with me to come, for a young lady that was very ill and also very disturbed. I left immediately. At the hotel I found a very sick young lady who from outward appearances did not have long to live. I spent some time talking with her and was eventually able to lead her to the Lord and to pray for her condition. As I left her brother-in-law and sister-in-law, who were with her, thanked me and assured me they would keep me informed as to her progress. Late the next day, having not heard from them and anxious to know how she was, I phoned the hotel and was informed that they had checked out that morning and were enroute to California which was their home. For the remaining years of my stay in Chicago I did not again receive any communication from them. I then moved to California where I became pastor of the Church of The Open Door in Los Angeles.

One Sunday afternoon after the service, who should come up to see me but the three people I had met at the hotel in Chicago those many years before. They told me that their leaving Chicago had been so sudden they had forgotten to advise me. That past week they had seen a church ad in the paper, had recognized my name and picture, and had come to thank me for my help and to apologize for not advising me sooner of what had transpired. The young lady especially thanked me for leading her to Christ and testified to the fact that her life had been wonderfully changed and that she now was using a special talent the Lord had given her in music, for Him. The talent was writing Gospel songs. With that she handed me a manuscript of a new song saying, 'I have written this especially for you in remembrance of the day that you introduced me to the most wonderful person I have ever known.' As I opened the manuscript I saw a beautifully written song which she had entitled "Jesus Is The Sweetest Name I Know.'

"As I read the words, I could tell the message of this song would live on. Through the years, since 1924 when this occurred, this has proven true."

I thanked Dr. Philpot for the story and asked him, "By any chance, did Miss Long tell you if any special portion of Scripture or a special story had been the spark which led her to write 'Jesus Is The Sweetest Name'?" He replied, "Al, I'm glad you asked, for she did and I think it is the most interesting part of the whole story. Here it is.

"A doctor, while in China as a medical missionary, made it a practice to give the Gospel story to all those who came for medical care before he would treat them.

"One morning before the clinic doors opened, he came out into the compound and saw a very old woman stooped with age. He could tell from the color of the dust that clung to her clothing, feet, and sandals, that she had come a long way. That morning as he presented the Gospel story to her, he knew that something was happening inside the woman. Soon, 'As the rose opens to receive the rays of the noonday sun,' so her heart opened to receive the Saviour. Tears began making little rivulets down her dusty cheeks. After the preaching service, the doctor's busy day began as he took care of the medical needs of the many people who had come. The day closed, as did many more in the weeks that followed. One morning before the doctor left home, there was a knock at his door and answering it, he found himself looking into the face of the old woman he had met weeks before. When he asked her what she wanted, her reply was, 'Sir, He has saved me and I know He lives in my heart. He has made my life so happy! But, Sir, I've forgotten His name. Could you please tell me His name again?' The kind physician then had the privilege of repeating over and over again, into the ears of the old woman, the matchless name of Jesus; and as he did, she too, echoed His name. After a short time the woman bowed low in oriental fashion, thanked the doctor, and headed back toward her village. As he watched her disappear into the distance, the assurance came to him that never again would she ever forget that precious name."

My visit with Dr. Philpot had come to an end but it had been a very inspirational and profitable one for I had gleaned two more stories for my Hymn Histories. ABS

Throw Out The Life-Line
E. S. U.
Rev. Edwin S. Ufford
Arr. by George C. Stebbins
1. Throw out the Life-Line a-cross the dark wave, There is a broth-er whom some one should save; Some-bod-y's broth-er! oh, who, then will dare To throw out the Life-Line, his per-il to share?
2. Throw out the Life-Line with hand quick and strong: Why do you tar-ry, why lin-ger so long? See! he is sink-ing; oh, has-ten to-day— And out with the Life-Boat! a-way, then, a-way!
3. Throw out the Life-Line to dan-ger-fraught men, Sink-ing in an-guish where you've nev-er been: Winds of temp-ta-tion and bil-lows of woe Will soon hurl them out where the dark wa-ters flow.
4. Soon will the sea-son of res-cue be o'er, Soon will they drift to e-ter-ni-ty's shore; Haste then, my broth-er, no time for de-lay, But throw out the Life-Line and save them to-day.
CHORUS
Throw out the Life-Line! Throw out the Life-Line! Some one is drift-ing a-way;
poco rit.
Throw out the Life-Line! Throw out the Life-Line! Some one is sink-ing to-day.

THROW OUT THE LIFE-LINE

"There is more electricity in that song than in any other I have heard," exclaimed Dr. Cuyler, a well-known preacher, after hearing Ira D. Sankey sing, "Throw Out The Life-Line."

Through the years it has remained a song that has done much in moving the consciences of men to go after the lost.

Its writing was prompted by a drill which Rev. Edward Smith Ufford witnessed at a life-saving station on Point Alberton, near Boston. To fortify the need for such drilling, one had only to look out into the ocean from the pier on which the drills were held. There could be seen a ship that had been wrecked years before in which several lives had been lost because no one was able to help.

The energetic action of the life-saving crew as they threw the life-line far out over the water, plus the realization of the lives lost in the wrecked ship, were the things that triggered the thought of the song into Rev. Ufford's mind.

When he reached home, he first wrote the words. These came very rapidly. He then sat down at his parlor organ and in fifteen minutes, he had composed the now world-famous melody. This was in 1888. That year he published it in sheet music form and sold it locally.

When Dr. Pentecost and George C. Stebbins came to Lawrence, Massachusetts, in 1890 to hold meetings, Mr. Stebbins was given a copy of the song. He was impressed with it, save for the fact that Rev. Ufford was not skilled in writing harmony and there were several harmonic mistakes in the sheet music which could do havoc, he thought, to the song's usefulness. He contacted Rev. Ufford explaining his suggestions for change. These were readily accepted and Mr. Stebbins submitted it for inclusion in the first *Male Chorus Book* published by Ira D. Sankey and Mr. Stebbins. It was also included in the next edition of *Gospel Hymns* and within a year had become known around the world. ABS

Trusting Jesus That Is All
EDGAR PAGE STITES
IRA D. SANKEY
1. Sim - ply trust - ing ev - 'ry day, Trust-ing thru a storm - y way;
2. Bright-ly does His Spir - it shine In - to this poor heart of mine;
3. Sing - ing if my way is clear, Pray - ing if the path be drear;
E - ven when my faith is small, Trust - ing Je - sus— that is all.
While He leads I can - not fall, Trust - ing Je - sus— that is all.
If in dan - ger, for Him call, Trust - ing Je - sus— that is all.
CHORUS
Trust - ing as the mo - ments fly, Trust-ing as the days go by;
Trust - ing Him what - e'er be - fall, Trust - ing Je - sus— that is all.

TRUSTING JESUS THAT IS ALL

The words of this fine song first appeared in a Chicago newspaper in the spring of 1876. They were clipped from the newspaper and given to Dwight L. Moody who, in turn, gave them to Ira D. Sankey with the advice to put them to music. Mr. Sankey said he would, if Mr. Moody would vouch for the doctrine taught in the verses. Mr. Moody said he would and thus Mr. Sankey was encouraged to write one of his earliest compositions. He included it in *Gospel Hymns #2* which he was, at the time, compiling with P. P. Bliss. The newspaper had, as they so often did in those days, neglected to include the name of the author and it was not until 1879, that the writer was found out to be Edgar Page Stites, a resident of Cape May, New Jersey, and a cousin of Eliza Hewitt of "Will There Be Any Stars In My Crown" fame. The revival of 1857 and 1858 plus the Civil War had a great influence upon the life of Mr. Stites. He became an active member of the Methodist Church and during the war, was stationed at Philadelphia where he had charge of feeding the troops that passed through that city. This position also allowed him many opportunities to speak with the boys in blue about their souls.

After the war, he became a Delaware River Pilot, but his love for Christ and his desire to win others eventually led him to become a local Methodist preacher. He was also very active in the newly formed Methodist Camp Meeting at Ocean Grove Assembly in New Jersey which was founded in the early 1870's. It was through hearing a very stirring message at one of the early assembly gatherings, on Job 13:5, "Though He slay me, yet will I trust Him!" that Mr. Stites was led to write "Trusting Jesus." A copy of this poem fell into the hands of a religious editor who sent it to the Chicago paper.

When Mr. Sankey contacted Mr. Stites to verify the fact that he was the author, Mr. Stites replied that he was, but would appreciate it if he would include only Mr. Stites first two names on the song. He felt his calling was that of a preacher and that he would not want to become known as an author. So for many years, the name Edgar Page was listed as the writer. This was also true of another of Mr. Stites' songs —"O Beulah Land." It was not really until a few years before his death that the singing church became aware of the fact that Edgar Page and Edgar Page Stites were one and the same person. ABS

When They Ring Those Golden Bells

WHEN THEY RING THOSE GOLDEN BELLS

The marker is found on a soldier's grave plot in Bluff City Cemetery in Illinois. It cost six dollars and contains the following — "Drum Major, D. A. Marbelle, 6th Infantry." Very few words for a man who had as many talents and lived as colorful a life as did Dion De Marbelle, whose real name was Daniel A. Marbelle. His life story reads like a legend.

Marbelle was born in France. For a number of years in his early life, he braved the rigors of the arctic seas aboard a whaling ship. The year 1847 found him in the American Navy, fighting Mexico. During the Civil War, he was a musician with the sixth Michigan infantry regiment. After the war, De Marbelle toured the country with an opera company, doing both acting and singing. When Mr. Bailey organized what is now the "Barnum and Bailey Circus" De Marbelle was one of its first performers. He then organized his own circus but tragedy struck by way of a fire which destroyed his big top and all of the other circus tents. We next find him helping Col. William Cody, better known as "Buffalo Bill," to start his famous Wild West Show and if you don't think this would be enough for one man, may I add that he was an outstanding public speaker who could speak on about any subject, was also a poet, a sleight-of-hand artist, and composer of popular ballads.

With all of these talents, De Marbelle should have died a famous, if not rich, man. But as is so often the case with those endowed with artistic gifts, he couldn't manage his business affairs. His last years were spent in dependence upon others for his keep. His home was an abandoned schoolhouse and, like the prophet Elijah, God fed him, but instead of ravens He used kind neighbors. It has been said that "our extremities are God's opportunities" and so it was with Marbelle, for each time he would give his testimony in the little Methodist Church near Elgin, Illinois, where he also sang in the choir, he would say, "For years I was so busy I didn't have time for God and so rich I didn't need Him. God had to slow me down and take my success away so that He could talk to me about the home beyond the river."

Is it any wonder that one day oblivious of his meager surroundings Daniel A. Marbelle, sinner saved by Grace, soared far beyond the pull of earth's ties and with the pen of an inspired oracle wrote:

There's a land beyond the river
That we call the sweet forever,
And we only reach that shore
By faith's decree.

After completing the words, he wrote a melody which winged its way far above and beyond anything he had ever written in his whole life. Friends published the song for him, but during his lifetime it never gained the popularity that it did when later it was republished in 1911 by Peter Bilhorn. This time it took on a new life and vigor that have made it one of the great favorites in the field of Gospel music. ABS

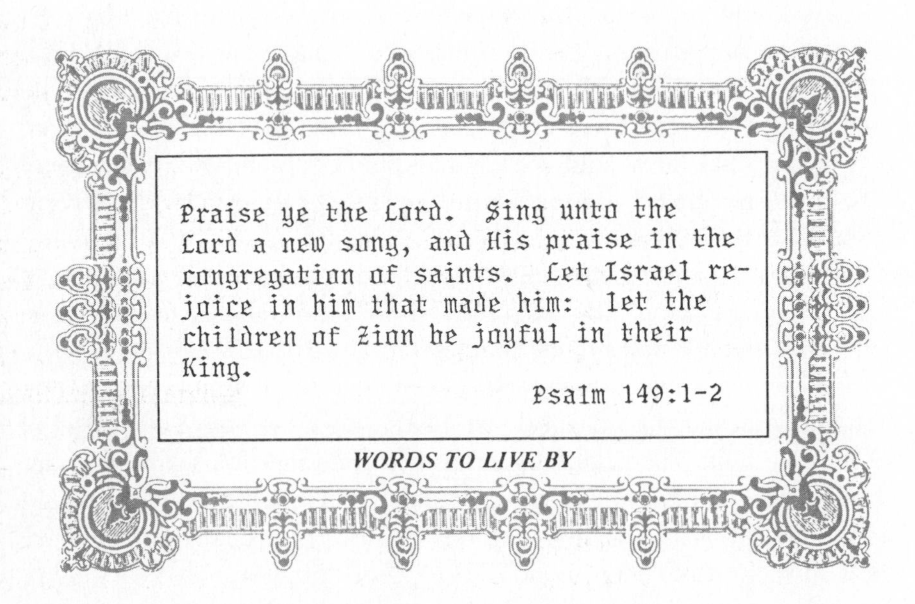

The Sweet Story Of Old
Greek Melody
Jemima T. Luke
Adapted by William B. Bradbury
1 I think, when I read that sweet sto - ry of old, When
2 I wish that His hands had been placed on my head, That His
3 Yet still to His foot - stool in prayer I may go And
1 Je - sus was here a - mong men, How He called lit - tle chil - dren as
2 arms had been thrown a - round me, And that I might have seen His kind
3 ask for a share in His love; And if I thus ear - nest - ly
1 lambs to His fold– I should like to have been with Him then.
2 look when He said, "Let the lit - tle ones come un - to Me."
3 seek Him be - low, I shall see Him and hear Him a - bove.

THE SWEET STORY OF OLD

"Dear Children, you will be men and women soon, and it is for you and the Children of England to carry the message of a Saviour's love to every nation of this sin-stricken world.It is a blessed message to carry, and it is happy work to do. The Lord make you ever faithful to Him, and unspeakably happy in His service! I came to Him at ten years of age, and at ninety-one can testify to His care and faithfulness."

These were the words of Jemima Thompson Luke, the writer of this lovely and famous song for children (and adults, too, I'm sure). They were sent to the young people attending the 1905 International Christian Endeavor Convention in Baltimore, Maryland, where the hymn was sung as part of the magnificent "Festival of Praise."

Jemima's father was a man sold on foreign missions and his enthusiasm rubbed off on his daughter too, for she was a wholehearted worker for the Lord. She was a gifted author and the editor of a magazine called "The Missionary Repository." This was the first Christian magazine ever produced especially for children and numbered among its contributors, David Livingstone, Robert Moffat, and James Montgomery.

One day as she was driving out to inspect a children's work in which she was interested, and because the journey was to take at least an hour, she decided to use the time in writing a hymn that had been singing in her mind for some time. It had to do with the blessed Gospel story that she so much enjoyed telling to boys and girls and particularly to those who had never heard the story before.

She would often remark to them how wonderful it would have been to have lived in Jesus' time and have had Him put His hands on their heads and bless them. The children would readily agree to this but then she was always quick to add — "But we can actually talk with Him now when we pray and we have His own precious promise that He has gone to prepare a very special place for us called Heaven. Someday all the boys and girls of the world — red, brown, yellow, black and white — who have trusted Him as Saviour will be living there with Jesus."

The song began to take form and as she developed it, it really became a children's Bible story in miniature. Jemima Thompson (for she had not yet married Rev. Luke) had been able to compress a 10- to 15-minute Bible lesson into four stanzas. She didn't realize it at the time, but she had written a song that would go on telling the sweet story she loved so well for years to come — even after she had gone to the beautiful place called Heaven that she had written about.

The poem was first sung to an already existing melody a short time after she had written it. It was at the Blagdon School where Miss Thompson, herself, taught the boys and girls. Soon children in Sunday schools all over England were singing it and before too long it was being sung in the Sunday schools of America as well. ABS

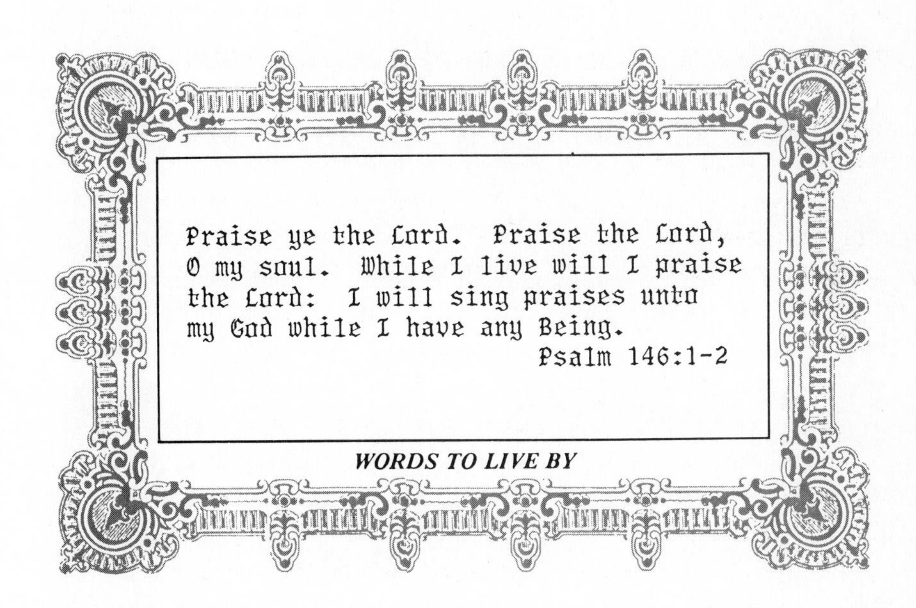

Jesus, I Am Coming Home

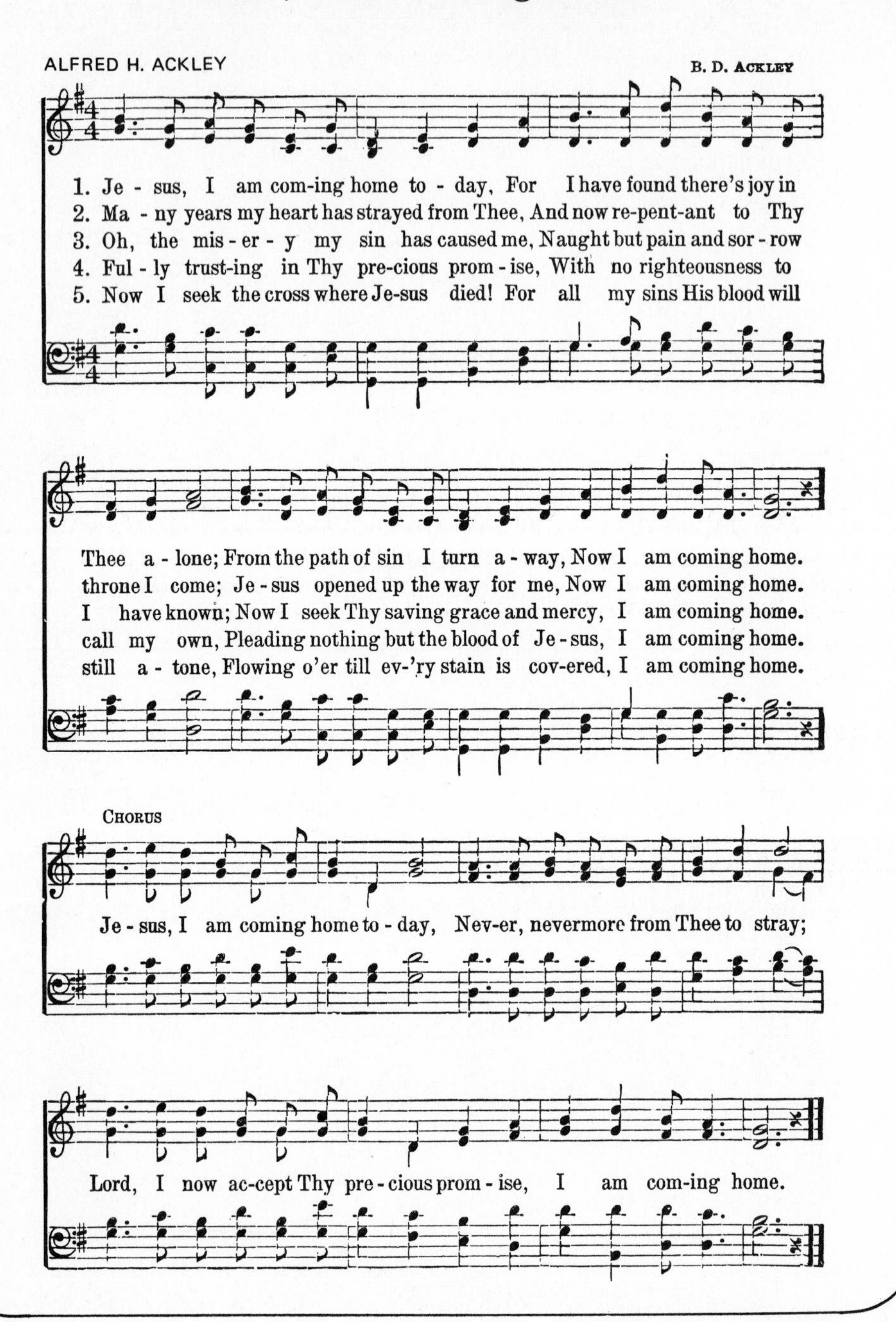

JESUS, I AM COMING HOME

"The clicking of the wheels on the rail joints, of a stuffy day coach in which I was riding, became so audible and had such a persistently intrusive note, that I found myself keeping time with the rhythmic clicks." It was Bentley D. Ackley relating to me how he was inspired to write the song "Jesus, I Am Coming Home." I shifted from one thought to another," he continued, "Seeking to find a suitable phrase to match the rail-rhythm. All this, without any definite ideas for a melody. Of course, the fact that I was hurrying home between meetings, focused my attention on my home. I would get to see my youngest daughter, then three months old. I could hardly wait. The old train continued to click away and all of a sudden it was saying to me, 'Well, I am coming home today. I am coming home today.' It was then the thought came to me. Our Heavenly Father is ever waiting for us to come home and with that, I jotted down the idea and the melody which accompanied it — suggested and beaten out by the car-clicking wheels on the rails. I then sent the melody and suggestions for the words to my brother, Rev. Alfred H. Ackley, who wrote them and thus completed the song." ABS

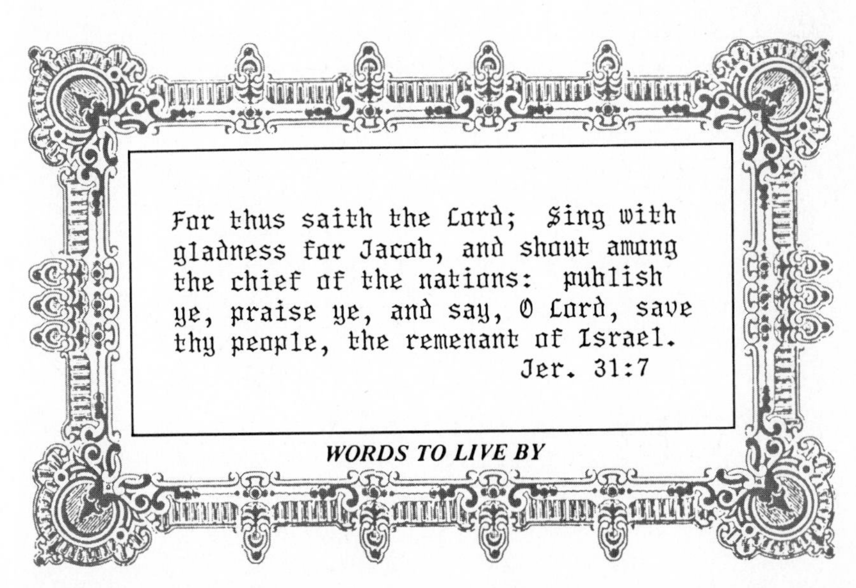

HOLD THE FORT

D. L. Moody, Major Whittle, and P. P. Bliss were attending a Sunday-school Convention in Rockford, Illinois. In one of his sermons Major Whittle told this action-packed historical incident.

It was October 5, 1864 and General Sherman had begun his famous "March to the Sea." For the moment his army was camped in the vicinity of Atlanta. In a carefully prepared movement the confederate General Hood passed the right flank of Sherman's army, gained the rear and immediately began to destroy the railroad. Heading north they burned blockhouses and captured many of the union soldiers.

Sherman's army was put in rapid motion pursuing Hood, to save the supplies and larger posts, the principal one of which was located at Altoona Pass. General Corse, of Illinois, was stationed here with about fifteen hundred men, Colonel Tourtelotte being second in command. A million and a half of rations were stored here and it was highly important that the earthworks commanding the pass and protecting the supplies should be held. Six thousand men under command of General French were detailed by Hood to take the position. The works were completely surrounded and summoned to surrender. Corse refused and a sharp fight commenced. The defenders were slowly driven into a small fort on the crest of the hill. Many had fallen, and the result seemed to render a prolongation of the fight hopeless. At this moment an officer caught sight of a white signal flag far away across the valley, twenty miles distant, upon the top of Kenesaw Mountain. The signal was answered, and soon the message was waved across from mountain to mountain:

"Hold the fort; I am coming. W.T. Sherman."

Cheers went up; every man was nerved to a full appreciation of the position; and under a murderous fire, which killed or wounded more than half the men in the fort Corse himself being shot three times through the head, and Tourtelotte taking command, though himself badly wounded — they held the fort for three hours until the advance guard of Sherman's army came up. French was obliged to retreat. Sherman's message and rescue had saved the day. Major Whittle's application of the story hit home — Christians should not capitulate to Satan and his power for we have the promise of Christ's coming.

Bliss was captured by the story. It's use that day by Major Whittle had been a wonderful illustration for his sermon but it had also given a new song to Bliss. This he wrote immediately.

The next day Whittle and Bliss held a meeting in the Young Men's Christian Association rooms in Chicago. Bliss went on the platform and wrote the chorus of this hymn on the blackboard. He then sang the verses for the first time in public, and the audience joined in the chorus. Soon after he had it published in sheet form. In a comparatively short time it had been adopted as the favorite Sunday school song of both England and America.

Mr. Bliss once said to Mr. Sankey, not long before his death, that he hoped that he would not be known to posterity only as the author of "Hold The Fort," for he believed he had written many better songs. However, on the tall shaft erected as a memorial to Bliss in the Rome, Pennsylvania, cemetery are found these words:

P. P. BLISS
Author of "Hold The Fort."

The boys and girls of the Sunday schools of America and England had sent in their pennies to Mr. Moody for this monument and they wanted the world to know that as far as they were concerned "Hold The Fort" was the best song Mr. Bliss had ever written. ABS

TAKE ME AS I AM

Moody and Sankey were holding great citywide meetings in Scotland back in the late 1800's. Great crowds were coming to the meetings and many were becoming concerned about their spiritual condition and realized that they must make a decision for Christ. One such person was a young girl, from the poorer section of Glasgow, reluctant to go forward at invitation time, went to her own minister for help. He replied to her saying, "Ah, Lassie, don't be so alarmed! Just read your Bible and say your prayers and everything will work out all right."

But to the poor illiterate and heartbroken girl this was impossible and she cried out, "Oh, preacher, I canna read, I canna write, I canna pray!" Then lifting her eyes toward Heaven she said, "Lord Jesus, take me as I am," and in this way she became a follower of the Lord Jesus.

Hearing of this heart-touching experience, Eliza Hamilton wrote the story in verse and sent them to a Christian magazine — copies of which, went to both Ira D. Sankey and Rev. J. H. Stockton. Both men saw the poem and put it to music. Both of their songs were published about the same time but it is Mr. Stockton's melody that is the one used most today.

ABS

Take Me As I Am

Eliza Hamilton
J. H. Stockton
1. Je - sus, my Lord, to Thee I cry, Unless Thou help me, I must die;
2. Help-less I am, and full of guilt, But yet Thy blood for me was spilt;
3. No prep - a - ra-tion can I make, My best resolves I on - ly break;
4. I thirst, I long to know Thy love, Thy full salvation I would prove:
5. If Thou hast work for me to do, Inspire my will, my heart re-new,
6. And when at last the work is done, The battle o'er, the vic-t'ry won:
FINE.
Oh, bring Thy free sal - va-tion nigh, And take me as I am!
And Thou canst make me what Thou wilt, But take me as I am!
Yet save me for Thine own name's sake, And take me as I am!
But since to Thee I can-not move, Oh, take me as I am!
And work both in and by me too, But take me as I am!
Still, still my cry shall be a - lone, Lord, take me as I am!
D. S.—bring Thy free sal - va-tion nigh, And take me as I am!
REFRAIN.
D. S.
Take me as I am, Take me as I am; Oh,

Going Down The Valley

GOING DOWN THE VALLEY

"Yea, though I walk through the Valley." At the Franklin Circle Church in Cleveland, Ohio, it was the custom of the pastor to announce the deaths that had occurred in the church families. He usually did this at the end of the prayer service. Jessie Brown was a faithful member of the church and had heard these announcements many times. Often she would visualize, in her mind, a long procession of people walking toward a dark valley — each one far enough apart so that they entered one by one and standing there to guide them through, was the Saviour.

At one particular service, several names were read and with a renewed emphasis, Jessie again saw the picture that she had so often visualized. After reaching home, she wrote the hymn.

It was set to music by composer J. H. Fillmore of the famous Fillmore Brothers. (Three men from the same family, who gained fame as Gospel songwriters.) ABS

AMERICA THE BEAUTIFUL

One of the best patriotic hymns is "O Beautiful For Spacious Skies," also known as "America The Beautiful." The year was 1893. Miss Katherine Lee Bates was on a trip westward across our great country. Her first stop was Chicago and the great Columbian Exposition with its gleaming white buildings. She said this scene made such a strong impression upon her and her patriotic feeling, that it was in no small degree responsible for the beginning and development of what was to be this much-loved song of America. Her allusion in verse four to "Thine alabaster cities gleam" stems from this Chicago visit. As she continued westward, she passed through the great fields of grain and fruited plains, on to the purple mountain majesties of Colorado. But it was on her trip to Pike's Peak, from whose summit she witnessed the far expanse of spacious skies and the sweep of amber plains, that she then and there began the opening lines:

"O beautiful for spacious skies
For amber waves of grain ..."

This hymn reminds America of her noble past, of the Pilgrims whose stern impassioned stress made a thoroughfare for freedom. ABS

America The Beautiful
KATHARINE LEE BATES
SAMUEL A. WARD
1. O beau - ti - ful for spa-cious skies, For am - ber waves of grain,
2. O beau - ti - ful for pil - grim feet, Whose stern, im - pas-sioned stress
3. O beau - ti - ful for he - roes proved In lib - er - at - ing strife,
4. O beau - ti - ful for pa - triot dream That sees, be - yond the years,
For pur - ple moun-tain maj - es - ties A - bove the fruit - ed plain!
A thor - ough-fare for free-dom beat A - cross the wil - der - ness!
Who more than self their coun-try loved And mer - cy more than life!
Thine al - a - bas - ter cit - ies gleam—Un-dimmed by hu - man tears!
A - mer - i - ca! A - mer - i - ca! God shed His grace on thee,
A - mer - i - ca! A - mer - i - ca! God mend thine ev - 'ry flaw,
A - mer - i - ca! A - mer - i - ca! May God thy gold re - fine,
A - mer - i - ca! A - mer - i - ca! God shed His grace on thee,
And crown thy good with broth - er - hood From sea to shin - ing sea.
Con - firm thy soul in self - con - trol, Thy lib - er - ty in law.
Till all suc - cess be no - ble - ness, And ev - 'ry gain di - vine.
And crown thy good with broth - er - hood From sea to shin - ing sea.

SILENT NIGHT! HOLY NIGHT!

High up in the Austrian Alps in the region known as the Tyrol — "the land in the mountains," are found the two little villages of Oberndorf and Arnsdorf. In Oberndorf lived a young 26-year-old priest named Joseph Mohr. In Arnsdorf lived his friend, Franz Gruber, church organist and village schoolmaster.

The year was 1818 the day before Christmas. Joseph Mohr had started the day making the last-minute preparations for the annual Christmas festival which would take place on Christmas evening.

There would be a lot of singing, for in that region among the Tyrolean peaks, every child seemed to be born with the love for music and it was the one thing they never outgrew. This was very evident at the Christmas song-fest.

Mohr and Gruber had often discussed how beautiful the music seemed to be at Christmastime but as far as they were concerned the "perfect" Christmas song had not yet been found. Joseph Mohr mused — "How wonderful it would be to have something brand-new for tomorrow." But this thought soon passed for someone came with the news that a poor wood-chopper's wife had just given birth to a child and he was needed to give his blessing. This meant that he must hurriedly finish as much of the preparations as he could and then leave for the wood-chopper's cottage which was located a very good distance from the little town.

That night Mohr was also to attend a Christmas party held at the home of one of his wealthy parishioners, a ship owner whose palatial home was located on one of the mountains overlooking the little village in the Valley. Because walking was Mohr's only means of travel it would mean that by the time he had finished visiting the wood-chopper's family he would have to go directly to the Christmas eve party and this he did.

It was late that night when he finally started on his homeward journey. It had really been a full day. He was tired but his mind like a slide projector kept reviewing the happenings of the day — the highlight of the day had turned out to be his surprise call to visit the humble home of the wood-chopper and bless the newborn son. It had not been a palace but he had found himself surrounded by Joy, Love, and Contentment. His heart and mind had been strongly moved as it was again at this moment of reflection.

As he approached the crest of the summit called Totenberg, overlooking his little village, he paused for a moment. The silence of the night, the starry splendored wintry sky, the twinkling of the village lights, the murmur of the Salzack River far below and the realization that tomorrow was Christmas overwhelmed him as they all united in calling forth a symphony of thought that had been crying for expression for a long long time.

As quickly as he could he descended to his house and tho' the hour was late he began to write. When he had finished it was 4 o'clock Christmas morning.

Early that day he hurried to Oberndorf and his friend, Hans Gruber. He wanted him to share in this moment of inspiration. As Gruber read the lines that had been written he was thrilled and exclaimed "My friend Joseph — you have found it. It's the song we have been looking for! Praise God!"

Because there were still some preparations which had to be made for that evening's festival Mohr excused himself leaving the words he had written with his friend.

Gruber took his guitar and began to sing Mohr's words. He was to say later that they really sang themselves for in a short time the beautiful flowing melody as we know it today had been composed. Their search was over — Joseph Mohr and Franz Gruber had found the perfect Christmas song. Later in the day Gruber took the completed song to Oberndorf where he and Joseph sang it together for the first time. That night, at the Christmas festival, the parish choir joined them as they introduced it to the villagers.

It would take another year before it would start on its mission to the world. This happened when the church organ broke down and needed repairing. The man called to do the job came from Zillerthal, a small village over the mountains from Oberndorf. His name was Fritz Mauracher. It was in November, 1819. He stayed the better part of two days working on the organ. When he had finished he asked Gruber to test the organ for his final approval.

I'm sure because Christmas was so near Gruber had no qualms about playing the Carol he and Mohr had written the Christmas before. From the organ there began to flow the melody that today is so familiar. To Mauracher it was some of the most inspiring music he had ever heard and he begged Gruber to give him a copy so that he might introduce it to his own little village. Soon the "Strasser Quartet," a well-trained group of women from his town, adopted it and through the years featured the song in their concerts. In 1831 they sang it at the Leipzig fair and in 1832 a musician named Friese heard them sing at Dresdon. He copied the song and used it for the next ten years in his organ concerts but it was not until 1842 that it was finally printed for the first time. In spite of all the years it was still without a name and was published simply as "The Tyrolese Song" because it had come from the Tyrolean Alps. In all, this had taken 24 years and it would take another 12 years before it was heard by Emperor Frederich at Berlin, Germany. He proclaimed it the perfect Christmas Carol and ordered it to be included in all of Germany's Christmas programs.

From that time on its future was secure and soon it was being translated into other languages and carried around the world. According to my records it was first published in America in 1871 by C. L. Hutchins in his *Sunday School Hymnal.* ABS

The following pages have been added for your convenience. They will, we trust, enable you to add more stories and songs as they appear from time to time in Christian periodicals and publications. A fill-in index has been provided on Page 308.

ADD-A-STORY • ADD-A-SONG • ADD-A-HYMN •

ADD-A-STORY • ADD-A-SONG • ADD-A-HYMN •

ADD-A-STORY • ADD-A-SONG • ADD-A-HYMN •

ADD-A-STORY • ADD-A-SONG • ADD-A-HYMN •

ADD-A-STORY • ADD-A-SONG • ADD-A-HYMN •

ADD-A-STORY • ADD-A-SONG • ADD-A-HYMN •

ADD-A-STORY • ADD-A-SONG • ADD-A-HYMN •

ADD-A-STORY • ADD-A-SONG • ADD-A-HYMN •

ADD-A-STORY • ADD-A-SONG • ADD-A-HYMN •

ADD-A-HYMN • ADD-A-STORY • ADD-A-SONG •

ADD-A-STORY • ADD-A-SONG • ADD-A-HYMN •

ADD-A-STORY • ADD-A-SONG • ADD-A-HYMN •

ADD-A-STORY • ADD-A-SONG • ADD-A-HYMN •

ADD-A-STORY • ADD-A-SONG • ADD-A-HYMN •

ADD-A-STORY • ADD-A-SONG • ADD-A-HYMN •

Add a Song a Hymn a Story
INDEX